WHY THINGS ARE

WHY THINGS ARE

Answers to Every Essential Question
in Life

Joel Achenbach

FOREWORD BY DAVE BARRY

BALLANTINE BOOKS ■ NEW YORK

All rights reserved under International and Pan-American Copyright Conventions. Published in the United States by Ballantine Books, a division of Random House, Inc., New York, and simultaneously in Canada by Random House of Canada Limited, Toronto.

The contents of this book originally appeared, in slightly different form, in The Miami Herald.

Library of Congress Catalog Card Number: 90-93227

ISBN: 0-345-36224-1

Cover design by James R. Harris
Cover photograph by Anthony Lowe
Interior design by Michaelis/Carpelis Design Assoc. Inc.
Manufactured in the United States of America
First Edition: July 1991
10 9 8 7 6 5

For Mary

ACKNOWLEDGMENTS

Surely, we told ourselves, it was the greatest journalistic enterprise on the planet: We were in this for the bigger truths, the deeper secrets, the grander epiphanies. Such was the organizing principle at *Tropic*, the Sunday magazine of the *Miami Herald*. It did not seem presumptuous in such a place to start a regular column called "Why Things Are." For their great attitude and editing virtuosity I must thank Gene Weingarten and Tom Shroder, who handled almost every word in this book. Naturally any errors, misstatements or omissions in this text are probably the fault of Gene or Tom. (Why would anyone rather be an editor than a reporter? Is the pay that much better?) Also I owe a great debt to Liz Donovan, who did a vast amount of the research and had the unfair advantage of knowing most of the answers off the top of her head. That this material cohered into a book is the handiwork of Betsy Rapoport and Elizabeth Zack, my editors at Ballantine Books. Many thanks also to Beth and Dave Barry, Philip Brooker, Ray Bubel, Janet Chusmir, Michael Congdon, Brian Dickerson, John Dorschner, Jeff Leen, Doris Mansour, Gene Miller, Susan Olds, David Von Drehle, Pete Weitzel, and especially to Mary Stapp, who probably never wants to hear another question that begins with "Why."

CONTENTS

FOREWORD

Why do books have forewords?

The main reason, of course, is that having a word like *foreword* in the language creates the opportunity for people to incorrectly spell it as *forward*, which gives the professional language snots yet another thing to be smug about. Or about which to be smug.

The other reason is that the foreword provides an opportunity for a friend of the author, such as myself, to tell you why you should buy this excellent book by Joel Achenbach. Although of course I expect to get my own copy for free. This is only fair, because I've been a major contributor to *Why Things Are*, not in the sense of doing any research or writing but in the sense of being a mentor (from the Greek, meaning "a person whose office is directly across the hall at the *Miami Herald*").

What happens is, sometimes Joel will be over in his office, wrestling with some complex philosophical issue that has puzzled the greatest thinkers for thousands of years, such as why Super Glue doesn't stick to the inside of the tube (see page 285), or why guy honeybees are willing to explode during sex (page 9), and I'll walk across the hall to take a look at the question on his computer screen. Very often the solution will come to me instantly.

"Joel," I'll say, in a wise and thoughtful mentor-style voice, "let's go drink beer and shoot some pool." And so we do. One time we were playing in Miami Beach and—this is a true anecdote—we got into a game with a man named Raoul, who taught us the following Spanish expression: A *todo chulo se le cae un moco de su lapa*. According to Raoul, this translates roughly to: "Every pimp drops a booger from his lapel." Raoul could not coherently explain what this expression means, but I have found it to be extremely appropriate in a wide variety of situations, so I thought I'd stick it in the foreword here as a bonus.

And that is just a tiny sample from the giant salad bar of vital information that you're going to find in this book. Joel has an amazing knack for thinking up questions that you would never think of yourself, but as soon as he brings them up, you find yourself smacking your forehead and saying, "Yeah! Why the heck *do* mosquitos live in the swamp, where there's nobody to bite?" (see page 5).

Yes, you're going to enjoy this book a lot, and when you're done reading it, you'll be able to spout so many amazing facts that, at parties, people will tend to edge away from you. The hell with them. A *todo chulo se le cae*, etc., that's what I always say.

—Dave Barry

INTRODUCTION

A snapshot, before we get to the Big Picture:
One Sunday morning a few years ago I was swimming in my backyard pool when I suddenly discovered a bee—an ordinary yellow-insect sort of thing with wings and a big behind—kicking and jerking in the water.

Normally I do not care about the lower orders, the smaller species, the bugs, but sometimes you suspend the rules, like on Sunday mornings. I decided, God-like, to save the creature's life.

Cupping my hands, I shoveled a bee-laden mass of water onto the deck. Peeking over the lip of the pool, I assumed he would quickly get airborne (immediately and without evidence I had assigned my bee a masculine gender). The wings would surely dry quickly in the hot Miami sun. I hoped for a Kitty Hawk scene: a few sputtering failures, then near-success, and finally a grand, soaring triumph. Instead the bee hobbled in my direction, as though he wanted to thank me up close or, heaven forbid, fall back in the pool. His left side appeared crippled and he tilted precariously to one side. He trembled and convulsed as though electrically charged. I looked for water to gush from his mouth, but instead what emerged was a hideously long red devil-tongue tapered to a fine point that rippled in tiny licking motions.

I did not know that bees had tongues.

About this time I noticed a small black ant approaching at great speed, but in crazy, zigzagging ant-patterns, as though dodging gunfire. The ant ran past the bee, checked both flanks, then dashed headlong at the bee, grabbed an antenna, and pulled with such might that the vastly larger creature momentarily lost his footing. My bee seemed stunned and outraged, and promptly yanked himself from the grip of this impudent pest.

The ant ran away, disappearing under a prickly fern.

The bee shuddered and lolled sideways. He was wracked with insectile pain.

I looked back toward the prickly fern.

Two ants appeared.

They sprinted across the deck. When they reached the bee, they circled for a minute like cats. One ant charged. He must have been the Rambo of ants because, although he was no bigger than a flake of pepper, he grabbed the tilting bee's left antenna and in a single astonishing motion *flipped him on his back*.

It was the greatest display of strength I had ever seen.

The bee quickly righted himself, but then a third ant appeared from under the prickly fern, and then a fourth, and then the party really cranked into gear, entire platoons of ants loping madly across the deck, weaving in complex attack patterns, twenty ants, thirty ants, forty ants. My bee went wild, twisting, rolling, bobbing, but he was besieged by dozens of creatures. They badgered his head, tugged at his wings, rocked him from side to side. It looked like college kids trying to turn over a bus during a spring riot. They pulled and pushed him away from the pool, back toward a seam in the deck that on a microcosmic scale must have seemed like a sharp cliff or a seismic fault line. They steered his head out over the precipice, then shoved him off.

On their level the sound must have been thunderous, though it was too quiet for the human ear. The ants then dragged the bee back up the vertical wall, got him to the top, and pushed him back off a second time. It seemed like overkill, but that's how ants are—ruthless.

By now the bee's devil-tongue looked dried up. He stopped moving. The ants began the long haul home with the carcass. I got out of the pool and pulled back the prickly fern just in time to see my bee disappear under a brown, decaying leaf.

Nature is cruel and efficient; there are no kindnesses for the weak.

End of story.

This minor drama immediately brought a host of questions to mind: Why are ants so strong? Why is nature so horrifying, yet so perfectly constructed? Why can't every species fly, if it's such a great thing? Why is the sky blue? Why isn't the summer solstice the hottest day of the year? Why doesn't the sun suddenly go *woof!* and explode, since it's a burning ball of hydrogen gas? Why is it taking so long for human beings to start scooting around the cosmos like they do on *Star Trek*?

Why is the universe here?

Why do we exist?

These are big, bruising questions. Some linger in our minds on a daily basis. Others—like, Why are cafeteria trays still wet after all these years?—percolate just beneath the consciousness. Still others—Why don't apes evolve into human beings anymore?—are questions that we would never ask ourselves, but that we *ought* to.

This book deals with "why" questions exclusively. Why is simply the best question.

This is not to insult those who handle what, where, when, and who, nor even the masters of how. But these questions are too often answered through pure description, the mere delivery of information, the recitation of facts, trivia, minutiae.

When you ask why, you are shooting much higher. This is a question that addresses the subtext of what and where and when and how, a question that challenges the enigma of the universe. I hope it is clear that *Why Things Are* is the most ambitious book ever written.

What makes "why" such a special question is that it is entirely human. "Why" is our own conceit. "Why" does not occur naturally in the universe. The universe just IS, from all appearances. You can describe what it is, and where it is, and even when things happen (though time, as we will explain later, is also somewhat of a human conceit). But if there were no people like us, there would be no one asking *why* these things are.

This book is not a scientific or academic work. What makes the Why Things Are staff so qualified to write a treatise of such epic scale is that we are wonderfully ignorant. We are blank slates, but insatiably curious. Our minds are facile and elastic, unburdened by postgraduate degrees, knowledge of jargon, or the need to impress our brainy colleagues. We don't wear tweed.

I am hesitant to reveal too many details about the Why staff, lest the glories of celebrity distract from the demands of research. Suffice it to say that the Why Things Are International Command Bunker is located deep in the earth, with a crew of seventy-five people grinding away day and night, faces illuminated by the ghostly green glow of computer screens. Everyone wears a headset and a red jumpsuit. There is a large central map, where someone is continually adjusting small red pins. As research director, my chair is attached to a narrow-gauge rail, permitting circumnavigation of the bunker without the need for ambulation. Even I, though, must answer to the Old One. That's all I can say at this time.

This book grows out of a column that began in December 1988 in the *Miami Herald*'s Sunday magazine, *Tropic*. In addition I've included some longer pieces, labeled "Special Reports." This is for people who want something heartier than the mental Jujubes and Goobers that make up the rest of the book.

We start by asking why ants are so strong.
We end by explaining why we exist.
Why Things Are will be utterly definitive.
Until the sequel.

WHY THINGS ARE

BUGS

(Ants. Bees. Tapeworms. Mutant bacteria. We solve the riddle of why the world is essentially disgusting.)

WHY ARE ANTS SO STRONG?

You say the lower orders of animals have stronger muscles? Not so. If you learn nothing else from the why book, learn this: A *muscle is a muscle is a muscle*. It's the Gertrude Stein rule of musculature. It doesn't matter if the muscle is human muscle, ape muscle, badger muscle, or ant muscle. It's all the same generic stuff: contractable tissue.

Ross Hutchins's book *Insects* states that there is "no correlation between absolute muscle power and animal size, and the apparently greater strength of muscles of small animals is an illusion."

In fact a test of jaw strength among humans and ants gave a slight edge to humans, according to entomologist James Lloyd of the University of Florida. Our mandibular muscles exert 6 to 10 kilograms of pressure per square meter, while the equivalent muscles in ants exert 3.6 to 6.9 kilograms.

Which means, of course, that the Spider-Man story is all wrong. According to Marvel Comics, mild-mannered high school science nerd Peter Parker was bitten by a "radioactive spider." As a result he developed "spider-strength" in his still-spindly arms. It's a factually unsound assertion! Insects, whether they be spider or ant, get their strength from having

3

lots and lots of muscles piled on top of one another. Bugs are like steroid freaks. Watch an ant long enough and you'll see that he's in some kind of 'roid rage.

We mistakenly think that events, even on a tiny scale, are analogous to those in our own world. When a few tiny ants body-slam a huge honeybee, the average human eyewitness jumps back in awe, if not in fright. We do a quick mental calculation to find the equivalent in human terms and conclude we'd have to be Superman, able to crush lumps of coal into diamonds with our bare fists, leap tall buildings in a single bound, and so on. It seems that nature is kicking sand in our faces, showing us how soft and weak and pathetic we are.

Insecurity is unnecessary. Bugs have an unfair advantage in life: Gravity barely affects them. They have no mass to speak of. Insects are such lightweights in relation to their overall surface area that they don't need to devote many muscles to holding themselves up. They can fall great distances without being hurt. (On a larger scale, though, a meaty tarantula *will* splat if it falls off a table; we found this out from a scientist who actually saw it happen.) The big concern among ants is not gravity so much as surface tension. An ant can get stuck in a drop of water, because the tension of the surface acts like Handi-Wrap. On the plus side, an ant can carry massive loads, such as an entire Wheat Thins cracker, up the sheer surface of a window.

The final reason that ants appear to be superpowerful is that they're clever. They work brilliantly in teams. Three army ants working together can carry a dead lizard that could not be carried by the ants individually, even if the lizard were cut into three pieces. Entomologist Nigel Franks has written in *The American Scientist* that there are two reasons for this "super-efficiency" of ant teams:

1. They balance the object perfectly. Normally an individual ant would labor against "rotational forces," or torque, created by the wobbling object.

2. Ants walk out of step with each other. Human soldiers use this same trick when they carry a stretcher. The idea is to keep more load-bearing legs on the ground at any given moment.

Let's be more specific. An ant has six legs, and it walks by moving three at a time, two on one side and one on the other. When carrying something by itself, it is using 50 percent of its legs at any one time to bear the load. But put three ants together and they act like a single organism with eighteen legs. This triple-ant takes one step at a time, so at any given moment there will be three legs moving forward and fifteen firmly planted. Thus for each ant the percentage of load-bearing legs has risen from 50 percent to about 83 percent. The ants can therefore carry heavier objects.

What is incredible is that these ants become totally stupid when away from the colony. Put one hundred army ants on a flat surface and they will march in a circle, endlessly, around and around, until they starve to death.

WHY DO SO MANY BILLIONS OF MOSQUITOES LIVE IN THE SWAMPS WHERE THERE'S NO ONE TO BITE?

N ot far from the Why Things Are International Command Bunker is the vast swamp known as the Everglades (though by the time you read this, it might be nothing but tract houses, golf courses, and Taco Bells). If you drive on the paved road into the sawgrass interior and get out of your car, your body will be coated instantly with bazillions of bloodsuckers. So what do they do when there aren't any motorists around? How do they survive?

They don't live off blood.

They drink plant juice.

Male mosquitoes don't even bite. Only females suck blood,

because blood plays a function in the gestation of eggs. The swamp is popular with these skeeters because of all the still water, and there are enough critters out there—for example birds—to supply the blood to keep the eggs a-germinating.

WHY CAN'T MOSQUITOES TRANSMIT AIDS?

This is one of those rare opportunities where we can conceivably start widespread global panic without straying from the truth: Mosquitoes *can* transmit AIDS.

Theoretically.

It probably won't happen in real life.

The AIDS virus won't replicate inside the mosquito the way a yellow-fever virus can, for one thing. Still, the mosquito's proboscis, dabbed with blood from an AIDS-infected human, could act like a flying syringe if the creature interrupted one of its blood meals and flew over to feed on someone else. The quantity of blood isn't much—about 100 to 1,000 times less than what you find on a junkie's needle—but still it's enough to make scientists want to check it out.

The main defense against bug-transmitted AIDS is the sparseness of the virus in human blood. The virus that causes anemia in horses is a million times more prevalent per milliliter of blood than the AIDS virus in humans. If a mosquito bites an infected person, it probably won't pick up any of the virus at all.

If it did, and then went on to bite another person, not all of that blood would be transferred. And then, even if an infected white blood cell were passed on, widespread infection is far from automatic. The cell could just die. A healthy person probably needs multiple exposures to the virus to get infected. Junkies may have such high rates of infection because they're sick and already weakened. Consider that among health-care workers accidentally pricked or cut by infected needles and instruments as of early 1989, only 0.5 percent, or 1-in-200, showed signs of AIDS antibodies.

Dr. Barbara Johnson, research biologist with the Center for Infectious Diseases in Fort Collins, Colorado, and an expert in mosquito-borne viruses, says, "My calculation is that it would take approximately four thousand mosquito bites, where each mosquito had fed on an AIDS patient, to have a *probability*" of the infection being introduced to a second person.

"It is at least theoretically possible that some insect transmission is going on," she said, but added, "of all the different ways that you can get AIDS, I don't think this is one that you should worry about."

Why Doesn't Nature Dispense with Male Creatures and Let Females Reproduce Asexually, Like Aphids?

Life, to be sure, wouldn't be the same without dudes. Dudes have given so much to the species, such as (a) the watching of TV sports while dressed only in white cotton briefs; (b) nuclear weaponry; (c) simulated flatulence using the armpit.

Despite these achievements, males are somewhat superfluous. They are deficient in the single talent most important in the scheme of nature: birthing babies. Forget what you've heard from sensitive guys, feminists, parental-care books, and the like: men don't have children. Men just stand around and watch and try to be something other than a total irrelevancy. A man is basically just a sperm delivery unit.

Sure it's fun! But it's not always essential. A lot of insects reproduce without fussing with sex at all; they clone themselves. Any gardener will tell you that aphids spread like mad, yet they abstain from sex completely. Their reproductive process, called parthenogenesis, is much quicker than the messy, difficult procedure that is employed by most creatures and cost Gary Hart the presidency, because every clone can make another clone, as opposed to a sex-based system in which half the offspring can't have children.

There is one virtue to sex: genetic variation. If you were to reproduce asexually by just spitting out a tinier version of yourself, your clone would suffer all the same foibles and weaknesses as you. But sexually produced offspring are unique; they'll have their own peculiar mix of mom-and-dad genes. These variations are critical to the Master Plan, giving creatures a hedge against changes in the environment and the brutal touch of natural selection.

That said, we should note that in most of nature, males are pathetically small and inferior to females. We think of males as being larger only because that is true among certain larger mammals, such as *Homo sapiens*. The reverse is true among insects. And in fact the largest creature on earth is a female blue whale.

Males are disposable parts of the reproductive engine. When a drone honeybee mates with a queen, his genitals explode. As you might imagine, this is a mortal injury. The male praying mantis is famous for being eaten by the female after copulation. And check out mites: Certain female mites will asexually lay a bunch of eggs containing only males. Within three to four days the males mature and begin mating with, egad, their mother. Then they die. No, not of embarrassment. They just have no other reason to exist.

You might also consider certain species of anglerfish that live in total darkness three to ten thousand feet beneath the open ocean (see "Why do some fish live in total darkness at the bottom of the sea instead of swimming someplace nicer?," page 247). The female is a couple of feet long. The male is only a couple of *inches* long, much of that being—if we can speak frankly—testes. He latches onto the hindquarters of the female, so that he looks like a dangling flap of skin, a misshapen growth of some kind, a diseased wart. His lips fuse to her body and he begins living off her blood. He ceases to function as an independent organism. He just hangs there, inert, waiting for his big moment, the moment when he delivers the sperm (no doubt shouting, "Take it all. baby, take it all!").

WHY ARE MALE HONEYBEES WILLING TO MATE WITH A QUEEN EVEN THOUGH IT MEANS THEIR GENITALS WILL EXPLODE? WHY IS NATURE SUCH A NIGHTMARE?

A drone honeybee will wait his whole life for one chance to mate with a virgin queen. The event itself is cataclysmic. According to A *Natural History of Sex*, by Adrian Forsyth, "As soon as the queen opens her sting chamber to receive him, he explodes, his genitals bursting forth like a detonating grenade." Or perhaps like a champagne cork. Plugged, the queen flies away. The drone falls dead to the ground, eviscerated. (But with a smile on his face.)

Why such horror?

One answer is this: In his death the bee has ensured his paternity. Not only has he filled the female with his seed. he's plugged her up and made it difficult for another male to inject any competing genes.

This unpleasant phenomenon exists only in species where there are far more males than females. If the females were more numerous, the male would cat around forever. But when females are scarce, the male figures he's lucky to have his one shot at glory.

Exploding genitalia might still strike us as irrational—after all the point is to keep the species alive, and impeding the female's future coital activities would seem to interfere with that goal—but we should remember that nature fosters behaviors that allow the strongest to survive. Nature is coldly logical, and sometimes the service of that logic requires a creature to do things that to a human are abhorrent. In this case the fastest, most enterprising males will find their mate, and the slow ones will get frozen out. (You might say the whole thing is done on a first-come basis.)

This also explains why "love bugs," those creatures that hover, coupled, over Southern roadways, remain stuck together for days at a time. The male is fulfilling his need for paternity certainty. Why they don't get out of the way of moving cars is another mystery (see "Why do fish hang around under bridges even though they see their friends getting yanked up out of the water with barbed hooks on their lips?" page 248).

Now let's go to the Bigger Picture:

Animals don't choose their behavior. Nor do they, over time, gradually learn that one strategy for survival is better than another. What happens is more mechanical than that: There is a competition among genes. A "good" gene doesn't win; it's just the one that's most successful. We might agree that a gene that causes a bee to explode is a bad gene; even the Creator might think so (though let's not slide into that area just yet). Yet it is perfectly obvious that the exploding-genitalia gene would win the contest because it literally drives out the competition. Nature rewards behaviors (genes) that impede or destroy rivals. In other words, Nature isn't nice.

A disturbing implication of this is that we do not use genes so much as they use us. Our bodies are merely instruments that service a gene. The exploding-genitalia gene is victorious and cares little that the victory comes at the cost of death for its carrier, the wretched, concupiscent drone.

Let's go to another example. *Why is a male praying mantis willing to make a move on a female even though he knows she is going to eat him?*

Can't live with 'em, can't live without 'em, that's the philosophy of mantis dudesters. When the male makes his advance on the female, they begin to copulate in their own buggy little way, and the female shows her gratitude by suddenly extending her large jaws and biting the head off her suitor and swallowing it. Then she eats the rest of the body and eventually becomes the head of a single-parent household.

Why does the guy tolerate this? Why not flee, shrieking, at the first sight of such a vicious harridan? Because if the male didn't mate, he wouldn't reproduce. Mantises that had a genetic code dictating caution and celibacy would not be able to pass their genes on.

Now, you might ask why the females are so mean. Simple: It's a free lunch. Since genes aren't "moral" and have no compunction against programming for what we humans would call cannibalism, it makes perfect sense that females would eat the males and save themselves the trouble of looking for food.

Secondly it might be noted that the females often bite the heads off the males even when the guys are still making the initial approach, prior to the mating itself. Incredibly the headless mantis can still perform his genetic duty. As Richard Dawkins writes in The Selfish Gene, "The loss of the head does not seem to throw the rest of the male's body off its sexual stride. Indeed, since the insect head is the seat of some inhibitory nerve centers, it is possible that the female improves the male's sexual performance by eating his head."

(Kids, don't try this at home.)

Extra Credit:
If you want to read about the brainless triumph of crazy genes, check out Forsyth's narrative on the astounding brain worm, Dicrocoelium dendriticum. This thing is about an inch long, flat, and lives in the livers of sheep, deer, and groundhogs.

First it engages in what passes, at the brain-worm level, for sex. Later it spits out some eggs, which wash down the sheep's bile ducts and intestines and then out onto the pasture. There the eggs sit until a dung-eating snail wanders up. (Evidentally there's more of them strolling around than you think.)

The snail eats the eggs, which then hatch into roundish things that drill through the snail's stomach into the digestive gland. Then they transform again into things called mother sporocytes. These are cloning machines. Asexually they fill the digestive gland with daughter sporocytes, which then transform once again into things called cercaria, which resemble sperm cells. These wriggle to the snail's respiratory chamber.

The snail gets a hacking cough. It hawks up a big gob of mucus-covered cercaria. Exposed to pasture air, the gob dries and suddenly resembles a snail egg. Inside, the parasite waits for the arrival of . . . a wood ant. (Yes, the ants are making a cameo appearance here, in case you haven't had enough of them.) The wood ant hauls the slime ball back to the nest, eats it, thinking it's a snail egg, and lo, within moments the cercaria are changing again, into metacercaria, which implant themselves in the ant's stomach and brain. The ant goes insane and, controlled by the parasite and suffering lockjaw, clamps motionlessly on the end of a grass blade.

Along comes . . . the sheep. Chomp. The sheep's pancreatic juices cause the metacercaria to hatch into . . . brain worms. The worms sniff out the liver and set up camp.

Another day, another dollar.

It is precisely this sort of thing that makes one agree with the Van Horne character in John Updike's *The Witches of Eastwick*: "This is a terrible Creation."

WHY CAN'T OUR INTESTINES DIGEST TAPEWORMS?

Human intestines don't digest much of anything. They only absorb nutrients that have already been broken down in the stomach. A tapeworm, which can reach thirty yards in length, can chill out in the guts without much worry. As for tapeworm eggs, which have to pass through the stomach, they're coated with an acid-resistant protein similar to what makes up our fingernails.

More common in humans than the tapeworm is a kind of roundworm known as *ascaris*, which is like an earthworm, only somewhat larger. Kids get these from eating dirt contaminated by human feces. The bummer about *ascaris* is that if you get a fever or take some medicine and the worm gets uncomfortable, it starts to migrate from the intestines. It tends to slither right out your nose or mouth.

"It's frightening and scary and makes everyone [who watches] very ill, but it's really very harmless," assures Dr. Richard Davidson, a University of Florida parasitologist.

How can you tell if you have these worms inside you? You usually can't. "Most parasitic infections don't cause any symptoms," says Davidson.

He also mentioned the mites that cover our entire bodies. But never mind.

WHY ARE FLIES ATTRACTED TO DUNG?

A pile of poop is a fly's idea of a singles bar. The guys go to scope out the babes. The female flies are looking for a place to lay their eggs, and a moist, malodorous meadow muffin is the perfect spot. Flies meet and mate in the same place that they raise their maggots, thus simplifying their lives greatly.

Dung is also loaded with nutritious bacteria. Maggots love the stuff. The bacteria account for about half the weight of a typical cowpie (the same with human feces), and give it the characteristic odor and coloration. (You want to know why it always comes out looking more or less the same no matter what you eat? Because the bacteria don't change.) Adult flies are also prone to dehydration, so they often lick the dung for moisture. But, contrary to appearances, as a general rule they don't eat it. *That would be gross.*

WHY DON'T GERMS GET DISEASES?

The repugnant truth is that sometimes bacteria get infected by viruses. These viruses are called bacteriophages, literally "bacteria eaters." Also, parasitic bacteria called bdellovibrio grow on other bacteria. Our scientific sources couldn't answer our most urgent question: Is it possible for a virus to infect a bdellovibrio bacterium as it sucks the life from a strain of, say, gonorrhea? And if so, wouldn't that be Gag City?

In any case it's clearly a jungle down there. Even viruses can get sick in a sense. A virus, as you know, is a spare little thing, a floating dust mote in miniature, and dead to the world unless it can get inside a living cell and begin to replicate. Our antibodies recognize these foreign bodies and coat them, preventing them from affixing to a cell. The virus doesn't exactly die, since it's not really alive, but eventually it dissipates. The amazing thing is that antibodies never go away; they always stay with us, looking for that same ugly face.

We should remember our scales. A human cell is between one thousand and one million times bigger than a bacterium, and a bacterium is one thousand to one million times bigger than a virus. Viruses that kill bacteria were first detected in 1915. These viruses attach themselves to the surface of the bacteria and inject their RNA or DNA genetic material directly into the genes of the bacteria. This causes the bacteria to start cloning huge colonies of viruses, until the bacteria eventually explode like that guy in the movie *Alien.*

These kinds of viruses have great medical potential for humans or farm animals. Bacterial infections are typically treated with antibiotics, but that requires continual dosages over many days or weeks. Instead the doctor could simply introduce a strain of bacteria-bursting viruses, and we could all sit back and watch the fun.

The only drawback is that sometimes when the virus tries to commandeer the genes of the bacteria, a new crop of mutant bacteria comes into being. These are supposedly not very dangerous, but of course that's what the typical mutant bacterium would *want* us to believe.

WHY HASN'T LIFE ON EARTH EVER BEEN WIPED OUT BY A NASTY MICROBE LIKE IN *THE ANDROMEDA STRAIN?*

You have to admit, it's pretty impressive out there in the woods. The big trees. The bunnies. The badgers. *Fabulous* moss. It all comes together in one incredible food chain—you know, the badgers eat the bunnies, the bunnies eat the trees, the trees eat the moss, and finally the moss eats stuff in the air. It makes you want to bring a lawn chair and just watch.

Sure, Nature has its horrifying side, as we've noted, but usually it's terrific. Why isn't there ever a breakdown in the system? A planet-destroying virus? A continent-coating slime mold? Why has life survived—nay, thrived—for so long?

The traditional textbook explanation is straightforward enough. Species that harm the ecosystem become extinct. Let's say you have a huge fish, a megacetacean, *Whalus humungus,* that is constantly hungry and has the genetic advantage of being able to eat and digest anything—grouper, starfish, coral, sea monkeys, you name it. The creature would be able to prosper for a while and do serious damage to the ecosystem of reefs. But as the reef environment worsened, the food supply would dry up and the superwhale would end up croaking (or whatever sound it makes when expiring).

The same holds true for microbes. It is not a profitable scheme to kill everything. Killers don't thrive. Adapters do.

But now let's get into a nontraditional explanation: the Gaia hypothesis.

This is the idea that all life on earth behaves as though it is a single living organism and that it regulates and sustains itself over time. The theory states that microbes and bacteria and even larger organisms like trees are taking an active role in regulating the environment, keeping the temperature and the chemical makeup of the atmosphere within a narrow range, maintaining the correct level of precipitation and cloud cover, and so on. Species are actually acting like individual cells in the organism of earth.

Biosphere management doesn't happen at the badgers-and-bunnies level so much as at the microbial level. For the first 3 billion years of life on earth, there was nothing more interesting than one-celled organisms. Only in the past 500 million years have fish and flowering plants and alligators and dinosaurs emerged. What were the microbes doing for 3 billion years? Preparing. Fixing things.

James Lovelock, the primary proponent of the Gaia hypothesis, cites as an example the manner in which the biosphere managed to stay cool when, several billion years ago, the sun's heat output increased dramatically. That heat might have been trapped by the thick veil of carbon dioxide in the atmosphere, but instead a new strain of blue-green algae flourished, sucking the CO_2 right out of the air, reducing it a thousandfold.

And then the slime became extinct. It changed the world and suffered the consequences.

Now you have to wonder: Did the algae do this intentionally? Can slime have a grand scheme for the world? Moreover would any organism willingly alter the atmosphere and thus ensure its extinction under the changed conditions?

Lovelock and Co. have never answered this to the satisfaction of most scientists. The biggest complaint against the Gaia hypothesis is that it isn't necessary—there's nothing in the way microbes behave that can't be explained by normal Darwinian models.

It is also unfortunate that some folks want Gaia to be more than a metaphor—they want to believe that the earth is quite literally an organism.

Organisms must be able to reproduce. And no organism can

eat its own waste. An organism is an open system—food in, waste out. The earth is a closed system, and childless.

But wait! We now come across a possible refutation (however laughable) to the assertion that the earth lacks offspring. Dr. Lewis Thomas, famed biology watcher and author of *Lives of a Cell*, wrote in *The New York Times* that such astronautical adventures as colonizing the moon and Mars represent the first tentative steps by Gaia to reproduce herself.

The truth is that people have gotten a little drunk on the Gaia concept. It fits wonderfully into holistic notions of oneness and Mother Earth without scaring any atheists. The New Agers love it. It's so . . . harmonic.

For reassurance we talked to Lynn Margulis, a University of Massachusetts microbiologist who co-wrote with Lovelock one of the first papers on the Gaia hypothesis. She's not thrilled that an important scientific concept has been co-opted by the pyramid-power people. She told us, "Of course it's just a metaphor. . . . The surface of the earth, the troposphere part, the part from the sediments to the atmosphere that you fly under, shows *properties* of life," but that doesn't mean it's actually alive like some kind of Swamp-Thing.

Still, in the age of the greenhouse effect and the ozone hole, Gaia is a useful idea. If there is a cancer in the biosphere, it is probably the human genome, in the freak strands of DNA that give us "consciousness," with the attendant logic, ego, and "farsightedness." The human ability to lay waste to rain forests and spew garbage into the atmosphere threatens to turn up nature's thermostat beyond our comfort zone. We may think we have mastered the environment, but then so did *Whalus humungus*.

GADGETS

(In which we take a look around the house and get confused.)

WHY DOES A THERMOS KEEP MILK COLD AND COFFEE HOT?

How does the Thermos know what to do?

The first thing to remember is that the word "thermos" comes from "Thermos," the brand name of a "vacuum bottle."

Second, realize that it is a container within a container. The inside container (that's three times we've used the word *container* now in two sentences—uh, four—but it's easier than thinking up synonyms that would only confuse the situation) is a glass bottle. Between the bottle and the outer container is a no-man's-land, with close to zero air molecules. A vacuum, almost. Vacuums don't transfer heat very well. If you don't care to know why, then skip to the last paragraph.

Heat is transferred in one of three ways: conduction, convection, and radiation. Conduction means that molecules are smacking into each other like dominoes, sending energy down the line. Since *vacuum* means "an absence of molecules," there are no molecules against which to smack, and conduction doesn't happen. Convection is when molecules cruise through traffic on their own, weaving and darting, trying to get across

19

town—kind of like steam bubbles rising from the bottom of a boiling pot. Inside a Thermos there aren't very many free, unattached molecules that can go convecting.

Radiation defies easy analogy. It's kind of like . . . beauty. There's a little bit of it in everything. The hotter the source, the greater the radiation. It comes at you in waves, piercing everything in its way, whether stone or flesh. Like light from the sun it can leap across a vacuum. There is a silver lining on the inside of the vacuum bottle to reflect much of the radiant energy from your coffee or soup and postpone the inevitable.

So what happens is, the vacuum and silvered side combine to prevent heat from escaping from the inner container if it's filled with something hot and to prevent heat from entering the inner container if it's filled with something cold.

But you knew that.

WHY DO MICROWAVE OVENS MAKE STUFF HOT EVEN THOUGH THERE'S NO DETECTABLE SOURCE OF HEAT?

No doubt it will not enlighten you to hear that microwaves are a type of high-frequency electromagnetic wave that penetrates food and causes atoms to agitate violently and become "hot."

Figure it like this: Right there in your kitchen is a radio station, KMWV. This station plays one rock group called Magnetron over and over. Magnetron's music is so stupid that only food can hear it. The little food atoms react by doing a dance. (This is called an extended metaphor.) First the atoms line up in rigid formation. Then they suddenly flip around, facing the opposite direction. Back and forth, back and forth, kind of like the Twist or maybe even the Time Warp. They do this a couple billion times every second. It's what you call a fast dance. All that dancing heats things up inside the food, while the atoms in the food containers, which don't respond to microwave frequencies, can't even get a slow dance going.

An exterminator told us that a microwave could not kill a roach. So we called an entomologist at the University of Florida to see if it was true. He did an experiment.

"There was never any reason to suspect that a microwave would not kill a cockroach. There is even less reason now," he said. "It blew up like a potato."

WHY DO REFRIGERATORS MAKE FOOD COLD EVEN THOUGH THEY RUN ON THE FLOW OF EXTREMELY HOT ATOMIC PARTICLES, THAT IS, ELECTRICITY?

You put a package of hot dogs into your refrigerator, and it gets cold. Your first question is, What are hot dogs, anyway? It turns out that they are nothing more nor less than bologna. Incredible. Next you wonder, Where does the cold come from? The answer is: The cold doesn't *come* from anywhere. The heat *leaves*. It goes into the air around the refrigerator.

You see, there are pipes in your refrigerator, holding "refrigerant," a liquid such as freon that is not actually cold until you make it cold. What is special about refrigerant is that it evaporates—goes from liquid to gas—at a fairly low temperature, as opposed to water, which must hit 212 degrees Fahrenheit. In order to evaporate, a liquid must draw heat from somewhere. That's why when you moisten your finger and wave it in the air, it feels cooler. The water is evaporating and drawing heat from your skin. The key to the refrigerator is that liquid refrigerant is turning to a gas in the pipes, and in so doing drawing heat from the interior of the box.

Now, if you're paying close attention, you'll realize that something's missing here. Why wouldn't all the liquid turn into a gas and just stay that way, thus ending the refrigerator's ability to cool down the next warm package you put into it? Because there's a thing called a compressor that runs on electricity. The compressor takes the gas and squeezes it until it's a liquid again. The liquid runs through the fridge, turns to a gas again, goes into the compressor, turns back to liquid, and so on. When your refrigerator breaks, turn to your spouse and say, "I think it's the compressor." This will usually be correct and, more importantly, will sound smart.

WHY IS A SAFETY MATCH SAFE?

Most tools seem complex but are actually fairly simple. Matches are the contrary. The humility of their design belies a deeper engineering genius. Consider: The common match was invented in 1805, nearly two hundred years after the first telescope.

There are two types of matches, the "safety match" and the "strike-anywhere match." For simplicity's sake, we will refer to the latter as the "dangerous match." The dangerous match can be ignited with your fingernail, or, if you're as tough as Clint Eastwood in those old spaghetti Westerns, your beard. The tip is coated with the chemical phosphorus. White phosphorus is so flammable it bursts into flames upon contact with the air. There is more than a pound of the stuff in a human body, in blood, muscles, bones, and teeth. Why don't your teeth burst into flame when you talk? This is a mystery too deep for the present volume. All you need to know is that the modern dangerous match uses *red* phosphorus, which is calmer than its white cousin. Rub the match on sandpaper or any rough surface and the friction heats the match to the ignition point. The flame then fires down into the match's "tinder," easy-to-burn chemicals like sulfur, potassium chlorate, and charcoal, melded together with glue and wax. There's also dirt and powdered glass to keep things under control. To make things more comfy for all concerned, the entire stick of wood has been soaked in a chemical that prevents smoldering. Still, the fact remains that this is a match that bursts into flame with the slightest frictional provocation.

The safety match is a radical departure. The thinking behind the safety match is that although the phosphorus and the "tinder" are wild and unpredictable when stuck together, they are harmless and mediocre when solo, like Lennon and McCartney. So the phosphorus is not even on the match; it's on the box, or the pack, or whatever you call it (you know—on that black, scratchy strip). To light the safety match, one simply has to press it against the strip, "close cover before striking," and yank, unless the match in question is the last in the pack, in which case it will not light no matter how many billion times you try.

Why Do Eyes Turn Red in Photographs?

This seems to be true of every Polaroid snapshot: The picture would have been perfect except that the subjects are staring into the camera with eyes that look as if they are possessed by Satan.

This is caused by blood.

The flash from the camera is being reflected on the rear of the eyeball, which is red from all the blood vessels. The problem can be solved by using a flash at a distance from the camera, or by getting your subjects to look somewhere else.

Another trick is to turn up the lights in the room, making them as bright as possible, which causes the subject's pupil to contract and admit less of the light from the subsequent flash.

WHY DO CREDIT CARDS HAVE SO MANY NUMBERS?

You're drunk. You stagger to a phone. You try to charge a call to your Visa account. Problem: Your Visa account number is 987-888002-191355-3333339999666 and your fingers just can't get it right. No call. Okay, fine, so there are actually just sixteen digits. But that's way more than necessary. Even if we gave every person on the planet his or her own account, we'd still only need ten digits. The extra digits, though, make it extremely unlikely that a store clerk will accidentally write down someone else's account number. There are 10 quadrillion possible sixteen-digit Visa account numbers, but only about 65 million actual Visa accounts. The odds that anyone could write down a real Visa number at random are therefore 65 million-in-10 quadrillion, or about one-in-150,000,000.

WHY DO PHONE CORDS GET SO HORRIBLY TWISTED?

You just know there's some sort of molecular twist memory in the cord that kicks in about two weeks after it emerges from the coiling factory. You know it. Because they do that by themselves, right?

We went to the supreme expert: George Reichard, the top phone-cord specialist at Bell Laboratories' Consumer Products Division in Indianapolis. He said he has always been concerned by the way they get twisted, and he has actually studied the phenomenon. Indeed, when we called and expressed an interest, he sounded deeply moved.

In admirably economic phrasing he explained precisely why the phone cords get twisted: "People tend to twist them." Unconsciously we follow set patterns of phone handling: Pick up handset. Turn 90 degrees clockwise and put under left ear. When left ear begins to hurt, move handset to right ear, employing subtle 180-degree clockwise twist. When call is over, turn handset 90 more degrees clockwise and hang it up. That's a full 360.

We studied dozens of phone cords around the Why Things Are International Command Bunker and tried to figure out why some were twisted clockwise and others counterclockwise. The obvious explanation would be handedness. A right-handed person will dial with the right hand and hold the phone with the left to the left ear. But it can also be that some people are right-eared and some left-eared. A right-eared person would switch the phone right-to-left and put a counterclockwise spin on it. But the patterns we saw were totally random. The twist may actually come from pacing while talking.

Reichard produced a great revelation: Phone cords become twisted because the phone company won't put a stop to it. It *is* possible to make a phone cord that doesn't twist. You need only a swivel at the end of the cord, similar to what is used to keep fishing line from twisting. Some gadgetry stores sell such swivels, but AT&T hasn't ever marketed them. Carl Blesch, spokesman for Bell Labs, said the reluctance to sell a nontwisting phone cord "is a business decision."

One might guess that the competition for AT&T these days is against low-priced, low-quality competitors, and since it already sells the upscale phones, it doesn't need to add on another expensive design feature. AT&T only makes a few zillion dollars a year as it is, and we wouldn't want to cut into that profit margin by insisting on phones that don't tie themselves into knots.

AT&T does make a thing called a Tuff Cord, which adds a coating of clear polyester plastic to the standard polyvinyl-chloride cord jacket. The cord is thick and stiff. "It'll take more spins before you exceed the torsional stiffness of the cord," Reichard comments expertly.

WHY DO TELEPHONES USUALLY START RINGING WITH A FULL, DRAWN-OUT RING BUT OTHER TIMES WITH ONLY A PARTIAL RING?

Let's think this through. Maybe there's a gadget underneath the phone that controls the ringing, and when you pick up the handset in mid-ring, it means that next time the phone rings, you'll only get a partial ring. We could actually check this out experimentally, except that we already know it's the wrong answer. The ringing comes from the central office of the phone company.

When we make a call, even to our neighbor next door, the signal first travels across town, over hill and dale (or, more accurately, over causeway and shopping center), until it reaches the nearest branch office of the phone company, with its switchyard of circuits. In that office will be a device, or maybe two devices, or in some cases a whole bunch of devices, that emit a ring-provoking signal in a constant cycle, over and over—two seconds of noise, four seconds of silence. This signal piggybacks onto your phone call and, using 100-volt bursts of electricity, triggers the bells on your neighbor's phone. If your call goes whizzing through the phone company office during the middle of one of these ring-triggering signals, your neighbor's phone will erupt in a partial ring.

Meanwhile you will hear a ring through the earpiece of your own phone. Sometimes it will seem as though your neighbor picked up even before it rang a single time. In fact the ringing you hear and the ringing your neighbor hears are totally unrelated sounds generated by different equipment. Only by coincidence would the ringing be simultaneous.

The real question is, *Why does the phone company blast us with that brain-frying three-beep tone whenever we misdial?*

The phone company calls this a special-information tone, though a better name would be "you-stupid-fool, you-can't-even-dial-a-phone tone." It's been universally adopted by phone companies since the breakup of Ma Bell. The technical description of this teeth-grinding sound is, according to a phone company source, "minus 13 dBmO thousand hertz (dBmO equal decibels relative to one milliwatt, measured at 0 minus dB transmission point) with a tolerance of plus or minus 1 to 1.5 decibel."

The purpose is twofold. If enough tones are sounding on one particular trunk of phone cables, it alerts the phone company that something has gone wrong, for example someone cut a cable, or a tornado hit, or whatnot. The second function is to tell the dialer that he screwed up. Why does it have to be loud enough to pasteurize raw milk? Because, says the phone company, a lot of people don't dial with the handset to their ear and the sound needs to be loud enough to alert them, no matter where the phone is. This strikes us as great logic: It does not matter if millions suffer, so long as that one person who dials the phone *underwater* can be informed that he must check the number and dial again.

WHY DOES NO ONE MAKE COFFEE ANYMORE IN THOSE OLD-FASHIONED PERCOLATORS THAT SOUND SO GREAT?

A percolator makes a sound sort of like ... *gurblurgle* ...., and then after a few more *gurblurgles* the pace picks up and builds to a crescendo of *urgl-urgl-urgl-urgl*. That's got to be the most wonderful music ever invented.

But the coffee itself is quite bad. The coffee bean is delicate; it shouldn't be boiled like a dang potato. This is how an old percolator works: Boiling water rises through a tube to the top of the canister, where it drips down through the grounds that sit in a metal filter. Fine so far. But then this weak protocoffee is boiled again and sent back up through the percolator, over and over, leaching all sorts of nasty oils and acids out of the grounds and resulting in a sour effluent. About twenty years ago the percolator vanished from the landscape with the arrival of electric drip machines, led by Mr. Coffee, in which boiled water is dripped just once through the grounds.

Want to become a coffee snob? Start by checking out Corby Kummer's four-part series in *The Atlantic*, which began in the May 1990 issue. Kummer, the magazine's food columnist, spent two years studying the bean and concludes that the best technique is the drip pot, not to be confused with electric drip machines. The drip pot is a three-tiered assemblage that requires you to flip it upside down when the water boils—or, more precisely, when the water is between 197 and 205 degrees Fahrenheit. There's so much to worry about!

Have your beans been kept in an airtight container with a one-way valve allowing gases to escape? Do you use the right proportion of arabica to robusta beans? Do you foolishly leave your coffee on a burner, or do you do the proper thing and transer it to an insulated pitcher? Do you brew with bottled water? Do you use a grinder with sharp burrs, or one with a whirring blade? Have you switched yet to brown, unbleached filters as a way of avoiding toxins in the white filters? You say you have? Well, haven't you heard yet about the superior oxygen-bleached filters?

Our advice: The next time you're in the home of a coffee snob who makes a big speech about buying whole beans instead of ground coffee, look bewildered and then utterly appalled and say, "You mean you buy your beans *already roasted*?"

CREEPING SURREALISM

(In which we explain the ultimate mystery: Why does nothing seem *real* anymore?)

We must bring the masses illusions.

—Adolf Hitler

These are cancerous times, and for proof of the disease you need look no farther than a package of Pepperidge Farm "Nantucket" Chocolate Chunk Cookies, part of the Pepperidge Farm "American Collection." Here's what it says:

"Only the bakers of Pepperidge Farm could pack so much scrumptious personality into classically American cookies. . . . They added a heaping measure of simple fuss and bother. That meant making each cookie one of a kind, with an individual personality all its own. So they gave them rugged, irregular shapes, just as if someone had lovingly shaped each cookie by hand."

What we have here, first of all, is the classic Humble Down-Home Multinational Corporation affectation. Pepperidge Farm is a massive corporate enterprise that is owned by Campbell's,

31

the world's largest soup company—yet they beg us to think of them as just regular folks who probably live in the woods in some gingerbread house. (This rivals, for sheer moxie, if not dishonesty, the old Bartles & Jaymes pitch. Your average low-wattage TV viewer may not have realized that the two old geezers on the Bartles & Jaymes advertisements were not real people. They were actors trying to sell a wine cooler made by Gallo, the world's largest wine company.)

What is most distressing about the Pepperidge Farm phoniness is that they designed a machine that makes cookies that look as though a human being made them. Then, incredibly, they admit the hoax right there on the bag. They *brag* about it. They say, "Yo, these cookies only *look* as though someone made them by hand."

One thinks of those loathsome AT&T commercials in which the camera jerks around as though controlled by a spastic. People are mumbling dispiritedly, like nonactors. We are supposed to think that this is reality so *stark*, so *naked*, that the camera has been frantically shoved in front of it—but with the budget for this ad campaign you could probably buy a nuclear submarine. One suspects that the camera is not hand-held at all but is attached to a complex machine that exactly simulates the jostling motions of human cameramen. Maybe it's the same machine that makes those cookies look handmade.

Something is horribly, detestably wrong. Maybe it is this: In modern America *nothing is real anymore.*

We have become comfortable with artifice, fond of the fake.

Yes, there's an actual trend out there. Let's call it Creeping Surrealism.

A goofy term, but you get the point. There are academic and philosophical studies of this general phenomenon, using varying nomenclature, perhaps the best being Jean Baudrillard's term *hyperrealism.* The hyperreal, Baudrillard says, is a world in which "illusion is no longer possible because the real is no longer possible."

The French have a way of overstating. Still, there's truth there.

Before we explain why this has happened, let's try to get a better fix on exactly what it is that is going on.

One classic example would be the effort in 1987 to get people to appreciate and celebrate the bicentennial of the U.S. Constitution. A Bicentennial Commission was appointed, headed by former Chief Justice Warren Burger. The commission decided to run a series of TV commercials—but TV networks don't like to run public-service ads that are longer than thirty seconds. What can you say about the old document in just half a minute?

A blue-ribbon Madison Avenue firm came up with some ideas. One of the best was this: Show military recruits taking their oath—which includes a vow to protect the Constitution. Steve Horn, a director who made the "Reach Out and Touch Someone" ads for AT&T (them again), visited an army office in Brooklyn to see how recruits were actually sworn in.

He was appalled. The army office was small, sterile, and poorly lit.

"I can't show that on television," he explained later. "People wouldn't want to watch the ad."

So he filmed the ad in a majestic vaulted room at a Catholic college on the northern tip of Manhattan. Light streamed in from windows on high. Smoke machines filled the room with dense, tangible atmosphere. The actors—attractive and demographically diverse—were spaced apart in the gloom, each one perfectly erect, hands over hearts, illuminated in Caravaggesque chiaroscuro.

Artistic license, Horn said. Everyone does it, he said: TV, newspapers, magazines.

"Everything is a lie," he said. The real army office can't be used, he said, because "that's such an undramatic room. So . . . I do what I do best [and] make it look good. I try to make it look dramatic and heroic. . . . Heightening reality makes things come across a little better. I think it helps to make it more real, more emotional."

In other words, Better Reality Through Television.

The brutal truth is that although most people can still tell the difference between the real and the artificial, they no longer think the distinction matters. They don't care! Our brains have been inured to falsity; we've made the necessary mental adjustments, just as we did as kids when we had to deal with the fact that, on *The Flintstones*, neither Barney nor Fred had a neck.

People magazine ran a cover story on the marriage of the *Miami Vice* characters played by Don Johnson and Sheena Easton. *People* magazine can, by definition, write stories on anybody, on any human being living or dead, yet it prefers to write about people who *do not actually exist*.

One of the great monuments to Creeping Surrealism is the modern Hollywood studio tour. In Orlando, Disney and MCA-Universal have built rival studios and, correspondingly, rival studio tours—but the studios were actually an afterthought to the tours. Market research showed both companies that the public would patronize a studio tour *even if it wasn't a real studio*.

Both companies decided to build the studios anyway, because, as one Disney official put it, "There's a certain amount of studio that we wanted just to make the entertainment areas credible."

At both Orlando attractions the companies have built old-fashioned back lots, with a simulated New York street, a Middle America courthouse square, and quiet Leave-It-to-Beaver neighborhoods. They say these are working sets, but that's a little snow-white lie. Directors don't *use* back lots anymore, except for the odd TV commercial. The sets are for tourists. So what we have is a situation in which the facades are themselves fakes—they're there to create the *illusion of facades*.

A year or two ago there was a TV commercial starring the actor who played Dr. Cliff Warner on the soap opera *All My Children*, in which he endorsed a brand of cough syrup, saying,

"I'm not a doctor, but I play one on television. . . ."

So why has this happened?

Because although the distortion of truth has always been integral to civilization, never before have the manipulators of truth been so powerful or ubiquitous. The technology of falsehood has outraced our judgment. Modern life has confused us. Alienated from nature, liberated from such barbaric responsibilities as the growing of food and the making of shelter, we have entered a mysterious phase in which we passively accept a cartoon version of reality projected upon us by unreliable, deceptive, and sometimes diabolical media.

The Why Things Are road staff once had a haunting encounter with Creeping Surrealism at the American Booksellers Convention in Washington, D.C. First there were the posters advertising the books from dozens of America's great bestselling authors—Bill Cosby, Tip O'Neill, Donald Trump, Barry Manilow, Chuck Berry, Meadowlark Lemon, Joe Theismann, Elizabeth Taylor, Ben and Jerry, and so on.

If there was one heavyweight in the bunch, it was Shirley MacLaine, the actress. She said her new book, *It's All in the Playing*, was a compendium of revelations that came to her while playing herself in the TV movie based on her previous best-seller, *Out on a Limb*.

"It uses the experience of playing myself to explore—well, the notion that we're all the writers, directors, producers and stars of our *own* drama. You can play your part *in real life* just as you can play your part in a movie."

It was obvious that she had her finger on the pulse of America: Why be yourself when you can be like someone in a movie? (Jay McInerney wrote in *Bright Lights, Big City*, "It was getting harder and harder to live as though you weren't in a movie.")

Naturally someone had to ask Ms. MacLaine the obvious question: Would there soon be a movie based on her book about playing herself in the movie based on her previous book? She hesitated. Then she said, "I don't think so."

But later her publisher's publicist, Stuart Applebaum, refused to rule anything out: "Nothing is impossible."

We live in a time so bizarre that it barely rates the privilege of being called history. It's more like antihistory, an aberration, like when the antipopes moved the papacy from Rome to Avignon.

Obviously some of this stuff is more humorous than dangerous. Still, you have to wonder if the battering that we suffer has taken a toll: Perhaps the phenomenon of fraud and falsity that has been masterminded by television and the advertising industry can actually penetrate into our interior lives—and our behavior will become so twisted that even the most primitive emotions, such as love and grief, will take on the stink of artifice and imitation.

In any case, the 1990s is already a banner decade for reality fabrication. One of the bestselling books of 1990 is *Millie's Book*, the memoir of a dog, as told to Barbara Bush. On television there are more jerking-camera ads than ever, including the ones for Levi's Cotton Dockers in which the golf buddies cavorting around the dewy greens are faintly overheard in random chatter—"look, folks, no script!" How much more authentic can you get?

The answer to that question comes from Dean Witter: Black-and-white newsreel-style footage, replete with scratches on the negative, of someone who is supposedly Dean Witter vowing that his company will measure success one investor at a time. We are supposed to trust these ads because they look as though they were made in the 1920s or so, long before Madison Avenue knew how to manipulate the truth. These ads are so honest they even have scratches!

The art world's answer to all this is Mark Kostabi, a New York painter who doesn't actually paint many of "his" paintings. He hires someone to do the painting for him, and he even hires someone to come up with the ideas. All he does is sign his name at the bottom. The paintings reportedly sell for upwards of $10,000. "Only a fool would buy a Kostabi," he has said, adding that this statement is part of his shtick. Obviously he is both parodying and exploiting a society in which value is a function of publicity rather than the other way around.

Into this broad, diabolical picture stepped the guileless, handsome, semitalented singers Rob Pilatus and Fabrice Morvan. They were Milli Vanilli. They admitted in November 1990 that they didn't really do the singing on their Grammy-winning first album, though this should have come as no surprise, since they had long acknowledged that they merely lip-synched their concerts. At a press conference after the scandal broke, Pilatus tried to apologize:

"We really love our fans. We just hope that they understand we were just young and we wanted to live life the American way."

The American way requires that they write a book about their lives, their dreams, their tragic downfall. There has been talk already about a book deal. Whether they will write it themselves is not a great mystery.

WORDS

(Oswald. The *S*-word. Jive turkeys. Why
Shakespeare is sort of like Elvis.)

WHY DO WE REMEMBER THE MIDDLE NAMES OF ASSASSINS?

*Whenever they took him down, he heard his name on the radios and
TVs. Lee Harvey Oswald. It sounded extremely strange. He didn't
recognize himself in the full intonation of the name. The only time he
used his middle name was to write it on a form that had a space for
that purpose. No one called him by that name. Now it was everywhere.
He heard it coming from the walls. Reporters called it out. Lee Harvey
Oswald, Lee Harvey Oswald. It sounded odd and dumb and made up.
They were talking about somebody else.*

—from the novel *Libra*, by Don Delillo

First, the cosmic explanation: Names are codes. In rolling a
name over in our mind we try to crack the code. Who is this
man Lee Harvey Oswald who would do such an awful thing?
Names encode the answer. Middle names in particular tend to
be strange, antiquated, formal, a nod to distant ancestors:
Wilkes. What kind of name is that?

Beyond the etymology there is a much simpler answer: Police blotters always use middle names to avoid misidentifica-
tion. There might have been a Lee Jehoshephat Oswald in
Dallas too. The news media invariably pick up the names ver-
batim. They know they cannot be sued for libel for accurately

repeating information from an official police report, even if it turns out to be wrong. So all heinous crime stories and Death Row stories take the full name right off the official documents.

What happens next is that the full name becomes a single expression, Leeharveyoswald, sort of like Sammydavisjunior. You would never say Lee Oswald. The Harvey is fixed in concrete. Same with Johnwilkesbooth. Markdavidchapman. Jamesearlray. Even Mehmetaliagca, the man who shot the pope. There is one modern exception to this rule: Sirhan Sirhan, who assassinated Robert Kennedy. What was his middle name? Dave maybe? Did his friends know him affectionately as Mac? Actually his middle name is Bishara; some of the first stories on the assassination identified him that way. He's since become simply Sirhan Sirhan. Why? Probably because Sirhanbisharasirhan is a tongue twister, too many sibilant sounds swooshing together. But perhaps it is also because the repetition of Sirhan Sirhan gives the name a formal weirdness, an enigmatic structure that fits the inexplicable nature of the crime. Sirhan Sirhan: a name so evil you have to say it twice.

WHY WERE CERTAIN PRESIDENTS KNOWN BY THEIR INITIALS, BUT NOT OTHERS? WHY DO WE REFER TO FDR AND JFK AND LBJ BUT NOT TO RMN OR JEC OR RWR OR GHWB?

Headlines. In the past many newspapers had eight columns per page, and the columns were a tight squeeze for a headline. Let's say you're working the copy desk and you've got to fit the president's name into a one-column head. Roosevelt? That counts 8.5 picas (capital letters and m count as 1.5; f,l,i,j,t count as 0.5; capital m and capital w count as 2.0; everything else is 1.0). So Roosevelt must be FDR. Carter? Six picas. No problem. Nixon? Ditto. Johnson? Seven-point-five picas. Gotta be LBJ. Eisenhower? Forget it. Ike (sounds better than DDE).

And so on. Every president known by his initials has a name of at least seven picas.

WHY ARE THEY CALLED "SPERM" WHALES?

It's a horribly embarrassing mistake! The early whalers found massive loads of strange waxy stuff in the whale's snout. Maybe they had been at sea too long, who knows, but they figured, *whoa*, this sucker can really bring it. They named the substance spermaceti, meaning "seed of the whale." The substance actually has no reproductive function, serving instead as part of the whale's sonar mechanism and possibly as a protective cushion against deep-sea pressures.

WHY IS THERE A ZODIAC SIGN CALLED CANCER?

So touchy is the word *cancer* that many Cancers now call themselves moon children. The word *cancer* comes from the Greek word for crab, a crab being the shape discerned in the constellation called Cancer. When the zodiac was established back in Roman times, the sun entered the constellation of Cancer on the 22nd of June, thus the origin of the name. The real question is, *Why is the disease called cancer*? The Oxford English Dictionary reports that this is due to the fact that the veins around a swollen area resemble the legs of a crab.

WHY DID JOHN HANCOCK AFFIX THAT GARISHLY LARGE SIGNATURE TO THE DECLARATION OF INDEPENDENCE?

He was the president of the Continental Congress, and thus had dibs on the first signature. In fact he was one of only two people who signed it on July 4, 1776, the other being the Congress secretary, Charles Thomson. Upon penning the big signature he reportedly said, "There, King George will be able to read that without his spectacles." But maybe he was revealing a personality defect: an oversized ego. We should recall that Hancock wanted to lead the Continental Army and was peeved at being passed over in favor of George Washington. He may have been sort of an Al Haig character. You know: "I'm in charge here."

WHY ARE THE DOG DAYS OF SUMMER CALLED THE DOG DAYS OF SUMMER?

The dog days run from the middle of July to the end of August. They are hot, sluggish, pestilential. We wish we could report that these days are called so because you feel like lazing around the yard like some sort of hound dog, but the truth is that this ancient term is derived from the brightest star in the sky, Sirius, "the Dog Star." During this part of summer in ancient times, Sirius rose in the morning just before the sun in the Northern Hemisphere. The ancients figured the bothersome heat had something to do with the combined radiation of Sirius and the sun. The ancients, in case you hadn't noticed, were wrong about virtually everything.

WHY IS AMERICA NAMED AFTER AMERIGO VESPUCCI INSTEAD OF CHRISTOPHER COLUMBUS?

America's name is based on a lie and a grave error. Vespucci claimed to have explored the New World in 1497, though this now seems to have been a fiction. He did make it in 1499—*way* behind the times. Still, a German mapmaker named Martin Waldseemüller thought Vespucci was the first man to reach the New World, and in 1507 he suggested the name America. Waldseemüller's confusion may be due in part to

Columbus's insistence that he had reached Asia, not a new continent. (See: "Why did Columbus miss the North American mainland even though he visited Cuba and the Bahamas," page 100.) That bit of foolishness cost him: Amerigo got two continents named after him. Chris got the capital of Ohio.

Why Is It an Insult to Call Someone a Turkey?

Turkeys have a bad reputation, which is not entirely deserved. The wild turkey is a savvy creature. The process of breeding and raising fat, white-meat domestic turkeys "has taken some of the inherent cunning out of the wild turkey," says National Turkey Federation spokeswoman Laurie Wilson. Contrary to popular myth, turkeys won't look up into the sky during a rainstorm and drown. But, lacking a mother's instruction, they don't know enough to find shelter in the rain, which can lead to sickness and death. They are foolishly fearless when approached by strange creatures, and yet they'll get panicked by a sudden rainfall and slam into each other. Because they are bred for heaviness, they lack agility, and a turkey in the center of the pile can suffocate or be trampled to death. We believe this is known as a "jive turkey."

Why Are Formulaic Books and Movies So Popular? Why Do We Exult When James Bond Says, for the Zillionth Time, "The Name Is Bond, James Bond"?

If novelty was the essential ingredient of modern art, then repetition is the hallmark of postmodern craft.

How would the funny-paper readers react if some Sunday morning Dagwood, realizing that he had missed the bus to work once too often, quit his job and started selling real estate out of his home? We can only guess, because it'll never happen. In his essay "Innovation and Repetition: Between Modern and Post-Modern Aesthetics," (*Daedelus*, Fall 1985), semioticist and novelist Umberto Eco argues that formulaic novels are pleasurable because (take a deep breath) "the readers continuously re-cover, point by point, what they already know, and what they want to know again; that is why they have purchased the book. They derive pleasure from the non-story (if indeed a story is a development of events which should bring us from the point of departure to a point of arrival where we never have dreamed of arriving); the distraction consists in the refutation of a development of events, in a withdrawal from the tension of past-present-future to the focus on an *instant*, which is loved precisely because it is recurrent."

What this means in English is that a good brainless paperback or a formulaic movie ("Yo, Rocky, you gotta *believe* in yoosef") temporarily suspends time. It alleviates the discomfort we feel as we're yanked through a worsening, changing world toward our ultimate termination. This is different from simple escapism. All entertainment, good or bad, provides an escape from day-to-day drudgery, but only formulaic entertainment takes us to a place we've been before, a comfortable, static little womb. The moment that Bond says "Bond, James Bond," time stops, and we are neither old nor young, neither rich nor poor, neither sick nor healthy.

Come to think of it, a Bond movie would be a lot more fun than reading "Innovation and Repetition: Between Modern and Post-Modern Aesthetics."

Why Is All Academic Writing Dull, Wordy, and Impenetrable?

We got to thinking about this the other day when we saw a friend reading a book called *Outline of a Theory of Practice*, by Pierre Bourdieu. Our friend said it is a very trendy book in Europe.

We didn't understand the title. We looked at the jacket blurbs and they were gibberish. Then we opened it up. Here's a sample sentence:

"Thus Levi-Strauss's use of the notion of the unconscious masks the contradictions generated by the implicit theory of practice which 'structural anthropology' accepts at least by default, restoring the old entelechies of the metaphysics of nature in the apparently secularized form of a structure structured in the absence of any structuring principle."

You have to admire that awesome burst at the end. This is impenetrability at its best. Obviously the major problem with understanding this is that the subject matter is of no interest to a normal beer-drinking human being. You can't get mental traction on any of it.

Why do academics write this way?

There are three possibilities:

1. They are precise. Academics use words the way a mathematician uses symbols, without regard to aesthetics or comprehension.

2. The writer simply can't write. In this case, the translation from the French may also be at fault.

3. The writer knows that the more baffling the prose, the greater his or her stature in the academic community.

Although all three are obviously factors at some level, we are inclined to suspect that the third is an inordinately major one. Steve Lagerfeld, senior editor of the *Wilson Quarterly*, concurs with us in this. Lagerfeld's job is to edit articles written by scholars and make them understandable to a general audience, since the scholars write in prose that only a few people can comprehend. Academics feel a disdain for popularizers, since time spent making a subject easily understood is time that might have been spent forging ahead into new territories of knowledge. No one gets tenure because they're popular with students or, gad, the public.

"There is a fair amount of artifice involved, in that to be a member of this select group, you have to speak the language. Generally the dynamic is that if other people can understand the language, it must not be so special, and we must not be so special," Lagerfeld said.

To be fair—oh, it's so painful—we should note that much of the academic writing that comes across our desk these days seems livelier than what we used to see in college. There seems to be a movement toward accessible, literate academic writing. So maybe our question is mean-spirited and factually inaccurate (though a lot can be said for this approach, we'd argue).

James McPherson, a professor of history at Princeton, wrote a lucid book on the Civil War called *Battle Cry of Freedom*, which sold well and won a Pulitzer Prize. He says he has detected a little scorn from a few colleagues. His next book, he promises, will be for a narrower audience. "I've tried to live with a foot in each door," he says, though he needn't worry too much. He already has tenure.

WHY DO FOREIGN LANGUAGES SOUND SO FAST?

All languages are spoken fast. If you know a language, it just *sounds* slower.

When we listen to a language in which we are fluent, we are listening and analyzing at the same time. We hear "a light housekeeper" and differentiate it immediately from "a lighthouse keeper" based on context. Same for "an ice box" and "a nice box." This takes effort. We are mentally slowing down what we hear, tweezing one word from the next, ungarbling the garbled.

When listening to a foreign language, there is sound but no analysis. And it sounds kind of like this: Sobreberissimiloch-errribiricochinearrrachaia.

Some languages are more bewildering than others. Staccato

languages like German and (less so) English sound more clear-cut to foreign listeners than soft languages like French. Cuban Spanish, where the ends of words, particularly ess sounds, are dropped regularly, sounds much faster than, say, Mexican Spanish, in which consonants are emphasized.

WHY DID WILLIAM FAULKNER SET MOST OF HIS NOVELS IN A FICTIONAL PLACE CALLED YOKNAPATAWPHA COUNTY, RATHER THAN IN A PLACE THAT'S EASIER TO PRONOUNCE?

O f all the great fictional places in English literature—Lilliput, Oz, Gotham City, and so on—none is tougher on the tongue than Yoknapatawpha County. But that's Faulkner: dense, difficult, kind of annoying.

Having written a couple of mediocre novels in the mid-1920s set in Georgia and New Orleans, Faulkner took the advice of novelist Sherwood Anderson to "write about your own little postage stamp of native soil," which happened to be a patch of northern Mississippi called Lafayette County (pronounced by the locals with the accent on the *fay*). Faulkner proceeded to set fourteen novels and dozens of stories there and needed at least a thin layer of fiction to take some of the slander out of his tales, which featured a heapin' helpin' of Southern degeneracy, sodomy, bestiality, murder, suicide, mutilation, necrophilia, nymphomania, and the really weird stuff like the kid in As I Lay Dying who thinks the putrefied corpse of his mother is a fish.

So Faulkner named his county Yoknapatawpha, after the original Chickasaw Indian name for a river that runs along the southern border of the county. Yoknapatawpha, meaning "muddy water flowing slowly through flat land," had been shortened by the white population into Yocona, which they pronounced Yocknee. Why Faulkner picked Yoknapatawpha and not something else is a mystery. He didn't seem to have much fascination with Indian culture. He may have just liked the word—liked how hard it is to say.

"Faulkner never tried to make anything easy for anyone," says Doreen Fowler, associate professor of English at the University of Mississippi in Oxford, Faulkner's hometown. "Maybe he was drawn to it just because of its difficulty."

After all, Faulkner was the kind of writer who did not hesitate to write a single sentence with more than 1,800 words—not once but twice. He wrote for himself, not the public. Once, in a guest lecture at the University of Mississippi, he was asked how he would rank himself among American writers of his day. He said second, after Thomas Wolfe, but ahead of John Dos Passos and Ernest Hemingway. Hemingway, he said (thinking no one would ever quote him), "has no courage, has never crawled out on a limb. He has never been known to use a word that might cause a reader to check with a dictionary to see if it is properly used."

His friends and neighbors were caught totally by surprise when he won the Nobel Prize for Literature in 1949. Faulkner had been worshiped in Europe as a great American genius, but in the United States only the racy 1931 novel *Sanctuary* sold well, and by 1945 almost all his books were out of print, with the original printing plates sold as scrap metal.

To make a living, Faulkner had to become a contract writer in Hollywood, tinkering with screenplays. When he left his job at Warner Bros., someone went to clean out his desk. Inside was an empty bottle and a long roll of paper with some words written on it. The words said merely "Boy meets girl," five hundred times.

WHY DID HEMINGWAY KILL HIMSELF EVEN THOUGH HE HAD AN EXCITING LIFE FILLED WITH ROMANCE, ADVENTURE, AND PROFESSIONAL ACCLAIM?

A popular myth has arisen that Hemingway took his own life because he realized he could no longer write. This jibes with the larger myth of Hemingway as a man of action, unwincing in matters of life and death, able to employ suicide as a final emphatic punctuation to a life sentence threatening to run on too long.

The truth is that Hemingway was mentally ill. He was afflicted with manic depression and paranoia in his later years, along with assorted other physical ailments (such as a bad liver) that contradicted his self-promoted macho image. In his final years he was frequently hospitalized and given shock treatments, but to no avail.

The most obvious contributor to his mental and physical breakdown was his alcoholism. It made for some great scenes in *The Sun Also Rises* (to be read only with Alka-Seltzer on hand), but as Kenneth Lynn notes in his biography *Hemingway*, "alcohol abuse alters brain-cell function, promotes nerve damage, shrinks the cerebral cortex, and so imbalances the hormonal system that it induces the body to shut off production of natural euphoriants, thereby robbing the alcoholic, as soon as his high wears off, of any normal feeling of well-being."

His physical ailments drove him to ridiculous public displays of manliness, such as playing war correspondent armed with a gun and traipsing around Africa on well-publicized safaris. Accident-prone, he had an unfortunate habit of getting bonked on the head, which might have contributed to his mental problems later in life. Mishaps to his skull dogged him throughout his life:

■ In 1944 he bashed his head into a windshield in a car accident, requiring fifty-seven stitches.

■ Later that same summer he suffered another concussion in a car accident while covering the war in Europe. This exacerbated his earlier symptoms of memory loss, slowness of speech, sexual impotence, dull headaches, and a tendency to write backward (okay, that's what the Lynn biography says, and we believe it even though we can't quite picture it).

■ In 1949 his car skidded off a wet road in Havana and slammed into a bank of earth. Another concussion.

■ In January 1954 he was in two plane crashes in Africa. In the second he escaped the burning plane by bashing his head against the aircraft door. "All of his contradictory wishes to live and die seem contained in the terrible, all-out lunges with which he inflicted another concussion on himself and made his way to freedom," Lynn writes. After the second crash Hemingway, seriously injured, attended a clamorous press conference with a bottle of gin in hand and said his luck was running good.

Hemingway had long been obsessed with suicide. His father had taken his life by gunshot. In For Whom the Bell Tolls the hero, Robert Jordan, bitterly recalls his own suicidal father as a "coward." By the start of the 1960s Hemingway's suicidal impulses became manifest and his behavior more erratic. Once, during a stay at a hospital for treatment of hypertension, Hemingway begged to go home to pick up some possessions. A nurse and another man insisted that they accompany him. They drove to the Hemingways' house, and then, writes Lynn, "the instant the car stopped, he raced inside the house in front of the others and before they could catch him jammed a shell into the breech of a shotgun and swung the muzzle under his chin." The two others managed to tear the gun away from him. It was a temporary stay of self-execution. On July 2, 1961, Hemingway took a shotgun and ended his brilliant, fascinating, and tragic life.

Why Did No One Write a Novel Before Miguel de Cervantes Wrote Don Quixote in the Seventeenth Century? Why, for Two Millennia, Did Storytellers Insist on Working in Verse, Rather Than Prose?

The novel had its glorious birth with the publication of the first part of Don Quixote in 1605, and nearly died of severe pretentiousness in 1968, when Norman Mailer subtitled his nonfiction book Armies of the Night "History as a Novel, the Novel as History." If film is the art form of the twentieth century, the novel would be the same for the nineteenth, a time that gave us Hawthorne, Melville, Austen, the Brontës, Dickens, Tolstoy, Dostoyevski, Twain, and Hardy. (The art form of the twenty-first century? Noise.) The question is, *Why was verse the dominant art form for two thousand years*? Why didn't anyone tell a story in straightforward prose?

First we should note that for much of human history, fiction was considered a pack of lies. Plato first articulated an antifiction philosophy, and the Christian church kept it alive during the Dark Ages. It was a bad time to be a poet, much less a novelist. Also, it may be that friars who preached for alms didn't like the competition from poets and bards; it was better to accuse them of heresy.

Second, we should deal with a sticky definitional problem. You could argue (if you were contentious and annoying) that the novel originated in ancient Egypt two thousand years before Christ. The most famous ancient Egyptian "novel" is titled Sinuhe, though we hear it's pretty dreadful. The ancient Greeks and Romans also wrote nonfiction prose, such as Petronius' The Satyricon and Apuleius' The Golden Ass. Some scholars say the first true novels were the works of Boccaccio in the fourteenth century, and others cite Rabelais' Adventures of Gargantua and Pantagruel, finished in 1534. There were also chivalric romances, originally written in verse, that were rewritten in prose form, with narratives long enough and complicated enough to seem novellike. Plus there's the hijinks back East—a Japanese noblewoman, Lady Murasaki, wrote *The Tale of Genji*, very much a novel, soon after the first millennium.

So why would we say that Cervantes wrote the first novel? Because as a general rule all these protonovels lacked the seriousness of purpose, narrative consistency, and realism that we associate with The Novel of the modern era. A novel has to be more than a prose rendering of myth and legend; a novel has to have some dirt under its fingernails.

The puzzle remains as to why the great masters pre-Cervantes worked almost exclusively in verse.

The answer (drumroll here): because they had a backup band. Sort of.

You see, back in the days of Homer (one of the most famous historical figures who might not actually have existed; why he or she or them was called Homer remains a good why question), storytellers spun their tales orally, singing and chanting the stories to an accompanying musical instrument. In general it is much easier to memorize large stretches of verse than big chunks of prose, and verse certainly sounds better if you have to sing. It's a rhythm thing. Check it out sometime at home. Put on a long guitar solo from Led Zeppelin and try, just try, to sing a riff from *Moby Dick*. Very difficult.

WHY IS SHAKESPEARE CONSIDERED SO MUCH GREATER THAN ANY OTHER WRITER?

B ecause he's English.

The Shakespearean myth spread across the globe, transported by British imperialism. The Bard became a touchstone for Anglophiles everywhere. To insult or ignore him would be to eschew British culture and civility. He was not just a great poet, he was England incarnate.

The playwright's notoriety then fed on itself. Shakespeare

became an industry. For the common man attention to Shakespeare proved one's high-mindedness; for the actor a new interpretation of an old Shakespearean role established one's skill and originality; for the scholar the ability to cite Shakespeare was indispensable for intellectual discourse. Thus you find otherwise sane people wasting their time scrutinizing the tedious extremes of the canon, such as *Titus Andronicus*, *Henry VI*, *Part 3*, and *Cymbeline*.

We offer these answers fully knowing that hard-core Shakespeareans will froth at the mouth and gurgle in bilious protest, citing the depth, breadth, and imponderable brilliance of everything Shakespeare touched, his humanity, humor, and honesty . . . but in the very ferocity of their attack they prove how far gone is the Shakespeare cult.

For our part we love the guy, except for *Hamlet*, which seemed to us to be full of horrible clichés (for example, "This, above all, to thine own self be true" and the supercliché "To be or not to be, that is the question"). Even if we cede the point that he is the greatest writer of all time, his reputation is still out of control. As in all fields of human endeavor, *it is possible to be the best and still be overrated*. Shakespeare is, quite frankly, the Elvis of literature.

Visit any library and you will see shelves—nay, whole wings—that creak with books dissecting and masticating every word that the dude quilled, our favorite being Henry Ellacombe's 1896 volume, *Plant Lore and Garden-Craft of Shakespeare*.

At one point we were thumbing through the October 1859 issue of the *American Journal of Insanity* (we saved our back issues) and found an article entitled "William Shakespeare as a Physiologist and Psychologist," by A. O. Kellogg, M.D. "Many [medical] facts not known or recognized by men of his age appear to have been grasped by the inspired mind of the poet," Kellogg writes. He cites Falstaff's reference to sherry-sack making the blood "course from the inwards to the parts extreme" as evidence that Shakespeare knew about the circulation of blood, which was not officially discovered until twelve years after his death.

We have to agree with Gary Taylor's book *Reinventing Shakespeare*: "Shakespeare himself no longer transmits visible light; his stellar energies have been trapped within the gravity well of his own reputation. . . . If Shakespeare is a literary black hole, then nothing that I, or anyone else, can say will make any difference. His accreting disk will go on spinning, sucking, growing."

WHY DO BRITISH ROCK 'N' ROLL STARS SPEAK IN COCKNEY ACCENTS BUT SOUND LIKE AMERICANS WHEN THEY SING?

British bands emulated the American accent because they grew up listening to American rhythm and blues and early rock 'n' roll. American opera singers, when they sing in Italian, use an Italian accent.

A less obvious reason is that singing tends to mute any accent. According to Rachel Lebon, music professor at the University of Miami and a singer as well, singing requires the projection of sound on a vowel, as opposed to a consonant. In daily speech consonants, more than vowels, get wrecked and abused by accents, or are dropped altogether. You can't do that as easily when you sing.

A reporter asked the Beatles at a 1964 press conference, "Why do you sing like Americans but speak with an English accent?"

John Lennon answered, "It sells better."

WHY IS THE *S*-WORD CONSIDERED OBSCENE, BUT NOT SUCH SYNONYMS AS *FECES* AND *EXCREMENT* AND *ORDURE*?

We venture into this etymological mystery with the purest of intellectual intentions. Any vulgarity has an equivalent word that is deemed acceptable in common speech. Why are some okay but not others?

It boils down to prejudices. And obsessions. And the linguistic necessity for vulgarity.

The famed scatological noun-verb beginning with *s* was not always vulgar. The original Old English noun was *scite*, and the verb *scitan*, meaning to separate from the body. Nothing obscene there. Over the years the word evolved into such variations as *schyt*, *sheitt*, and the uneconomical *scheitte*. The past tense of the verb is particularly interesting, ranging from *scat* (similar to the Greek *skatos*, from which comes *scatology*, which means "the study of the *s*-word") to the wonderful *schote*, which really ought to be used even today, if you ask us. *The Oxford English Dictionary* cites a number of casual, undirty uses of the word, such as in the Old English version of *Aesop's Fables*: "The wulf . . . shote thryses by the waye for the grete fere that he had." Translation: He was scared s-word-less.

By the 1600s the word had taken on its present form, but not until the late 1700s did it vanish from polite speech.

"About that time there was a sort of cult of delicacy in the late eighteenth and early nineteenth century, and anything involving bodily functions became taboo," reports Margaret Fleming, a University of Arizona English professor who has studied the origins of the word.

So why aren't those other words, such as *excrement*, considered obscene? Probably because they are of Latin origin, as opposed to Anglo-Saxon. The Anglo-Saxon language was spoken in the Middle Ages by the lower classes in England, the *vulgus*, while the aristocracy spoke French. Anglo-Saxon words were deemed crude. They also have a punchy, explosive quality, so that when it came time to purge the language of vulgarities, it was those four-letter Anglo-Saxon words that were judged obscene.

The s-word isn't particularly vulgar in other countries. But they, too, need to express themselves in a shocking and dramatic fashion. So how do they cuss? They have their ways. The world is divided into three types of people with three types of obscene oaths, according to Reinhold Aman, editor of *Maledicta*, a journal of profanity and curses (once again, there is an expert on every subject).

The White Anglo-Saxon Protestants use body processes as the basis for cusswords. Most Catholics in Europe and South America erect curses around religious blasphemies (Aman gave examples, but none are printable). In Asia, Africa, and Polynesia curses involve family members, variations on such comments as "Your mother wears army boots."

Says Aman, "Other people are not as fixated as white Americans are, as WASPS are, on bodily products and copulation."

Why Is Elvis's Middle Name Misspelled on His Tombstone at Graceland?

The expert on this Mystery for the Ages is Gail Brewer-Giorgio, author of the scholarly, almost Talmudically researched text Is *Elvis Alive*? One of the key pieces of evidence that the King is still with us (other than a cassette tape of an Elvis-sounding person mumbling that he faked his death and moved to Hawaii) is that the tombstone says Elvis Aaron Presley, even though everyone knows Elvis's middle name is Aron. Brewer-Giorgio writes, "If Elvis did not die on August 16, 1977, then it makes sense not to tempt fate by putting one's name on a tombstone if one is still alive—and you don't have to be superstitious to believe this. To misspell the name could be a method of saying, 'It's not me.'"

Indeed one would feel that one should actually call Graceland to get one's final answer. We did. Graceland said that Elvis's middle name is spelled "Aaron" on his tombstone because that was, in fact, his name, being written as such on his birth certificate. (Oh, *that* old ruse!) He used Aron throughout his life for mysterious hillbilly reasons, such as the fact that his dead twin brother's name was Garon, and Aron was the same thing without the G.

WHY IS THERE NO GENERIC GENDER-NEUTRAL PRONOUN IN ENGLISH THAT CAN BE USED INSTEAD OF THE SEXIST HE OR THE WORDY HE OR SHE?

The average American, having started a sentence with an expression such as "the average American," may suddenly find himself hitting a verbal pothole on his way to the period. Should he choose the masculine pronoun, he not only will risk imprecision but will sound sexist, archaic, reactionary. But should he choose exactitude and fairness—saying, "the average American may suddenly find himself or herself hitting a verbal pothole on his or her way to the period"—he will sacrifice brevity and grace. A decent sentence becomes unwieldy and comical, sounding as if the average American does not know his or her gender unless he or she looks into his or her shorts.

No one actually talks this way. Good writing, as a rule, should be easily spoken. Also, "he or she" is still latently sexist, with its masculine-before-feminine construction. Yet to say "she or he" is distracting, a screaming advertisement for social concern.

One might decide to experiment with the word *one* in one's compositions. This is not sexist. Unfortunately this makes one sound like a pompous *arse*; no one speaks in such a way except lords in powdered wigs and William F. Buckley, Jr.

A strident egalitarian will insist on writing *s/he*. This vomitive confection resembles a typo and defies speech altogether.

The easy solution is, of course, to say *they*. We received a piece of junk mail from American Express saying, "Give someone something solid they can build on. Credit in their own name." This is not sexist, but it is also not English. *They* and *their* in this ungrammatical context clang harshly upon the educated ear. That famed little book of English usage, *The Elements of Style*, by William Strunk, Jr. and E. B. White, confidently decrees that in all such situations, "use the singular pronoun." What is the singular pronoun in English? He.

Sometimes, though, *he* is *not* quite right. To prove this point, we have as an example a dilemma that drove *The New York Times* to abandon any semblance of proper writing. *The Times* reported on June 30, 1990, that a Texas journalist had gone to jail for not naming his sources. The article said that, according to the jailed journalist, one of the sources "is a private citizen who has expressed fear for their life if they are identified." Though atrocious in its present state, the sentence is a tough one to rewrite, because we don't know the gender of the mystery source, and it would sound strange to say that this citizen has expressed fear for his or her life if he or she is identified—no one would ever express such a fear unless they suffered severe gender confusion.

Which is why it would be nice to have a gender-neutral pronoun. Some languages do. In the Tagalog dialect of Filipino, for example, there is no way to make a gender distinction in third-person pronouns. Either way the word is *siya* (see-AH), or *sila* (see-LAH) in the plural. The language has no words for *he* or *she*. This solves one problem but diminishes the verbal ammo. There ought to be a word, in addition to *he or she*, that means *s/he* or *his/her*. In fact there is one, in some parts of England. The local dialect uses *a*, pronounced AH, as a gender-neutral pronoun.

No neutral pronouns have caught on for a broader usage.

Dr. Victoria Neufeldt, editor-in-chief of Webster's New World Dictionaries, says she occasionally hears of attempts to invent such a pronoun, but every movement has been futile. The success of the title Ms. is owed to its simplicity: It is a modest revision of Mrs. and Miss and is easy to say. There is no such shortcut with *he or she*.

So for the time being we are stuck with either the repugnant *he* or the cacophonous alternatives. Or as a last resort, we can use the glib, informal, hypervernacular second-person; the average American knows that you can talk any way you want.

Why Do Radio Stations Play Hit Songs Long After We're Utterly Sick of Them?

Market research is to blame for this, and for most other things in life. Radio stations no longer pay much attention to record sales, since most teenyboppers don't even buy records. Instead stations constantly do their own surveys. At any given time a station might have a dozen researchers trying to figure out what the audience wants to hear. And for the most part, people want to hear something familiar. "Familiarity breeds con*tent*," says one radio-station manager. Now here's the cruncher: The average listener listens to only about fifteen minutes of radio a day. A trifle. To give this listener a chance to hear a song again and again, it must be put in the "power rotation," which means it might play once every two hours. If you're getting nauseated, you're listening to more than your share of radio.

WHY DID PRUFROCK SAY, "I GROW OLD . . . I GROW OLD . . . I SHALL WEAR THE BOTTOMS OF MY TROUSERS ROLLED"?

The line is the dramatic, quirky zenith of T. S. Eliot's *The Love Song of J. Alfred Prufrock*, one of those excruciatingly important literary lines that high school students are supposed to analyze at term-paper time *with original insights*. Naturally there's not a jot of meaning that you can detect in the thing, so you are forced to consider suicide, truancy, drug abuse, and teachercide before finally settling for simple plagiarism. What you need is help from the Why Things Are Literary Bureau (a division of the Why Things Are Department of Words). We're like *Cliffs Notes*, only more credible and funnier.

First of all we have to wonder why this quote is even memorable, much less significant. The obvious reason is that the mantra "I grow old . . . I grow old . . ." is the most economical statement about the essential tragedy of life, and therefore of literature. You can't condense the pain of mortality any further. (Of course you could wipe out the ellipses, but they're crucial, a hint of longing that turns factuality into mournfulness.)

Then you come to the kicker, the payoff, and it's unforgettably silly: "I shall wear the bottoms of my trousers rolled." What a goofy rhyme! How Mother Hubbard of him! But it's perfect. It's like a Herman's Hermits song: You hate it but can't get it out of your mind. It actually reads, at a quick glance, like the first thing he could come up with on a tight deadline. (We would have chosen, "I shall wash my dirty underwear with Bold.")

Traditionally students have been told that Prufrock will need to roll up his trousers when he gets old because he'll be thin and shrunken and won't want his pants to drag on the ground. That's a tedious argument of insidious intent. Eliot is making a much more profound statement.

Prufrock is a brilliant, pompous, self-pitying dude who wants to put the hit on women but doesn't have the nerve. He's letting life pass him by. He's getting old and going nowhere. He's not a tragic Hamlet figure, just a fool. He's worried about going bald. He knows he's a stuffed shirt and even describes his oh-so-traditional clothing, talking about his morning coat, his starched collar, and his conservative necktie. How can he score if he's dressed like a banker? He needs a fashion transfusion.

This is where the slacks come in. One of our unusually literate readers/sources, Bob Dattoli, has unearthed a passage from Jules Romains's *Men of Good Will*, which describes the fashions of the early twentieth century: "A fold at the bottom of the trouser-leg, simulating a cuff, was regarded as a rather frivolous elegance or a fashion for young men."

Prufrock, at the height of his despair—"I grow old"—suddenly shifts, as almost comic relief, into a darkly humorous vision of himself reinvented as a dandy: "I shall wear the bottoms of my trousers rolled." He'll be a fashion plate, shallow, trendy, un-Prufrockish. Then he goes on to think of how he'll comb his hair to cover his bald spot and how he'll do dashing things like walk on the romantic shore in his suddenly nifty trousers.

A contemporary version of the same idea might go something like this (without the rhyme): "I grow old . . . I grow old . . . Hey! Maybe I'll start dressing all in black! And moussing my hair! And disport myself doing the proverbial wild thing!"

MICROCOSMS AND MACROCOSMS

(Atoms. The earth. Space. In which we explain how the world is put together.)

WHY ARE WE SO SURE THAT ATOMS EXIST, WHEN WE CAN'T SEE THEM?

The Greeks, specifically two characters named Leucippus and Democritus (first names: Bob and Jim), first floated the idea that matter might be made up of discrete, indestructible units, building blocks for everything else. The Greek word *atomos* means "uncut" or "indivisible." The opposing view, which remained dominant for two millennia, held that matter could be infinitely divided—that it's just a lot of *mush*.

The debate shifted dramatically in the early 1800s, when a British scientist named John Dalton came up with the first modern atomic theory. He showed that when you mix elements in different proportions to make different chemical compounds, the ratio of the weights of those elements can always be expressed in small whole numbers. Huh? Okay, try this: If you add nitrogen to oxygen, you get a certain kind of gas. If you double the amount of nitrogen, you get a different kind of gas.

There are five kinds of gas, total, that you can get from mixing nitrogen and oxygen. In each the ratio of oxygen to nitrogen can be written in nice, neat whole numbers, that is, 1:1, 1:2, 1:3, and so on. The implication is that these elements are made up of discrete units—otherwise you'd have elements with ratios like 1:1.764532.

New "field-emission microscopes" can now directly observe large atoms such as tungsten or uranium. What is seen are the electron clouds, the network of electrons whizzing around the nucleus.

The nucleus itself, which is a million times smaller than the atom as a whole, cannot be seen. Atoms of course are not *atomos* after all: They have smaller components—protons and neutrons—not to mention those little orbiting electrons. The "elements" of the periodic table (hydrogen, helium, carbon, uranium, californium, byzantium, sputum, and so on) are distinguished only by the number of protons and neutrons and electrons that they have. If it's got one proton and one neutron, it's called hydrogen. Double that number, you got helium. What this means is that the entire world is just a showcase for all the various ways you can arrange protons and neutrons and electrons—it's almost as amazing as how many ways a good cook can fix chicken.

Protons and neutrons are thought to be divisible even further, into fundamental units of matter called quarks. Some theorists think the scale may recede even further, so that the smallest units are tiny loops, which are called superstrings, so tiny that one decillion of them—a million billion billion billion— laid end-to-end stretch to only one centimeter.

And what are strings made of? We have our own theory: Mush.

Why Is It That When We Touch Something, Like a Table, Our Finger Atoms Don't Get Mixed Up With the Table Atoms?

In fact why don't we gradually dissipate into the environment during the course of the day? Why don't we fuse to things the moment we touch them?

Stay calm. Your physical integrity is safe. Your atoms are fixed fairly rigidly into place, forming the internal girding of your molecules, which are in turn solidly woven into your tissues. There are no loose parts. The binding is due to things like electron-sharing, electronegativity, and covalent bonds—stuff you don't really need to understand, except insofar as covalent bonds have nothing to do with Wall Street.

Our fingers don't mix with the table for the same reason that oil doesn't mix with water. At the molecular level there is no force, no energy, no nefarious agent provoking the finger (or oil) molecule to rip itself from its brethren and infiltrate the table (or water) molecules. With a blowtorch you might be able to fuse hand to table, but we don't recommend that you try it.

Why Doesn't the Ocean Get More and More Disgustingly Salty as a Result of Whatever the Process Is That Made It Salty in the First Place?

The ocean is salty because rivers erode the salt out of rocks and wash it into the sea. That's way oversimplified, but good enough. The question that no one ever remembers to ask in elementary school is why the ocean doesn't get saltier and saltier over time. After all, ocean water keeps evaporating, raining back onto the continents, eroding some more, and so on. Seems like eventually all the oceans should become like the Great Salt Lake, ridiculously salty and devoid of life except for the occasional Mormon.

In fact the ocean has had a fairly constant level of saltiness for a billion years, according to University of Miami marine geologist Garrett Brass. It doesn't change much because of the various salt flats on the coasts of hot places like the Persian Gulf. With big tidal flats and lots of hot weather, the water evaporates so fast that it leaves behind massive deposits of salt. The ocean thereby becomes less salty than it would otherwise be. This is why there are salt mines under the Gulf Coast of the United States. There aren't many naturally occurring salt flats, but neither is there much salt coming into the ocean via streams and rivers.

WHY DO SUNRISES LOOK DIFFERENT THAN SUNSETS?

The geometry of dawn is identical to that of dusk, right? The angles and so forth? So why aren't they identical? You say you don't get up that early and don't know what we're talking about? Trust us, sunrises are to sunsets what Cream of Wheat is to Baked Alaska. You say you've never eaten either Cream of Wheat or Baked Alaska? Let's just say sunrises, though filled with hope and promise, are slightly insipid. They are gentle, sweet, skewed toward yellows and lavenders, with nice even layers like you see in One-Two-Three Jell-O. Sunsets are wilder, more unpredictable, and the real cymbal-crashing spectaculars feature incendiary oranges and reds.

Before we explain why this is so, we should deal with one of the all-time-behemoth why questions, straight from the Curious Child Hall of Fame:

Why is the sky blue?

Because blue light is scattered, which is to say reflected, by tiny particles in the air. Red and yellow and green and all the other colors are more likely to be absorbed by the particles. Thus more blue light bounces into our eyes.

It is the larger particles—stuff like dust—that scatter red light.

And that's the first reason that sunsets are more dramatic than sunrises:

1. There is more dust at the end of a busy day. The dust comes from car exhaust, kids kicking tin cans down the road, dogs scratching themselves, and so on. Where you live is also a factor. Residents of Long Island get great sunsets by looking through the wretchedness of Manhattan; the reverse effect would apply for sunrises in Long Beach or Santa Monica.

2. The humidity is higher in the morning. It's so high that the air becomes saturated with suspended liquid water. This foggy stuff doesn't scatter light as much as dust, though common sense seems to indicate the reverse should be true. The mystery is solved when you realize that a dusty afternoon sky is made up of lots of small particles, including eensy bits of gaseous water, while the morning dew is filled with relatively large, and relatively few, liquid droplets (though not so large that they fall to the ground). The morning haze looks thick, but it's really kind of thin. To a sunbeam it's smooth sailing.

3. There are more clouds in late afternoon. The clouds form as the earth heats up and the water vapor evaporates. You need good clouds for a really killer sunset.

WHY DO THE CLOUDS HANGING AROUND AT THE END OF THE DAY ALWAYS DISAPPEAR BY MORNING?

Like, where do the clouds go?

The answer is perhaps the single most astonishing piece of knowledge imparted in this slim, modest volume: Clouds vanish into thin air.

Not only that, but they do it quickly. It is a measure of the fleeting attention of human beings that we never notice that those little puffy cumulus clouds in the sky suddenly disappear without a trace.

These clouds are born fast, and they die fast. Dr. Richard Pasch, a former meteorologist for the National Hurricane Center in Coral Gables, estimates that a cumulus cloud condenses in about ten to fifteen minutes and then disappears within half an hour. There's no mystery to the phenomenon; the condensed water gradually mixes with the surrounding, drier air and converts to its invisible, gaseous state, what we call water vapor. (We all tend to think that clouds are made of water vapor, but we're mistaken. Vapors are gases and can't be seen. Steam, for example, is a gas. It exits a teakettle or smokestack and is perfectly clear for a few millimeters or a few feet, depending on the situation, and then the water vapor condenses into a visible liquid. Clouds are made of suspended liquid water, not water vapor.)

After dark, as the earth cools and the convective mechanism that creates puffy, white clouds shuts off, the existing clouds keep disappearing at the normal rate, but now they don't get replacements, so by morning the sky is clear.

WHY DOESN'T THE SUN RAPIDLY BURN UP, SEEING AS HOW IT IS A BALL OF HYDROGEN GAS AND OUGHT TO GO WOOF! LIKE THE HINDENBURG?

Hopefully you are still sitting down: The sun is not on fire. Repeat this to yourself. The sun is not burning. It is "fiery" only in the loosest use of the adjective.

We naturally assume that it is on fire because it is hot and bright and, in close-up photos, has what looks like jets of flame shooting off the surface. But if it were on fire, it would have burned out billions of years ago.

Indeed until the late 1800s the burning-sun notion provided a major argument for a literal interpretation of the Book of Genesis, which would put the age of the earth at about five thousand years. That fit nicely with calculations of the sun's size and mass, which indicated that the sun should consume itself in about fifty thousand years—assuming that it was burning just like a regular campfire, only bigger.

Eventually solar astronomers realized that the sun is largely a ball of hydrogen gas and lacks the key ingredient for fire as we know it on earth: oxygen. No oxygen, no fire. The "flames" are bright streamers of hydrogen shooting out into space.

The heat and light come from a process vastly superior to that old-fashioned chemical reaction that we call fire. It's the secret of the H-bomb: thermonuclear fusion. This is a trick that can be accomplished only where you have extremely high temperatures and pressures, such as the center of the sun. The outer layer, the part we can see, isn't hot enough. At the infernal core the usually repulsive—and we mean this in a nice way—atoms of hydrogen are fused together, forming helium. This transformation is rather complicated and involves lots of side effects, such as the emission of gamma rays and neutrinos and so forth, which taken together give you quite an explosion of energy. The liberated energy radiates and convects its way up to the surface of the sun, bubbling up in huge eruptions. The surface gives off heat and light as would a steel rod pulled from the furnace. We wouldn't say the rod was on fire; neither is the sun.

But hold on one gol-durned second. If all this explosive stuff is happening, if the sun is clearly giving off so much energy that even we, 93 million miles away, can live off just the tiniest fraction that we happen to intercept, then why does the sun seem so stable? Why is it taking so long to burn up that hydrogen? Why do we think we have another five billion years of this free energy?

Partly this leisurely pace is the result of the size of the sun, which is 333,000 times bigger than the earth, and thus has plenty of hydrogen to burn. Still, the sun's energy is also slightly deceptive. Surely, you figure, a finite blob of hydrogen *that hot* is going to use itself up pretty quickly. What our mental calculus forgets is that the sun's method of producing heat is much more efficient than what we do with a campfire. The sun gets more out of its gallon of gas. To stick with this metaphor, your car can go twenty miles when it burns a gallon of gasoline, using old-fashioned oxygen-fed fire. But if your car had a nice little fusion reactor, that same gallon of gas would propel it for millions of miles.

But, please, check your tires first.

WHY ARE WE SO NONCHALANT ABOUT THE POSSIBILITY OF BEING HIT BY A LARGE ASTEROID LIKE THE ONE THAT KILLED OFF THE DINOSAURS?

As far as anyone knows, the only human casualty due to meteorite impact was a certain Mrs. Hewlett Hodges, age thirty-two, of Sylacauga, Alabama. She was lying on the couch in her living room on November 30, 1954, when a grapefruit-sized meteorite crashed through the roof, bounced off the radio, and struck her in the arm.

She was treated for bruises.

One boo-boo in all of human history: pretty fair odds, right?

Chew on this statistic: A human being has about a one-in-a-million chance of dying from asteroid impact, according to our source at NASA. Though "one in a million" is vernacular for "impossible," it is actually a rather high risk, and the government routinely regulates other hazards that are statistically less risky. The reason the odds aren't more remote is that an asteroid impact would have a huge death toll; in other words, although it is extraordinarily unlikely that an asteroid will kill anybody this year, if one does hit, the chances are a lot of people would die. A truly giant asteroid hitting the ocean would boil off so much water that the entire planet would be steam-cleaned, wiping out life as we know it and raising the ultimate question "How will the New York Post find headline type that's big enough?'' (GOD TO EARTH: ''DROP DEAD'')

It is now widely accepted that an asteroid about five miles across hit the earth at the same time that the dinosaurs disappeared, about 67 million years ago. (Don't confuse the extinction of dinosaurs with the disappearance of megafauna which, as we will mention in chapter 16, humans may have had a hand in. Dinosaurs are cold-blooded reptiles, while megafauna are warm-blooded animals, such as the woolly mammoth which vanished from the earth about ten thousand years ago.) Most likely the impact raised a cloud of dust that darkened the earth for many months, shutting down much of the photosynthesis—the best guess for touchdown is a spot near the town of Manson, Iowa, where geologists have found traces of a huge buried crater. Not only did the dinosaurs die: Fully two out of three species on the planet went extinct.

There have been worse extinctions. About 225 million years ago, some 95 percent of marine invertebrate species died in what is known as the Permian extinction. A meteorite impact is suspected.

Now, we don't want anyone to get panicky just yet, though it has crossed our minds that a good scare might boost the ''Why Things Are'' readership. An object the size of the one that killed the dinosaurs probably strikes the earth only about once every 100 million years or so. More likely we'd be hit by a smaller object a few hundred meters across, like the one that just missed us in early 1989 by a scant six hours and half a million miles. Called 1989fc, it was several hundred meters across and had a kinetic energy you wouldn't believe—a speed of twenty miles a second, capable of puncturing the entire depth of the atmosphere faster than you can say ''late-Cretaceous extinction.'' The impact would have been equal to about twenty thousand good-sized hydrogen bombs. True, that's not all bad, if it hits Los Angeles, but otherwise you can envision serious problems.

If these things are rare, why worry? Because one could strike tomorrow, and we probably wouldn't even see it coming. There's no statistical reason why it couldn't. But wait! you say. We'd see it coming, right? We've got people out there, astronomer types, scouting the skies, right? We're on the lookout, right?

Negatory. In the entire country, only Eugene and Carolyn Shoemaker, of Flagstaff, Arizona, have been engaged in any systematic, full-time search for asteroids. They have a low-budget operation that uses a borrowed telescope.

A 1982 conference in Colorado on asteroids determined that a kilometer-wide object could be diverted from hitting the earth with a very small nuclear device. The problem is, you have to see 'em before you can shoot 'em. An asteroid is typically made of dark, carbonaceous rock that reflects little light. And if it's bearing down on earth, it won't show any "proper motion" against the background of stars.

"The one with your name on it, you probably wouldn't see at all," says physicist James Trefil of George Mason University.

Dr. Bevan French, program scientist of NASA's Solar System Exploration Division, says, "Enough warning means several years. . . . You have to intersect it at the distant orbit and not near the earth. If you make a small nudge at a distance, you can divert it. If you wait until it gets close to the earth on a collision course, you're really going to have to hit it hard, and it might not be possible."

Unfortunately our government has too many other important and worthwhile things to spend money on and cannot bother with something as inconsequential as saving civilization from instant extermination.

WHY DO OBJECTS FALL AT THE SAME RATE TOWARD THE EARTH REGARDLESS OF THEIR WEIGHT?

You would think that Orson Welles, if dropped from the top of the Empire State Building, would hit the ground before a paper clip that was dropped simultaneously. But (discounting any possible effects from wind or air resistance) they land at the same time.

Try an experiment.

Pick up the paper clip. Now pick up Orson Welles. Orson Welles is definitely heavier. What do we mean by "heavier"? We mean that, holding the deceased director of Citizen Kane by the lapels, we can detect that he is subject to greater gravitational force. But Orson Welles has another distinct feature: He is hard to move. The more massive an object, the greater the force needed to move it from a state of rest. This is true whether you are rolling someone down the sidewalk or dropping him from a skyscraper.

The hard thing to realize is that objects don't fall "because there's nothing underneath them." It's not a matter of geometry (unless you're talking in extremely sophisticated Einsteinian terms, in which case geometry is exactly what it's all about). Objects fall because they are being *moved* by gravity. You do not, in fact, "drop" Orson Welles; you just place him in a point in space. Since there is no structure to support him, gravity can move him without encumbrance.

The point here is that heaviness is a two-sided coin. As you get heavier, gravity pulls harder, *but it is also that much harder to budge you*. So weight doesn't make you fall faster or slower. That's your answer.

Theoretically if you had unbelievably sensitive instruments, and if you dropped Orson Welles and the paper clip in separate experiments instead of simultaneously, you might be able to show that the cinematic giant hit the ground a fraction of a fraction of a microsecond more quickly than the paper clip.

This is because the late spokesman for Paul Masson wine exerts his own gravitational attraction and pulls the earth toward him as he descends. So, for that matter, does the paper clip, but less so.

This is worthless cogitation, though. Gravity is the weakest of the four known forces in the universe (except perhaps on Mondays), and even the porcine *War of the Worlds* hoaxster doesn't have much gravitational attraction.

WHY DOESN'T THE AIR FALL TO THE GROUND?

Air doesn't fall to the ground because it's too hot—in a sense. "Hot" in this context means that the air molecules, such as oxygen and nitrogen, are moving rapidly. In fact they're rocketing around as though fired from a rifle. Gravity, as we have noted above, is an exceedingly weak force, and has relatively little effect on an oxygen molecule that's hurtling through the sky. Gravity is so weak it can't even pull down the tiny particles of *liquid* water that form clouds and that are buffeted about by the gross motion of the air.

Gravity does have enough of an effect to keep the air from escaping into space. Most of it, in fact, settles near the ground. The atmosphere is like a big ocean, with the pressure—the concentration of molecules—greatest at the bottom.

Air molecules *do* hit the ground all the time. Some bounce back into the sky. Others stick. Some linger on the ground until they get hot and then rise up.

One last thought: If the temperature were ever to drop to absolute zero, about 273 degrees below zero Celsius, the air would freeze and fall to the ground. It would litter everything, a thin coating of atmospheric debris. On the bright side, we would no longer have to remember the difference between ozone depletion and the greenhouse effect.

WHY ARE TREES ABLE TO SUCK WATER FROM THEIR ROOTS, AGAINST THE FORCE OF GRAVITY, EVEN THOUGH THEY DON'T HAVE MOVING PARTS?

Water molecules are shaped in such a way that they bind to one another like magnets and form long, one-molecule-wide chains that extend from the roots up through the narrow veins, or capillaries, of the tree, all the way to the leaves. As a molecule of water evaporates from a leaf, it pulls up the rest of the chain. The tree doesn't need moving parts, because water does all the work.

SPACE TRAVEL

(In which we explain that it's going to be a
long time before we boldly go where no man
has gone before.)

*Nor could the future even be seen until one could answer the obsessive
question: Was our venture into space noble or insane, was it part of a
search for the good, or the agent of diabolisms yet unglimpsed?*
—Norman Mailer, *Of a Fire on the Moon*

A few miles north of the Rose Bowl, where the flat valley
floor of the Los Angeles basin suddenly banks upward into
sagebrush mountains, there is a thick forest of buildings
clinging to the hillside. Some of the structures have no windows. Acres of corrugated metal rise four or five stories, squar-
ing off abruptly without overhangs or cornices. They look like
giant air conditioners. That this place is special is revealed by
the dish antennae on the roofs, by the guards at the gate, and
by the pale men and women who fill the fluorescent interiors
and speak the precision tongue of scientists.

This is NASA's Jet Propulsion Laboratory, a monument to
the power of machines, and we had come here, to Pasadena,
to ask some sixties-vintage questions that might have been
embarrassingly fanciful had not the space shuttle just blown
up over the coast of Florida.

We wanted to know:

Is our destiny in space?

Will human beings ever reach the stars?

Why send people into space at all, if machines can do the job better?

Why isn't space travel as easy as we thought it would be when we first watched *Star Trek*?

Pasadena is the perfect place at which to inquire. Space travel at interstellar distances is largely a simple arithmetical function of speed, of thrust, of getting there, of propulsion; and propulsion, as one would suspect, is a subject on which the people at the Jet Propulsion Laboratory can speak at length.

The search for answers begins in Building 233, which, like all buildings at the Lab, has only a number, no name. There is a man here named Jim French, surrounded by charts of gravitational tides on Mars, in a windowless office that is maybe one body-length square. One wall is dominated by a map of the moon, and on top of the filing cabinet is a model of a sister ship to the starship *Enterprise*. And a pair of enemy attack ships. Klingon. Romulan.

"The solar system isn't as much fun as it was in the science fiction stories, there being no Martians, and Venus turning out to be boiling hot," French starts out.

This is the difference between the romance and the reality of space travel. The romance holds that space is quite literally a frontier, a New World thick with stars, awaiting our modern conquistadors. The reality is that for most human purposes the solar system is too hot, too cold, too harsh, too dead; it is filled with desert worlds, worlds that have no surface, worlds where toxic gas rains from the sky. Not much fun.

French is a big, rangy guy, with a permanent look of mischief on his face. He wears cowboy boots and a large brass belt buckle that says "Mission to Mars." You could scuff your boots clean on his Astroturf hair; he looks like he should be named Buzz.

"I wanted to be the first guy to land on the moon. I was glad that it was done, but I'd have rather it been me than Neil Armstrong. I'm sure there are a lot of people in this profession who feel the same way but won't admit it."

French fits into a special category: He is what is known as a Visionary. When a stodgy scientist refers to a colleague as a Visionary, there is often a slight tonal modulation in the word, to indicate a degree of contempt. You can tell the Visionaries by sight—they're the ones who look like they're set to be suited up for the next launch, the Buck Rogers types. French, unlike many of his more earthbound colleagues, thinks sheer adventure is reason enough to go into space; merely sending machines doesn't satisfy his deeper urges.

"If your sole justification is science, then probably the unmanned exploration is justified. But I feel the reasons for manned exploration are considerably beyond just the scientific knowledge. I think a certain selected subset of the human race really has an itch to go out and plant their own feet, to start a colony, just as the Europeans started colonies in the New World. Some people will say we already have enough problems right here on earth, and that we should just sit on it and not go anywhere. To be crude, that's a lot of crap. You can't quit trying to expand. History is littered with the bones of civilizations that have refused to explore and expand." (Note: For the counterargument, see "Why did the Roman Empire decline and fall?," page 95.)

Then his voice gets a pained edge to it. For stargazers, cosmic enlightenment has had its disappointments. Mars was supposed to be alive. Space travel was supposed to become more commonplace. The Jim Frenches who came of age in the sixties thought star-trekking would be easy and inevitable.

"It's not as easy as Flash Gordon made it look," French says.

As the interview ends, he scrunches up one eye.

"Have you talked to Bob Forward?"

Bob Forward. We'd heard of him. We'll hear of him again.

On to Building 183. Photographs of the moons of Uranus are tacked to corkboard along a hallway on the seventh floor. Rich Terrile, an intense young astronomer, is talking with Fisher Dilke, a tweedy science correspondent for the British Broadcasting Company. They are ruminating about the recent *Challenger* disaster and wondering why so many people want to send living beings into space when machines can do the job just as well and often better.

"We sacrificed seven lives and two billion dollars' worth of spacecraft to launch a communications satellite," Terrile says of the *Challenger* disaster. He is arguing the case for unmanned space travel. He says that by looking through the eyes of *Voyager*, "I've flown the dark side of Uranus, out of communication with earth; I've seen the rings of Saturn backlit by the sun; I've seen erupting volcanoes on Io. I've been to so many places where I would have died from radiation poisoning. . . . There is romance in *our* type of science. Very few people understand that."

Dilke, agreeing, says, "You're really interested in what the places are like, not what kind of personal adventure someone is having while getting there."

By this time Torrence Johnson, another astronomer, has walked into the hallway.

"I'm a Trekkie," Johnson says, "and given my druthers, I'd like to visit these places on the bridge of the *Enterprise*. I love dashing down black holes and across warps in space. But my opinion is that the light barrier is a major problem. It may be built into the fabric of the universe. And that's discouraging to real-life Star-Wars-dashing-about."

The light barrier: We will hear more about that.

The scientists end their conversation with a suggestion: Talk to a guy named Bob Forward.

Building 180 is a tall, glassy obelisk, not unlike a giant silicon chip, so wafer-thin it could almost serve as a Hollywood studio back-lot facade. This is the administrative headquarters, center of the 6,500-employee complex. A little old man with wispy eyebrows has slipped into the public affairs office and says to the PR man, "I need a videotape of *Ranger* 7 crash-landing."

The little old man turns out to be William Pickering, the seventy-six-year-old former director of the lab, the man who oversaw the launching of Explorer 1 in 1958. "That was way back in the days when it was easy to do things," he explains. You could put something on the end of a rocket, shoot it skyward, and if it blew up, nobody would care but the insurance company. In Pickering's day the Jet Propulsion Lab blew up and crash-landed rockets like a kid playing a video game.

Pickering has given up on space; as of this writing he manufactures fuel pellets in Idaho. Sometimes he lectures. In this case he has to give a talk on Ranger 7 at an aerospace conference.

The videotape arrives, and Pickering quickly leaves the building and enters a cluttered storage room. He loops the tape through a machine called a previewer module. The pictures, taken in 1964, are in black-and-white. A photograph of the moon's surface appears on the screen, then another one from slightly closer, then another, descending to the pocked lunar surface, where craters lie within craters. A narrator speaks: "One hundred miles to impact . . . Fifty miles to the moon . . . Twenty-five miles . . ."

The last picture is from one and a half miles up.

Then: FOOM! The Ranger 7 is no more, its mission fulfilled.

Pickering looks happy. Those were the days, with the craving to go into space so feverish you could smash machines with impunity.

Failures? Pickering saw loads of them. Explorer 2 never made it off the launchpad. The first Pioneer probe rose ten miles and blew up. Pioneer 2, Pioneer 3, Pioneer P-3, and Pioneer P-30 all blasted off successfully, bound for the moon, but each one crashed into Africa. Pioneer 4 was supposed to take pictures of the moon but went thousands of miles off course. Pioneer P-1 exploded during a launchpad test. Pioneer P-31 climbed nine miles and blew up.

Ranger 1 went into the wrong orbit. Ranger 3 was supposed to hit the moon but missed by 22,862 miles. Ranger 4, as planned, smashed into the moon, but it did not manage to send back any data. Ranger 5 suffered a failure of the "switching and logic circuitry" and missed the moon by about 500 miles. *Ranger* 6 hit the moon a mere 15 miles from the aiming point, but the camera failed.

Mariner 3 was supposed to go to Mars, but it ended up in orbit around the sun. *Surveyor* 2 was supposed to soft-land on the moon, but it began tumbling out of control and smashed to the surface near the crater Copernicus. *Surveyor* 4 was supposed to soft-land in the same area, but two and a half minutes before touchdown it suddenly blipped off the control screens back on earth, for reasons that are still unclear.

And on the space program went, as though driven by instinct. Because the perpetuation of the species disallows the memory of pain. Because there were also great successes. And because, in any case, these were just machines.

> "What are we doing out here anyway? We bring pain and trouble with us. What are we doing out here in space? Good? What good? If man was meant to fly, he'd have wings. If he was supposed to be out in space, he wouldn't need air to breathe, wouldn't need life-support systems to keep from freezing to death. We don't belong here. It's not ours. Not ours."
>
> —Joey, *crewman contaminated by mysterious brain disease*,
> *Star Trek* episode "The Naked Time"

There is something peculiar about the Lab. People here are talking about raw, crude, subtle, arcane, empirical knowledge. They are talking about science. And that is strange to hear in the context of space travel, because of all the reasons that America has been going into space since 1958, there is hardly a one that has anything, anything at all, to do with science.

There were more pressing reasons. National pride. Military superiority. Adventure. The transfer of tax dollars to large aerospace corporations.

History tells us that all great voyages come during a country's cultural upswing, and that there must be both the ability and the will to explore. In the sixties this was a better description of the United States than the Soviet Union. So we reached the moon and they didn't.

The golden age of space travel ended almost as soon as Apollo 11 returned to earth. A Vietnam-induced malaise set in, a disenchantment with the expenditures, with the linkage to the military, with those big, bomblike rockets. With the exception of Skylab and the Apollo-Soyuz mission (a stunt on behalf of détente), the manned space program petered out. NASA's budget, which had reached $5.6 billion in 1966, bottomed out in 1974 at $3.2 billion. The emotional nadir came in 1977, when, after a stunning technological success, the two Viking landers scratched the surface of Mars and found only sand.

The renaissance came in 1981. The space shuttle Columbia blasted off, and suddenly spaceflight was starting to become the way the visionaries had dreamed it—casual, regular, ubiquitous, not even front-page news. Ronald Reagan was another reason for the renaissance. His plan for a Star Wars nuclear defense required great strides in aerospace technology. NASA's budget in 1985 set a record at about $7.3 billion. In 1984, in his State of the Union address, Reagan set four major goals for the United States, one of which was "to build on America's pioneer spirit and develop our next frontier—space."

Reagan focused on the construction of a permanently manned space station, NASA's next big project. He hoped the station would enable the nation "to follow our dreams to distant stars, living and working in space for peaceful, economic and scientific gain."

To distant stars . . .

Then the space shuttle blew up.

At a memorial service three days later in Houston, the president said, "The frontier is space and boundaries of human knowledge. Sometimes when we reach for the stars, we fall short. But we must pick ourselves up again and press on despite the pain.

"Man," he said, "will continue his conquest of space."

When the white man rolled across the North American continent and wiped out the native population, the justification was codified in a simple term: Manifest Destiny. It was the white man's destiny, granted by divine Providence, to occupy this land, and the heathen be damned.

Of course we don't believe in Manifest Destiny anymore. At least no one calls it that.

Pickering marches back out to the courtyard and stops in front of a large diagram that shows the path of the two Voyager spacecrafts. The diagram is for visitors, a place for snapshots. The board shows Voyager I slanting away from Saturn into the void beyond the solar system. Voyager II is curling past Uranus. A sign says,

Voyager II
Speed Rel Uranus 33,106 mph
Speed Rel Sun 44,192 mph

Voyager II is traveling at two different speeds, at the same time. It just depends on how you look at it.

Einstein is the cause of this confusion. Einstein destroyed, once and for all, the notion of fixed space. His two theories of relativity revealed that time and space—and motion, velocity, acceleration—are "relative" values. We say that a walking child is moving and the sidewalk underfoot is stationary, yet Einstein told us that it is no less accurate to say that the child is stationary and the sidewalk moving. At the dawn of the modern era Einstein eradicated the world of absolutes.

Einstein's special theory of relativity is an idea very hostile to space travel. To state the case in its most dramatic terms, Einstein is one of the two great conspirators in trapping the human race in the Near Universe. The other is God.

Let us start with him and come back to Einstein in a moment. God made the universe too big. The stars are too far apart. The distances are insuperable. There is too much void.

To illustrate the immensity of this scale in terms of space travel: The Pioneer 10 spacecraft, launched in 1972 to take pictures of Jupiter and Saturn, didn't make it out of our solar system until 1983. It carries a plaque with drawings and codes that tell aliens about earth. At the rate it is going, it will make its closest approach to the nearest star in 26,135 years.

The next generation of spacecraft will be faster. They will probably use what is called nuclear-electric propulsion. Instead of a ten-minute rocket burst, these spacecraft will accelerate slowly over time, building up speeds many times greater than *Pioneer* 10. That will cut the trip to the nearest star down to about 5,000 years.

Light itself—hustling along at 186,000 miles per second—takes more than four years to get to the nearest star, Proxima Centauri, which unfortunately shows no sign of having planets or supporting life. To get to Beta Pictoris, the nearest star most likely to have a planet or two, it would take at least fifty-two years. One way.

Nothing can move faster than light. Nothing ever will. This is one of Einstein's revelations. He realized that 186,000 miles per second is the speed limit of the universe.

Space cadets are quick to point out that the relativity theory raises the possibility of one-way time travel. Einstein showed that a spacecraft nearing the speed of light will experience a compression of time, so that, although years may pass on earth, up in the spaceship the astronauts will age only a few months. Unfortunately you have to be extremely close to the speed of light for there to be any noticeable effect. (At the speed of light itself, there would be no sense of time at all. A spaceman could point himself at an object five billion light-years away, a third of the distance across the known universe, and suddenly just be there.) But Einstein showed that nothing could accelerate to the speed of light, because it would take an infinite amount of energy to make that final push. One-way time travel, even if theoretically possible, has major practical problems. If we ever did travel five billion light-years across the cosmos, the folks back home couldn't appreciate it: The sun would have become unstable, expanded, shed its outer layer in a huge explosion, destroyed the earth, and then shrunk back to a tiny, slowly darkening ball of white fire.

The truth is very simple, or at least it appears very simple: God and Einstein have confined the human race to one small corner of a certain spiral galaxy. The view is very good, but there is only one decent place to live.

> KIRK: *Phaser banks, lock onto the enemy vessel.*
> SULU: *They must know we're after them. They've gone to Warp 6 also.*
> KIRK: *Warp factor 7.*
> SPOCK: *A sustained Warp 7 speed will be dangerous, Captain.*
> KIRK: *Thank you, Mr. Spock. I aim to catch them.*
> SCOTTY: *We'll either catch them or blow up, Captain. They may be faster than we are.*
> KIRK: *They'll have to prove it.*
> SULU: *Alien ship now at Warp 7.*
> KIRK: *Warp factor 8.*
> (*Spock, Scotty, and Sulu stare at Kirk in amazement. Music pounds.*)
> SULU: *Aye-aye, Captain.*
>
> —*Star Trek* episode "Arena"

Maybe Einstein's wrong.

This would be the first comment of the many people who believe—who passionately hope—that *Star Trek* will come true.

Richard Arnold, the curator of virtually all existing *Star Trek* prints at the Paramount studio in Los Angeles, a man who goes to eighty *Star Trek* conventions a year, gets very defensive if someone questions the scientific veracity of his favorite show. He's touchy about warp drive (Warp 1 is the speed of light, Warp 2 is the speed of light squared, Warp 3 the speed of light cubed, and so on). He says, "Everything in *Star Trek* was thoroughly researched by scientists."

Asked about the light barrier, Arnold insisted that waves have been discovered that travel faster than the speed of light. He said he learned this on "some show that Carl Sagan was on."

Alas, it is not a fact.

What is true is that scientists have conceived of (as opposed to discovered) particles called tachyons, which travel faster than the speed of light. Tachyons never slow down enough for us to see them. They are therefore undetectable and, you could also argue, irrelevant. Now, if someone could figure out how it would be possible to accelerate up to, and then exceed, the speed of light, that would be something. But it would also mean junking Einstein. It ain't gonna happen.

So what about hyperspace?

What about bending space?

We went up to the seventh floor of Building 180 to see a senior staff scientist named Al Hibbs. Hibbs is one of the few Lab employees who are trusted to go on television, because he talks like a normal person. He was the voice of *Voyager*.

Hibbs says all the young turks at the Lab want to go to the stars.

"Every young engineer who comes here has looked at that idea on his own and has always been frustrated that the answer [to how long it would take a ship to get to the nearest star] comes out to be five thousand to ten thousand years."

But what about warp drive?

"We don't know what the words mean."

Hyperspace? Bending space?

"Just words."

Some of the ideas of science fiction are well founded but others aren't. Anything that violates Einstein's cosmic speed limit remains, for the moment, in the harebrained category.

The danger in writing about the future of science is that any prediction seems to stand a better chance of being wrong than being right. A hundred and fifty years ago no one dreamed of going to the moon. So how can we presume to know what will happen next?

But that may be too cautious. A lot of scientific advancement has occurred in the past one hundred years, and we are better than ever at knowing the kinds of breakthroughs that we might see in the future. Physicists now seriously discuss the possibility that they may eventually have an essentially complete understanding of how the universe works (though probably not why it exists).

Since Einstein's day the most vigorous quest has been for a "unified field theory" that would interconnect the four major forces in the universe—gravity, electromagnetism, and the strong and weak nuclear forces. Since those forces explain just about every phenomenon that can be observed or experimentally created, no one expects to discover a major new force (say, "thought power") that would change the nature of space travel. At this point space travel is looking more and more like a problem not of physics but of biology. We don't live nearly long enough. (Suspended animation, you say? It can't be done to humans.)

A common rule of thumb in anticipating scientific advances is this: If a scientist says a given venture can't be done because it is too costly, then there is still hope. Costs change. But if the scientist says it can't be done because, say, it would violate the second law of thermodynamics, then there is not much hope.

Even if there is some secret force or power out there awaiting our inspired gaze, there remains another obstacle to star travel: national will. A society has to be fairly healthy, fairly happy, to make an investment in space. Consider this: We have the technology to send people to Mars, but we haven't done it. We may in the next decade. The aerospace community is gung-ho. But there remains the question of will, inextricably linked with a stickier issue: Why go to a dead world?

And then there is space colonization, dogged forever by a paradox: A society so desperate and troubled that it would need to expand into space couldn't afford to do so. And if it could, would the problems be left behind?

Space travel is like a Great Society program, in that it asks the federal government to assume a task that is purportedly in the best interest of mankind but for which there seems to be no private-sector incentive. Despite the bluster about the economic bonuses of space travel (such as the manufacture of drugs in zero gravity), it is still a losing venture financially.

Al Hibbs, for one, always thought we'd have made it to Mars by the mid-1980s.

"The schedules that we conceived when this all began were much more rapid," Hibbs sighs. "Space travel," he says, "is more difficult, technologically, than we anticipated."

But Hibbs, as if not to close the door altogether, says, "There's a guy you should talk to, named Bob F—"

Right, right.

We find Bob Forward by driving west on the Ventura Highway, down the length of the San Fernando Valley, then south into the mountains that guard the coast. Past the crest, through a tunnel in the rock, the road rounds a spur in the mountain and suddenly opens up into a view of the Pacific far below. And just then there is a driveway on the right, and a T-shaped building, jammed into the side of the mountain, several hundred feet above the village of Malibu. This place is called the Hughes Research Labs, and it is where Bob Forward works.

He is waiting at the entrance. He has a big pink face, shocking white hair, and an ample waistline. His suit pants have a sheen that suggests *Miami Vice*, but then there is his vest, which is psychedelic, striped in every mod color. He wears a white bow tie. Bob Forward could be a tour guide for children at a candy factory.

He has many jobs here. But there is one thing he does that makes him unique. He is supposed to think about a question and try to answer it:

Will mankind ever reach the stars?

After a warm greeting he goes to his office and plops down behind a video display terminal. His office is filled with his publications, with such titles as "Anti-Proton Annihilation Propulsion" and "Roundtrip Interstellar Travel Using Laser-Pushed Lightsails." He has argued that it is theoretically possible to drive a ship with large amounts of negatively charged antimatter, which turns into almost pure energy when it touches regular matter. He has also proposed the placement of a giant laser around the sun, which would shoot a beam of light to a five hundred–kilometer lens hovering between Saturn and Uranus, which would in turn narrow the beam sufficiently to reach a solar-sailing spacecraft at Alpha Centauri. There's nothing wrong with his math. The engineering—and the money and the patience—just isn't there. The materials would have to be too lightweight, too strong; antimatter has been produced in labs, but there is no way to store more than the most minute amounts.

We tell him that we came to find out the answer to a question: the question of man's destiny in space, the question of reaching the stars.

He listens attentively and then says, "We were very lucky that God put the moon where he did, because it made that first step so easy. It would be nice if there was a star about a tenth of a light-year away, with some planets around it, because we could go visit it in less than the lifetime of a human being. Unfortunately the stars are not that close. If we were living in a typical globular cluster, they would be. But we're living in the boondocks.

"I don't see an unmanned interstellar probe going for fifty years. I'd like to see it happen before I die, but I don't think it will."

He walks outside and leans against a railing. The sun is obscured by a February haze, but the view to Malibu is clear. The Pacific barely ripples, true to its name. He says, "It's going to be about two hundred years before human beings go to the stars. By then we'll be a lot smarter and wiser."

Ah, the wise man has said that the destiny of human beings is in the stars.

But then he clarifies himself. He looks far beyond the shore and says, "I really prefer to think of myself not as a human being but as an intelligent being. I happen to be made out of meat and bone and blood, and I happen to use ionic currents to do my thinking. A couple of hundred years from now we will finally have intelligent beings that will be using silicon and gallium arsenide to do their thinking.

"They will probably be smarter than we are because they'll think faster than we do. The intellectual community is ultimately going to have intellectual children, but they're not going to be made of meat and bone. They will do the exploring."

Bob Forward is talking about robots.

Captain Kirk will be a machine.

There is a disturbing conclusion—suspicion, rather—that comes from talking to the Visionaries, and from comparing the cosmological facts that we see on paper with the cosmological spectacle that we see up in the sky: Space has tricked us.

So hypnotic is its beauty that we tend to forget the harshness of it. When the movie 2001: A *Space Odyssey* showed a large space station slowly orbiting above earth while the soundtrack played Johann Strauss's "The Blue Danube," the viewer had to wish that it would come true, so powerful was the image. Yet what kind of environment is space? Space is literally the absence of anything. There is no air. No resources. The temperature borders on absolute zero. There is no pressure. The solar radiation is lethally intense. The empty continent of Antarctica is a more hospitable environment for a colony. In space only massive feats of engineering could keep a person alive. That engineering prowess, that commitment of energy, could go toward the saving of the earth.

Space has hypnotized the human race into believing that what we see at night is an unlimited frontier. Yet there seems to be no way for mortal man to breach the void beyond our own star system. The indestructible light wave can travel a billion light-years, ten billion, fifteen billion, travel the void from the edge of the universe, from the beginning of time itself, until finally it reaches the lens of our most powerful telescopes, beckoning us to go where we cannot.

The universe is lovely to look at, but it is accessible only by sight. You can't get there from here.

HISTORY

(In which we fill in the gaps of the human drama, from cavemen to Nixon.)

WHY DID NEANDERTHALS DIE OUT EVEN THOUGH THEY WERE HUGE AND STRONG?

We killed them.

For much of "human" history, starting with the emergence of *Homo sapiens* about half a million years ago, there were three distinct populations of premodern people. In southern Europe and western Asia lived the brutish Neanderthals, with their prominent brow line, stubby limbs, and oversized but unsophisticated brains. In Africa lived the middle–Stone Age Africans, who more closely resembled modern humans but who still used primitive tools. In eastern Asia lived people who resembled neither Neanderthals nor Africans, though the fossil record is incomplete and little is known of them.

About 35,000 years ago something happened. In Spain and France a new entity appeared, now called the Cro-Magnon man. He was us. He could walk into any bowling alley in America and no one would blink an eye. (As Jared Diamond noted in a story called "The Great Leap Forward" in *Discover*, you could probably teach him how to fly an airplane.)

Neanderthals didn't evolve into Cro-Magnon men. The Cro-Magnon men probably evolved from the Stone Age Africans, and at some point in that process they arrived in Europe, home

93

of the Neanderthals. The Cro-Magnon men might have been physically weaker than the Neanderthals, and their brains weren't as large, but they had other mental gifts, mainly an advanced ability to speak, so they could articulate the complexities of, say, interspecies warfare.

So they killed the Neanderthals—maybe. There's no actual proof of this. For a long time anthropologists didn't want to admit that noble savages might not be so noble. But the last Neanderthals died off about 32,000 years ago, shortly after the modern humans arrived. Hmmm . . .

WHY DO WE THINK JESUS CHRIST WAS BORN ON DECEMBER 25?

There's a 1-in-365 chance that this is the real birthday of Jesus Christ. No one knows the year of Christ's birth, much less the day. The Bible doesn't specify.

(Those who do not accept the divinity of Jesus can still accept Jesus' historicity. There are a couple of secular references to Jesus by the historians Josephus and Tacitus. More importantly, the Gospels are not exactly chopped liver. New Testament scholars say that the synoptic Gospels in particular— Mark, Luke, and Matthew—carry historical heft because of the similar, but not identical, accounts they give of Jesus' life. The Gospel of John is thought to employ a bit more literary license.)

The first known Christmas celebration took place in the fourth century A.D., after Emperor Constantine replaced paganism with Christianity as the official religion of the Roman Empire. December 25 was chosen because of its significance as a pagan holiday, which was called the Feast of the Unconquered Sun (Sol Invictus, in Latin). It marked the winter solstice, when the length of the day begins to get longer again and the sun proves it hasn't been whipped. One theologian we talked to quipped that the Feast of the Unconquered Sun could now be called the Feast of the Unconquered Son. Those zany theologians!

WHY DID THE ROMAN EMPIRE DECLINE AND FALL?

"Lead poisoning" is the answer we're aching to give.

A number of Roman skeletons have been found with high concentrations of lead. The Romans were known to have lined their aqueducts with lead to prevent seepage. Some scholars suggest the Romans slowly went toxic and turned into raving, degenerate lunatics.

This is history at its best: horrifying but humorous. The lead-poisoning theory is also the type of tidy, compressed theory that the time-poor modern pseudointellectual craves, fitting neatly into a mental pigeonhole between "in fourteen hundred and ninety-two, Columbus sailed the ocean blue" and "Benjamin Franklin discovered electricity." Life is vastly improved if we all agree to keep things simple, and forget about all this history jazz. After all, history is nothing more than a bunch of wars and plagues and kings named Louis. (Mostly it's a bad memory. As some wise man said, he who is condemned to remember history is liable to repeat it.)

But those of us in the Information Retrieval crusade can't ignore an empire that lasted more than a millennium, (actually two millennia, if you want to be generous) and whose collapse triggered a very, very bad time called the Dark Ages. You might well ask, "Why did the Roman Empire last so long?" There's never been anything else so dominant, so awesome to behold, save perhaps the '72 Dolphins. So here goes:

The lead-poisoning theory is poppycock. There is no solid

evidence for the lead theory. For example there are no con-
temporaneous accounts of Romans going mad, unless you
count the time Caligula married his sister and appointed his
horse to the Roman Senate. Or maybe he married his horse—
it's one or the other.

The real reason Rome fell is . . . well, it's kind of hard to say
why, because it's not even clear *when* Rome fell. The date A.D.
410 is often given, because that's when the Goths sacked
Rome. But this is an iffy milestone, since by that time Rome
was a quaint backwater and the real power of the empire was
far to the east, at Constantinople, or wherever the military
emperor decided to set up camp. Moreover Rome was quickly
restored to Roman rule that year.

The other major sacking was in A.D. 476. This time the barbarians were Vandals, and they installed a Vandal emperor.
But to declare that event the end of the Roman Empire is mere
barbarian-phobia. The barbarians were normal people too;
they didn't eat live babies or anything, and in fact most were
believers in Aryan Christianity. They were Roman wannabees,
who let the bureaucracy and other vestiges of the Romans
remain intact. So to say that the Roman Empire collapsed in
476 is not only arbitrary, it's snooty.

Even after Rome fell, the eastern Roman Empire flourished
in Constantinople. In the sixth century, Emperor Justinian managed to reconquer Rome and reunite the western and eastern
empires. Then the Moslems invaded, and much of southern
Europe became a colony of the Arab world. The Roman Empire lived on in the east, a.k.a. Byzantium, preserving Christian
culture and Roman law until Constantinople fell to the Ottoman Turks in 1453, by which time the Renaissance had started
in Italy. If you want to get really picky, you could argue that
the glory of "Rome" lasted until 1806, when Napoleon compelled Francis II to declare the Holy Roman Empire null and
void.

So, you see, it's a mess. That's history: a headache. Oh, and somewhere in there France had several kings named Louis.

So let's give up the question of when and just acknowledge that over time the Rome we all know and love—chariot races, dueling gladiators, planned cities with straight roads, guys with laurel branches in their hair—disappeared. Next question: Why the decline?

Christianity has often been blamed. The voluble historian Edward Gibbon speculated that Christianity, adopted as the official religion of the empire by Constantine in A.D. 325, promoted a pacifist streak among the Romans and sapped their will to fight. This theory is so improbable, however, that even Gibbon eventually spat on it. For one thing Christians historically could be pretty fierce in the war department. More significantly, the empire had been in decline when Christianity was still an outlawed religion and Christians were lion chow in the Colosseum.

A better explanation is that the empire simply had too much border to defend, too much frontage. This is the general reason that empires fall apart.

By the time the Roman Empire celebrated its millennium, in A.D. 248, there was increasing pressure on its frontiers from Germanic barbarians, who were themselves pressured by Huns and other nomads from the Asian steppe. The Romans should probably have invaded and pacified what is now Germany, but after the heyday of Augustus and Trajan and Hadrian they fell into a prolonged period of complacency, just trying to keep up appearances and maintain the borders. Not a winning attitude!

The empire was an administrative nightmare. It stretched from northern Africa, up through Asia Minor, and all the way to England. It hosted a parade of incompetent emperors. There was constant conniving over succession. The large populace in the east continually complained about paying taxes to support military efforts far to the west. Finally, in A.D. 284, Diocletian divided his domain into separate eastern and western empires, but this sapped the tax base of the military in the western empire. Hence, to save on costs, the empire started offering reservations of land within the empire to barbarian tribes. Eventually the military accepted barbarians into the armed forces. When the hordes invaded, some of the Romanized barbarians switched sides and fought against the empire.

This is where Christianity comes in. By the early fourth century some Roman leaders felt the empire could recover its past glory only if it adopted a new state religion. There were all manner of religions to choose from, ranging from Egyptian-style sun-god worship to Manichaeism, which saw the world Reaganistically as a struggle between Good and Evil. Before Constantine became emperor, he was a big promoter of Mithraism, a heresy popular in the rival Persian empire, in which the faithful became purified through the slaughtering of bulls in caves. But later he chose the more popular Christianity, at the time considered a Jewish heresy.

Had Constantine stuck with Mithraism, wrote Hugh Trevor Roper in *The Rise of Christian Europe*, "the pagan ceremonies which so quickly crystallized round the teaching of Christ would no doubt have accommodated themselves instead to the cult of Mithras, and the taurobolium, the baptism with bull's blood in underground caves, would have replaced the crucifixion and the sacrament of the Last Supper at the center of European worship."

WHY DOES CHINA HAVE SUCH A HUGE POPULATION?

The question, really, is, *Why is China so much more densely populated than areas of similar size and antiquity, such as Europe?*

Bountiful fertile lands may be one part of the answer; Confucian emphasis on the family may be another. But the major factor is probably the phenomenon of war and peace.

Since the start of the Shang Dynasty, about 1500 B.C., China has had many long, uninterrupted periods of centralized rule and political stability. Sure, you had your odd Mongol invasion, your bothersome famines, your annoying despots, and your unpleasant floods. But compared with life in the Western world, living in China was a breeze.

Europeans killed one another. They hacked, lanced, crossbowed, and keel-hauled each other at the drop of a codpiece. Empire-wise, the center of power kept shifting. One day the Egyptians run the world, and the next thing you know they're out of business and the Macedonians are on top, then the Romans, then the barbarian hordes, then the Moslems, and so on.

Fiscal, political, and economic centralization were first realized in the Roman Empire. About the same time the Han Empire ruled China. Although both empires eventually collapsed they continued to serve as a theoretical model for running a large and diverse area. China was much more successful than Europe in reconstituting the empire in the Middle Ages, purging the Buddhist monks of power and giving way to bureaucrats, who had to compete for jobs with what amounted to civil-service tests. Europe, however, was fragmented into small states. Hence mayhem.

Populations increase more rapidly in peacetime (witness, for example, the U.S. postwar Baby Boom). Between the mid-1700s and the mid-1800s the population of China doubled from 200 million to 400 million. China's human surplus gave it less incentive to replace human labor with machine labor in the Industrial Revolution. While Europe urbanized, China remained rural, with lots of crowded countryside. Urban families are smaller than rural families.

China held a census in 1982. The count: more than a billion people. A fifth of humanity. Communists.

Why Did Columbus Miss the North American Mainland Even Though He Visited Cuba and the Bahamas?

B rilliant but a little wacky, Columbus insisted to his dying day that he *had* discovered the mainland. He figured it was Asia. It was in fact the island of Cuba. Columbus explored both sides of the island on separate voyages but stopped just short of navigating the western cape, which would have proven that he was wrong. At one historic point, after discovering Trinidad, Columbus stepped on the mainland of South America, but insisted it was just an island, and took off for Asia . . . er, Cuba. When he finally ventured to the west and saw the mouth of South America's Orinoco River, with its massive outflow of water and detritus, he knew for sure that he was at the edge of a great continent, but he then became convinced it was one of the four mythological continents of Paradise, located at the top of a pear-shaped world.

Columbus never reached Florida because his maps told him that Japan would be about three thousand miles due west of the Canary Islands, off the west coast of Africa. So he went there, hit the Bahamas, and learned from the natives of a grander, mountainous land to the southwest where he might find gold—Cuba. It was only natural for the gold-crazed Spaniards to go hacking their way toward the treasures of the

Incas, Mayas, and Aztecs of South and Central America, since Florida did not yet have its tourist attractions.

WHY ARE ASIA AND EUROPE CONSIDERED TWO CONTINENTS EVEN THOUGH A QUICK GLANCE AT THE MAP REVEALS THEM TO BE ONLY ONE?

T hings got off on the wrong foot when the ancient Greek cartographer named Hecataeus of Miletus—actually we have no idea how old he was; we mean that he lived in the sixth century B.C.—divided the world into two equal parts, Europe being one and Asia the other.

The early cartographers knew that Europe and Asia were joined by land, and the great Eratosthenes even complained about the artificiality of "continents." But from the vantage point of Athens or Alexandria, the Eurasian landmass seemed virtually sliced in two by the line of water running from the Aegean Sea through the straits known as the Bosporus and the Dardanelles, to the far shore of the Black Sea. The world map of Eratosthenes, circa 240 B.C., shows Europe and Asia joined only by a narrow isthmus of land between the Black Sea and the Caspian Sea, the latter being depicted as an arm of a vast northern ocean. The land link was a technicality, like the juncture of Asia and Africa at Suez. (The early mapmakers also called Africa Libya back then, to give you some idea of the problem.)

In any case Europeans were not about to surrender their continental status. To this day when people talk of a "continental" breakfast, they mean something small and unnourishing like they serve in Europe.

WHY DOES GERMANY SEEM TO HAVE THIS THING ABOUT STARTING WORLD WARS?

This is one of a long list of inquiries that might be generally termed the German Question. Why did Germans support Hitler even though he was clearly a madman? Why did they commit the greatest genocide in history? Why did these war crimes happen in Germany as opposed to somewhere else?

These big questions challenge the elasticity of the Why staff. We can offer only a few minor thoughts:

1. Germany's history of warfare is largely a result of geography: It is at the crossroads of Europe. Check a map.

2. Germans aren't innately any more belligerent than anyone else. The history of every civilized country is filled with warmongering. The First World War was prefaced by demands for war among the civilian populations of almost every European power.

"Agitation for war was a universal phenomenon," says Gordon Craig, the Stanford historian who has written several books on Germany and the Germans. Craig goes so far as to say that mass education and the spread of literacy played a key role in the origin of several European wars. People suddenly could support numerous high-circulation newspapers, and they liked the excitement of colonial wars abroad. Newspapers fomented international tension: It sold. Craig says the press helped incite the 1854 war in Crimea, the 1870 war between France and Germany, and finally the First World War in 1914. (To this day it's hard to discern what the War to End All Wars was actually *about*.)

3. Hitler caused World War II, not the German people.

The question of a German national guilt may never actually be resolved. Putting it onto one guy, however Mephistophelian he might have been, seems a slight cop-out. But here's the argument:

Hitler initially appealed to the masses for the same reason any leader would appeal to Americans: He mobilized the economy that had been moribund under his predecessor because of the overly harsh conditions of the Treaty of Versailles after World War I, increased prosperity and employment, and inspired a renewed nationalistic fervor. Hitler cultivated the longstanding anti-Semitism and antimodernism of the masses, who saw Jews as representatives of modernity, socialism, liberalism, and big cities. Hitler spoke of a worldwide Jewish conspiracy. "The Jews became socially-allowed hate objects," the West German leader Philipp Jenninger said in a 1988 speech that, due to misinterpretation, caused his ouster. No one could anticipate in 1933 the enormity of the crimes that would be committed in 1941, but neither was the attack on Jewry a secret. "The essentials were known," Jenninger said. "The Jews stood alone. Their fate met blindness and cold hearts."

Still, German citizens did not have a monopoly on racism, nor did they crave war this time around or order the construction of extermination camps. Hitler started his diabolical jeremiad ostensibly as an attempt to win "living space" for his Thousand Year Reich, but in truth he hoped to glorify himself and destroy his imagined Jewish, Anglo-Saxon, and Bolshevik enemies. His confidant Albert Speer speculated that Hitler hated everything that he secretly admired.

4. Nazi leaders of a less sadistic nature (relatively speaking) were able to stomach the Holocaust through self-deception and bureaucracy.

These German leaders tried to avoid confronting the supreme evils of the day. Speer, Hitler's aide, wrote in a memoir that when Hitler announced to a table of senior German officials, "I want to annihilate the Jews in Europe," people acted as though they didn't hear, or as though Hitler did not mean his words literally: "We lived in a tightly shut world of delusion isolated from the outside world (and perhaps also from our respectable selves)."

Perhaps indeed! Another way to avoid acknowledging this great war crime was to hide it in bureaucratic language. There is no single directive ordering the Final Solution, only jumbled documents, such as the 1941 instruction by Hermann Goering to the secret police saying, "I herewith commission you to carry out all necessary preparations with regard to organizational, substantive, and financial viewpoints for a total solution of the Jewish question in the German sphere of influence in Europe." And so forth. Hitler's intent was plain, though. He once said, for example, "The Jew must get out of Europe. If he does not leave voluntarily, I see no solution other than extermination." Once the genocide had begun in earnest in 1941, the Nazi SS leader Heinrich Himmler told his followers, "This is an unwritten and never-to-be-mentioned page of glory in our history."

It's clear from the record that German leaders knew their acts were criminal, but obviously they were planning on writing all the history books themselves.

WHY DID NO PRESIDENT RUN FOR A THIRD TERM PRIOR TO FRANKLIN ROOSEVELT?

There are three reasons:

1. Modesty
2. Total incompetency
3. Sudden health problems (for example, Lincoln's catching a show at Ford's Theater).

At first the "Washington precedent" proved dissuasive. George Washington chose not to run for a third term. Thomas Jefferson, in deference to Washington and for ideological reasons, also stepped down after his second term, saying that anything more would be the equivalent of a rule-for-life, with the accompanying stench of dictatorship. James Madison, James Monroe, and Andrew Jackson, the other early-American two-term presidents, hewed to the same line.

Eventually the Washington precedent became moot, because after Jackson there was a run of boneheads who tended either to get sick and die in office or prove themselves such losers that no one would nominate them for a second term, much less a third. Moreover for many years vice-presidential nominees were lightweights picked from the political faction that opposed the presidential nominee, the idea being to build a coalition; but if the president died, the vice president wouldn't have much popular support and would fail to win his own party's nomination in the next election. Let's take a quick peek at the Loser's Gallery:

■ Martin Van Buren. As soon as he moves into the Oval Office, a major depression wracks the nation. So long.

■ William Henry Harrison. Gets sick at inauguration; dies a month later.

■ John Tyler. Pathetic former veep. Not renominated.

■ James K. Polk. Decent president, if you like territory-crazed Manifest Destiny types. He vows to serve only one term, and does.

■ Zachary Taylor. Gets sick and dies one year into office.

■ Millard Fillmore. Pathetic former veep. Not renominated.

■ Franklin Pierce. Alcoholic, depressive, tragedy-prone, he is not a good president and loses his own party's support. Not renominated.

■ James Buchanan. Described by one orator as a "bloated mass of political putridity," he does nothing to stave off the Civil War. Possibly the worst president in history.

■ Abraham Lincoln. The greatest American. Slain.

■ Andrew Johnson. Nearly pathetic former veep. Survives impeachment by one vote. Not renominated.

Finally we get to Ulysses S. Grant. He wins two terms and, with George Washington long gone, gears up to go on for three. But he has been nearly as bad a president as Buchanan, plagued by no fewer than five major scandals. Grant's support evaporates and he loses out to James Garfield.

Some more losers:

■ Rutherford B. Hayes. A party tool who slips into office on a narrow and perhaps fraudulent electoral-college majority despite losing the popular vote to Samuel Tilden. Wants only one term. Not renominated.

■ James Garfield. Shot dead in office.

■ Chester A. Arthur. Decent former veep. Not renominated.

Then you have Grover Cleveland, who wins two terms, separated in the middle by a diversionary four years with the extremely average Benjamin Harrison. Cleveland is denied a third nomination in 1896 because the Democratic party wants silver coinage while Cleveland wants to stick to gold. William McKinley wins two elections but is shot dead.

Teddy Roosevelt takes over in 1904 on the pledge that he won't seek a third term. He keeps the pledge for a few years but gets the itch again in 1912, stating, "My hat is in the ring," and arguing that he meant he wouldn't seek three *consecutive* terms. He is unable to wrest the Republican nomination from President William Howard Taft and runs on the third-party Bull Moose ticket, which merely siphons away Republican votes from Taft and puts Woodrow Wilson into office. Wilson would have liked a third term but is debilitated by a stroke in 1919.

Warren Harding dies in office and then Calvin Coolidge, after one and a half terms, calls it quits, possibly because he foresees the coming depression. Herbert Hoover is a disaster, and then you come to Franklin Delano Roosevelt.

Roosevelt was the first president in nearly 150 years who suffered from neither modesty nor unpopularity. In 1940, with the war raging in Europe, he decided to go for the hat trick, which prompted opponents to adopt the slogan, "Washington didn't, Grant didn't, Roosevelt shouldn't." He made it four in 1944.

WHY WAS THE SECOND ATOMIC BOMB DROPPED?

F avorable weather conditions, mostly.
   For years scientists had worked on "the bomb." The top Allied leaders never seriously questioned or debated the idea of using "the bomb." Truman wrote in his memoirs, "I regarded the bomb as a military weapon and never had any doubt that it should be used." What with all the manpower and brainpower and money being poured into the Manhattan Project, a powerful force of inertia took hold, and it would have been hard to stop everything at the last second and say, "Whoa, we're not going to actually *use* this thing, are we?"

Historians are divided as to whether Japan would have surrendered without the bombing of Hiroshima. Truman and Secretary of War Henry Stimson passionately voiced the consensus view that without the bomb we would have had to invade Japan at the cost of a million American lives. This has a certain agonized drama to it, but in truth it seems unlikely that a superpower, with the atomic weapon bulging from its pocket, would have rushed into such a bloodbath. Japan was not one monolithic kamikaze pilot. Peace feelers had emerged from the empire as early as June. After Iwo Jima and Saipan, Japan knew it had lost. The key condition of surrender for the Japanese all along was that the emperor be allowed to keep his title—a condition later granted without hesitation amid the terms of "unconditional surrender."

In the spring of 1945 there was an occasional discussion among the American leaders of alternatives to atomic holocaust, such as a "demonstration" of the bomb over unpopulated territory. But there was concern that the full terror of the device would be lost. Another idea was to warn the Japanese that we were going to bomb a certain city, so that civilians could be evacuated. But what if the Japs moved American POWs to Ground Zero? Another factor entered into America's thinking: the Russians. The Cold War had already started, and it would be handy, from a diplomatic standpoint, to show the Soviets that America was number one. The use of atomic force seemed to violate every known conception of the rules of war, such as discrimination and proportionality. But there was a very good argument against such moralizing, one that is regularly used today by advocates of nuclear weapons: We had already killed *just as many innocent people* by dropping thousands of conventional incendiary bombs on such cities as Dresden and Tokyo.

After disposing of all the arguments against using "the bomb," the members of what was called the Interim Committee decided upon the fundamentals: We would drop the bombs as soon as they rolled off the assembly line, until the Japanese surrendered. We would hit military targets. And most importantly, we would tell the Japanese in advance that we possessed a new breed of destructive weapon and were prepared to use it.

Sometime between May and August the idea of warning the Japanese got lost. The "military targets" became cities with large amounts of military industry: Hiroshima, Kokura, Niigata, and Nagasaki, in order of military importance. It was presumed that air-raid sirens would sound and that maybe twenty thousand people would die. On July 24, Truman ordered the bombing command on the island of Tinian to drop the first bomb as soon as weather permitted "after about 3 August 1945." Truman said he gave a final order some days later, though no record of that exists.

It was pretty much up to the commanders in the Pacific. The bombing mission comprised only three planes, flying without radio communication; for such a humble detail, no sirens sounded in Hiroshima. About 100,000 people died, not counting those that suffered genetic damage from the radiation.

No separate order was given to drop the second bomb. No meeting took place to discuss whether it was necessary. The bombing command on Tinian had planned to drop the second bomb on August 11 on the city of Kokura, but a storm was brewing and the mission was rescheduled for the 9th. That same morning Russia invaded Manchuria and declared war on Japan. We will never know if just the first atomic bomb and the entry of the Russians into the Pacific theater would have given the Japanese peace factions sufficient leverage to end the war— because a few hours later, having passed three times over the cloud-obscured city of Kokura, an American bomber flew on to Nagasaki, saw the city through a hole in the clouds, and incinerated it.

WHY HAS NO ONE EVER FIGURED OUT FOR CERTAIN WHO KILLED JOHN F. KENNEDY AND FOR WHAT MOTIVE?

Frankly we at the Why staff aren't confused at all. Oswald killed Kennedy. He was almost certainly acting alone. End of story.

What's that we hear? Vile curses in the air? The sound of this book being shredded? Okay, so we can't be absolutely sure. It's possible there was a conspiracy. It's also possible that the *Apollo* 11 landing on the moon was a hoax filmed in the Arizona desert. We've spent hours poring through JFK assassination documents, and the single thing that leaps out at the reader is that the evidence for the lone-assassin theory easily outweighs that for a conspiracy.

Just for example: When Congress asked a panel of forensic pathologists to review the autopsy photos and X rays of Kennedy's head, the panel concluded emphatically that he was shot from the back, consistent with the position of Oswald. Only one of the pathologists, a vocal conspiracy theorist, dissented. He held fast to idea that Kennedy was shot from the front, from the famous "grassy knoll." Whom do you believe? The many? Or the one?

Okay, so now you're screaming about all this supposed evidence that the Mob and Castro conspired to hit Kennedy. There's no question that they had a motive, what with the CIA's efforts to topple or kill Castro, and Attorney General Robert Kennedy's crackdown on the Mafia. Oswald was a Castro sympathizer. And on the surface, Jack Ruby's killing of Oswald looks like a classic Mafia rubout. But there are gaping flaws in this scenario:

1. Neither Oswald nor Ruby fit the mold of Mob hit men. They were bozos. Oswald's great anarchic achievement was taking a potshot at an army general and missing. For an operation this important, the conspirators would have wanted someone swift, sure, quiet, trustworthy, and, most of all, experienced.

2. Oswald got a job at the Texas School Book Depository—the building from which he fired the fatal shot—in October 1963, many weeks before Kennedy's handlers decided to route the motorcade right past the depository during Oswald's lunch hour. Kennedy went to Oswald; Oswald didn't go to Kennedy! It was pure, tragic coincidence—no one has ever turned up a shred of evidence of any inside job by Kennedy's aides.

3. The only time Oswald was exposed to the public was when he was transferred out of the police station. At the scheduled moment Ruby was at a Western Union office, wiring money to a friend. There is an exact record of this. He wandered by the police station an hour later. Because of the late arrival of a detective, Oswald's transfer had been delayed. Ruby meandered into the basement garage at precisely the right time and shot Oswald. One would presume a real Mob hit man would have arrived on time.

Two years of investigation by the House Select Committee on Assassinations turned up no evidence for a conspiracy except in an analysis of acoustics in Dealey Plaza, which purportedly revealed a second gunman. That analysis was later convincingly debunked by a government panel of scientists.

So, if there's so much evidence that Oswald was a lone gunman acting on his own twisted motives, why does the Kennedy assassination still seem so perplexing, so full of ambiguities and mystery? Simple. Whenever an epic event is closely scrutinized, with hundreds of witnesses and thousands of documents, contradictions arise in increasing numbers as the scrutiny grows closer. People are bad witnesses. Reality is elusive. It's what we learned with quantum mechanics: The universe is built upon principles of uncertainty.

WHY DIDN'T WE GO ALL-OUT IN VIETNAM AND WIN THE WAR?

When Ronald Reagan campaigned for the presidency in 1980, he drew cheers for saying, "Never again must we commit the immorality of sending our young men to fight a war that we're afraid to let them win." The line cleverly danced on both sides of the issue: Doves might conclude that Reagan was against the American intervention, while hawks would recognize Reagan's acceptance of the conservative interpretation of the war, that we suffered a failure of *will* rather than a pure military defeat. As the totalitarian horrors of the Vietnamese and Cambodian communist regimes have come to light, the conservative, revisionist view of Vietnam has gained momentum.

But could we have won that war? Why did we lose?

The second question first. South Vietnam ultimately fell to the Communists because in 1974 Congress refused to commit money and arms to the South Vietnamese regime. The January 1973 peace accords had guaranteed the existence of an independent South Vietnam after the withdrawal of American military troops, but everyone knew the ineffectual government of South Vietnam could not survive without U.S. aid. The North Vietnamese army seized upon the American abandonment of South Vietnam and, with shocking speed, rolled into Saigon in April 1975, sending the last American advisors scrambling for a chopper out.

So why'd we give up? Why did we lose heart? Why didn't we just kick butt, take names, and bomb them back to the Jurassic?

First let's deal with the bombing. Hawks claim that our reluctance to bomb Hanoi and the port city of Haiphong was the greatest single failure of will in the war. The American political leadership prohibited the military from dropping bombs within ten miles of the center of Hanoi or within four miles of the center of Haiphong. They feared that the massive destruction of cities and civilians would rekindle memories of the Dresden and Tokyo firestorms in World War II, incite the wrath of the Soviets and the Chinese, and possibly lead to nuclear war between the superpowers. Was this wise or gutless?

Gutless, says General Victor Krulak: "We didn't do it just from a lack of courage."

That's a military man talking. Here is a wake-up fact: America dropped more than six million tons of explosives on the two Vietnams, an area the size of Texas. That's *three times* the amount dropped by every nation in Europe, Africa, and Asia during World War II. General William Westmoreland wanted to go the final step and drop nuclear weapons, and President Nixon contemplated it. Nixon writes in *No More Vietnams*, "If we had chosen to go for a knockout blow by bombing the dikes [causing flooding and famine] or by using tactical nuclear weapons, the resulting domestic and international uproar would have damaged our foreign policy on all fronts." (Also, it would have been mean, but that was never one of Tricky's hang-ups.)

The hawks often ignore a fundamental fact: War is not fought for its own sake. War is just a tool of a policy. Theoretically the United States had enough firepower to smash North Vietnam to itty-bitty pieces. But would that have really "won" the war? No, because Vietnam was not just a battle over a plot of land; it was more of a proxy war in the larger superpower struggle between capitalism and communism. If the conquest of North Vietnam came at an unacceptable price—say, humanity-destroying nuclear war, leaving the planet dominated by Saint Bernard–sized radioactive vermin—we would all agree that it wouldn't be much of a victory.

Carl von Clausewitz, the great nineteenth-century war philosopher, wrote, "Subordinating the political point of view to the military would be absurd, for it is policy that creates war. Policy is the guiding intelligence and war only the instrument."

For exactly that reason we didn't invade North Vietnam. Not only would huge numbers of Americans have died, not only would it have been a major hassle to occupy and pacify a country filled with rabid nationalists, not only would it have been *expensive*, but we'd probably have only heightened our conflict with the real enemy, the Godless Reds of Russia and China.

So it *was* reasonable to want to limit America's aggressiveness. The problem is that you usually can't win a war that way. War must be fought brutally or not at all. Clausewitz defined war as an act of force designed to compel the enemy to do our will. War is not a fight over real estate.

A key to winning, Clausewitz said, is the principle of the Offensive. American military leaders mistakenly thought they were conducting an offensive war (repugnant would be a better word) by killing Commies in the jungle, but in fact we were being defensive all along, fighting a war of containment.

The American strategy in this war without fronts was "counter-insurgency." As in the Civil War, we were not concerned so much with the conquest of territory as with the killing of the enemy forces; we wanted to search out Charlie and destroy him, rack up a big body count. General Westmoreland stated that his goal was to "attrit Viet Cong and North Vietnamese forces at a rate as high as their capability to put men into the field." That didn't happen. Half a million Communists had died by 1970, but there were always more willing to fight.

This fact baffled the American leaders and astonished the American public. When the first 3,500 Marines splashed down in Da Nang in 1965, President Johnson downplayed the intervention of troops as merely a small skirmish. The public didn't bargain for a major war. That's why the Tet Offensive, in early 1968, though a major tactical military victory for the United States and South Vietnam, proved nonetheless to be an enormous *strategic* victory for the Communists (*tactical* refers to individual battles, *strategic* to the larger war). The unexpected strength of the Communists shocked America and triggered the erosion of our will to prosecute the war.

Our attitude toward Vietnam reflected an underlying racism and an obvious ignorance of Vietnamese history. We figured Vietnam was just à backward corner of the globe, part of an area our maps labeled French Indochina. In fact Vietnam was one of the oldest and proudest nations on earth. The Vietnamese had won independence from China in A.D. 946 and held onto it almost without interruption until the French conquest in the mid-1800s. In the closing days of World War II the Vietnamese nationalists led by Ho Chi Minh hoped that America would support their rebellion against the French, but they were disappointed. At the Yalta Conference in 1945, when the victorious Allies were dividing up the world, President Roosevelt asked China's leader, Chiang Kai-shek, "Do you want Indochina?" Chiang replied, "We don't want it. They are not Chinese. They would not assimilate into the Chinese people." Chiang recognized the Vietnamese's sense of national pride.

So why didn't the U.S. pull out as soon as it realized it was not going to win the war? The "general-in-chief" of the Vietnam war, Secretary of Defense Robert McNamara, supported the direct intervention in 1965–66 of 400,000-plus U.S. military troops, but, by his own testimony, "reached the conclusion that the war could not be won militarily no later than '66."

So why keep up the pretense? Because it would be humiliating to pull out, to renege on our promise to South Vietnam. President Johnson, the old-fashioned fighter from Texas, couldn't stomach such cowardice. Gung-ho generals in Vietnam itself couldn't conceive of giving up the war. And behind the scenes, the military-industrial apparatus cranked out the hardware, to no small profit.

Thus hundreds of thousands of young Americans were sent, year after year, to a faraway land, to die or be maimed fighting a war that our leaders *knew* they couldn't win.

WHY DID NIXON TAPE HIMSELF DOING ILLEGAL THINGS?

The only thing Nixon forgot to do was videotape himself receiving brown paper bags of cash from suspected underworld figures known to be close friends of Frank Sinatra. You would think a man smart enough to get elected president of the United States would realize that tapes and cover-ups don't mix.

There are several potential explanations for Nixon's talk-and-tape fiasco:

1. The hidden mikes slipped his mind.
2. He sincerely did not believe he was doing anything wrong.
3. He figured he could edit or destroy the tapes later.
4. His brain seized up on him in a fit of illogic.

We can probably dispense with the first. In 1971, barely a year before the Watergate break-in, Nixon directed an elaborate expansion of the taping system that had been used by his predecessors. Obsessed with his place in history, Nixon bugged himself in order to provide a record of his tenure and to protect himself from "revisionist histories," as he wrote in his memoirs. Stephen Ambrose, author of *Nixon: The Triumph of a Politician* 1962–1972, writes, "Anyone who listens to the tapes quickly realizes that Nixon often is speaking for the record."

The second possibility, that Nixon didn't feel he was doing anything wrong, is belied by his own taped comments. Sometimes he was just sneaky and conniving, like when he said, four days after the June 17, 1972, break-in at Watergate, "Every time the Democrats accuse us of bugging, we should charge that we were being bugged and maybe even plant a bug and find it ourselves!"

At other times he's more blatantly criminal, such as in his critical June 23 meeting with Chief of Staff H. R. Haldeman. On the tape Haldeman tells Nixon that the Watergate investigation will follow a trail directly back to Nixon's reelection campaign and to Attorney General John Mitchell. So Nixon and Haldeman summarily decide to tell the CIA to order the FBI to pull back on the investigation. It's as though obstruction of justice is second nature to them—and it is also clear that Nixon is fully aware that he is doing something illegal.

Haldeman says, "The way to handle this now is for us to have [the CIA tell the FBI] 'Stay the hell out of this . . . this is, ah, business here we don't want you to go any further on it.' . . . They'll stop if we could, if we take this other step."

"All right. Fine," Nixon responds. He suggests that the CIA claim that further investigation of the burglars will reveal national security secrets involving the Bay of Pigs. Nixon says the CIA should say, "Don't go any further into this case, period!" And then he comments, craftily, "I don't want them [the FBI] to get any ideas we're doing it because our concern is political."

"Right," says Haldeman.

There it is! The cover-up! This brief excerpt doesn't capture the extent of their plotting or the enormity of the crime, but when the full "smoking gun" transcript was released under Supreme Court order in 1974, it killed the last of Nixon's support. Nixon's own White House aides were so shocked by the revelation of the president's duplicity, of his blatant lies, of his betrayal, that they vowed to quit unless Nixon complied with the Court's order and turned the transcript over to Congress. He did and was out of office a few days later.

(Nixon says in his memoir In the Arena that his decision to ask the CIA to stop the FBI investigation of the Watergate burglary was an "inexcusable error," but claims he was legitimately concerned about protecting CIA secrets. He adds, "I thought that would also prevent the FBI from going into areas that would be politically embarrassing to us." Mitigating this mistake, he says, is the fact that the CIA did not actually inter-vene with the FBI. Nixon writes, "No obstruction of justice took place as a result of the June 23 conversation"—through no fault of his own, he should add.)

The third explanation—the "tape now, edit later" hypothe-sis—is the most likely. Nixon never thought he would lose con-trol of the tapes, and to this day his lawyers have managed to keep the vast majority under seal even though they have been processed by the National Archives to edit out national secu-rity matters.

Nixon's faith that the tapes would remain confidential also explains why he never burned them. In fact he thought they would be his political salvation, and said so to his coconspir-ators. Many times, "speaking for the record," as Ambrose puts it, he made statements clearly designed to exonerate himself, such as his famous statement to John Dean, "That would be wrong." Nixon was taping himself disapproving a $120,000 hush-money payment to E. Howard Hunt—but in the same con-versation he approved the payment several times.

"Selective use of the tapes absolutely exonerates Nixon," Ambrose states.

And there is some evidence that Nixon actually began to edit: Nixon's first in-depth conversations about Watergate with Haldeman have an infamous eighteen-minute gap. Haldeman has speculated that when the existence of the tapes was re-vealed in July 1973, Nixon set out to erase the damaging evi-dence, but, realizing that the job would be too enormous, gave up.

The idiocy of Nixon's actions—taping himself plotting a cover-up and being generally despicable—brings up the fourth possibility, the mental breakdown, which seems unlikely but is fun to discuss nonetheless. Psychoanalyst Leo Rangel writes in his book *The Mind of Watergate* that certain dubious acts are motivated "not by the neologic of rational adult behavior, but by the paleologic or primitive modes from earlier periods of psychic functioning." In other words, Nixon's brain was operating in caveman mode. True, there is something vaguely *australopithecene* about the man, even if he did go to China.

Perhaps the tapes are merely Nixon's way of returning to the scene of the crime. They say all crooks want to be caught, and Nixon offers no evidence to the contrary. In addition to paranoia, Nixon displayed signs of narcissism, particularly the related symptom of exhibitionism. The tapes are his exhibit. Nixon dropped his trousers and begged History to look.

THE EVENING NEWS

(The political world explained at last, with a special emphasis on Commies, bombs, and those daffy royals of England.)

WHY DID RUSSIA AND THE UNITED STATES KEEP BUILDING NUCLEAR BOMBS LONG AFTER THEY HAD ENOUGH TO REDUCE THE WORLD TO CINDERS?

The United States and the Soviet Union have more than ten thousand nuclear warheads apiece, enough to drop a hundred of these babies on every one of the one hundred largest and/or most annoying cities in the enemy nation. Chattanooga, *blam!* Des Moines, *zak!* Orlando, *phfftt!* When you figure that the average one-megaton hydrogen bomb has the equivalent power of 200 million salvos from a World War I field artillery gun, the overkill factor becomes clear.

Why the redundancy? Because our goal is not simply to blow up the enemy but to be able to blow them up *after* they've blown us up, after they've attacked us with the full fury of their arsenal and reduced our nation to a broad plain of oatmeallike carbon flakes. We want to be able to take 'em with us.

Thus the key desire of the military strategists is to have a survivable arsenal. The military presumes that the Soviets would be able to destroy about 80 percent of our silo-based missiles. So we have to make sure that a mere *fifth* of our arsenal—the 20 percent not destroyed—is sufficient to inflict intolerable damage on the enemy.

This "deterrence" philosophy requires the leaders of the respective nations to insist they are willing to commit senseless mass murder—senseless because once the bombs are on the way, the point of having them in the first place would disappear. The only motive for firing back would be sheer insatiable thirst for vengeance. This crazy psychological game only works if everyone agrees to ignore how crazy it is.

This is the Nuclear Game, where the conflict has nothing to do with politics, and everything to do with the existence of the bombs themselves. When a reporter asked President George Bush in September 1989 if he would support a moratorium on testing new nuclear weapons, Bush replied, "As long as we are dependent for a deterrence based on nuclear weapons, I would have difficulty eliminating all testing . . . it's important that these weapons be safe, it's important they be sound." In other words, the bombs exist to protect the bombs.

Ideology has completely vanished amid game theory. You say the Soviets are no longer our enemy? It doesn't matter. The game goes on. No country is going to dismantle its arsenal and try to forget the technology of destruction. The gap between nuclear strategy and meaningful political policy has never been so obvious as it is today, at the end of the Cold War: The United States and the Soviet Union may be cozy, but soldiers *still* sit in underground silos waiting for the command to annihilate the "enemy."

The weapon counters in the Pentagon and the military defense industry are in an unholy alliance to perpetuate the game. They are obsessed with keeping up with the Jonesevitches. They don't see the political change in the East so much as the improved accuracy of Soviet ground-based missiles. They insist that we make our forces more survivable, and suddenly we are paying hundreds of billions of dollars for the mobile

MX, the Stealth bomber, and the huge Trident submarines—weapons that have virtually no use other than deterrence. The only real function of these weapons is to be scary. It's like having a sign on your house saying Beware of Dog, only more expensive.

WHY DID THE UNITED STATES SEND THE 82nd AIRBORNE TO DEFEND SAUDI ARABIA, RATHER THAN SENDING, FOR EXAMPLE, THE FIRST AIRBORNE, OR THE SECOND AIRBORNE?

The main thing you need to know about the Army is that the smallest organized combat unit is the fire team. Then comes the squad, the platoon, the company, the battalion, the brigade, the division, the corps, the Army, the Army group, and finally the theater of operations. The "82nd Airborne" is a division—about 15,000 men and women, by present standards. (A division in World War I was 28,000 soldiers.)

The shocking, appalling news is that the unit numbers are kind of nonsensical. If the Army wants to parachute soldiers into a combat zone, it has no choice but to use the 82nd Airborne Division, because that's the only parachute assault division we have. The only other airborne division is the 101st, which uses helicopters. Those two divisions, together with the 24th Infantry, make up the 18th Airborne Corps. These numbers are deceptive, because the entire Army actually has only eighteen active divisions (and remember, a division is smaller than a corps).

The numbering system began in 1917 when the United States entered World War I. The idea was that divisions one through twenty-five would be permanent Army divisions, twenty-six through fifty would be National Guard, and fifty-one and higher would be "national Army" divisions specially raised to fight in

World War I. Over the years some numbers were retired, just like a ballplayer's, and a few high-numbered World War I divisions became part of the permanent regular Army, which is why the 82nd is still around long after the kaiser lost his war. To make things more confusing, there are three divisions that claim the number 1: First Infantry Division (Mechanized), First Armored Division, and First Cavalry Division. (*Cavalry* doesn't mean they still ride horses; in Vietnam they used helicopters, and since 1976 they've used tanks—just like the First Armored Division! The term *cavalry* is kept for sentimental reasons.)

It would be possible to simplify all this by returning to sequential numbers. But that would only make it easier for the accursed enemy to keep track of us. Better to be baffling. "It's a matter of deception," says John Wilson, historian for the U.S. Army Center of Military History.

It's also a matter of history. There's something about the number of a military unit that mists the eye. As Hemingway wrote in A *Farewell to Arms*, "Abstract words such as glory, honor, courage, or hallow were obscene beside the concrete names of villages, the numbers of roads, the names of rivers, the numbers of regiments and the dates."

WHY DON'T COMMUNIST LEADERS EVER GET ASSASSINATED?

Because they don't kiss babies.

There's a direct correlation between baby kissing and crumpling over with a lone nut's slug in your gut. Unbeholden to electoral requirements, Communist leaders don't press the flesh, so they don't get exposed to the Hinckleys and Oswalds out there. In East Germany, for example, the members of the ruling politburo didn't live in Berlin, but in a private, supersecure community called Wandlitz, about fifteen miles north of the city. Your average run-of-the-mill assassin couldn't get anywhere close to the place.

"The top elite do not go out among the crowds. And when they do, they're undoubtedly endangered. That's why they don't do it. East German [leaders] have always been afraid of their population," A. James McAdams, a Princeton professor and expert in Communist-bloc politics, told us prior to the fall of the Berlin Wall in November 1989.

One of the arguments by Communist hard-liners against the wave of reforms is that Western-style freedoms are more trouble than they're worth, allowing crack addicts, crime in the streets, and political assassinations. The common thread among several U.S. assassination attempts in recent years has been that the targets were campaigning: JFK was in Dallas on what was essentially a campaign trip in advance of the 1964 election; Robert Kennedy and George Wallace were both campaigning when they were shot, in 1968 and 1972, respectively. So there is that downside to Western freedoms. (On the other hand, our stores are filled with merchandise and we aren't forced to drink soup made from beets.)

Another factor to consider is that Communist countries do not tolerate the goofier elements of society. The state is the sacred body of society, not the individual, so there is a tradition that when one person's demeanor or habits come into conflict with state goals, it's Hello Gulag. In contrast is the case of Lee Harvey Oswald, a known kook who had defected to the Soviet Union, was repatriated to the United States, and made a spectacle of himself by handing out pro-Castro literature in New Orleans. In America you can't be jailed just because the government thinks you might be the type to shoot the president. Otherwise they'd have to lock up half the journalists, for starters.

"It's much easier to be nutty in our society," McAdams says.

"The burden of proof lies with the state in our society, and the burden of proof lies with the individual in a socialist society."

There are some exceptions to the rule that Communists don't get shot. Lenin was shot twice by an assassin in August 1918. He survived, but one of the bullets remained in his neck for four years. Rosa Luxemburg, a famous Polish Socialist, was slain in January 1919. The most radical Communists used the Lenin and Luxemburg incidents to justify increased vigilance against internal dissent, a philosophy that led inevitably to the doctrine of Communist party omnipotence and then to the Stalin dictatorship. Stalin may have arranged the assassination of his top deputy, Sergei Kirov, in 1934 as a pretext for starting the purges that took as many as ten million lives.

Someone tried to kill the Bulgarian dictator Zhivkov in the mid-1960s, but that may have been part of a coup attempt. And a few years back East German leader Erich Honecker's car was driven off the road. That anyone would use a cheap B-movie technique to kill a leader shows how backward those people are in assassination skills. Which reminds one of the Trotsky case: Leon, the famed Bolshevik, was dispatched by a Stalinist operative in Mexico in 1940. The weapon: an ice pick.

WHY DID THE COMMUNIST WORLD COLLAPSE?

The FAX machine.

Sure, political repression had something to do with it. Sure, people were tired of having only one shoe per person, requiring them to hop in a comical fashion. But it is also no coincidence that Chinese students organizing demonstrations in the spring of 1989 were doing so by FAXing documents to each other, usually via the United States. The FAX machine is symbolic of two trends in communist-socialist countries: decentralization and modernization.

It is hard to believe, but just a few decades ago the Soviet Union was an economic marvel. Its gross national product was increasing far faster than that of the United States. Why? Because it had a simple goal: Build BIG THINGS. The Soviets built big steel mills. The Soviets built big power plants. The Soviets built big subways to get people from the big factories to the big apartment buildings.

But then it came time, eventually, to build the little things, the myriad consumer products and devices of modern technology. This is nigh impossible in a system where no one can figure out a proper price for, say, a microchip. In the West we rely on free-market prices to determine value. But in the Soviet Union government officials assign prices, so you have absurdities such as farmers feeding baked bread to their animals because it's cheaper per pound than grain.

Centralized economies just don't work. Soviet citizens have virtually no incentive to be entrepreneurial or work hard; they don't get to keep any of the fruits of their labors.

This speaks to the underlying flaw of communism: It goes against human nature. Communism is an ideal, beautiful in its way, but when exposed to harsh reality it becomes just another Bad Idea. Why did people support it anyway? Because from Marx and Engels to the present day, most of the leading proponents of communism have been young "intellectuals" from wealthy backgrounds—the kind of people who can spout and defend Bad Ideas and not have to deal with the consequences of being wrong. Long after everyone else realized that the Soviet Union, China, East Germany, and the lot were totalitarian horror shows, campus intellectuals were still finding avenues of apology. "The supreme irony of Marxism was that a fundamentally humane and egalitarian creed was so dominated by a bookish perspective that it became blind to facts and deaf to humanity and freedom," the conservative economist Thomas Sowell writes in *Marxism: Philosophy and Economics*.

It's been years since Marxism-Leninism had any real intellectual heft within the Communist world. People in communist societies realized in the eighties that they were stuck with fifties technology and forties wages. To try to catch up, their governments began to decentralize their economies—which meant, for example, increasing access to telephones, computer data bases, photocopy machines, FAX machines, and so on. With information decentralized, people could finally communicate with each other. They all realized they hated being under the thumb of the Communists and took to the streets.

That's the FAX, Jack.

WHY DO WE ALWAYS HEAR ABOUT THE FAR EAST AND THE MIDDLE EAST BUT NEVER THE NEAR EAST?

The Near East is the Middle East; there isn't a Near East anymore. We start in the Middle, then go to the Far.

For centuries the term *Near East* referred, sensibly enough, to everything from Morocco to the Persian Gulf. The Middle East extended from there to Southeast Asia. The Far East included the nations along the Pacific. When World War II broke out, Britain transferred its Middle East military command from India to Egypt, to be closer to the action. The new station kept the old name. Gradually almost everyone picked up the new British nomenclature.

It's obvious where this is going: China and Japan will eventually become part of the Middle East too. The Far East will move to California, where it will change its name legally to Far Out.

WHY IS RUSSIA SO BIG?

The Soviet Union greedily takes up one-sixth of the world's landmass and stretches across two continents (right: Australia and South America). The fact that an essentially European nation sprawls to within a hair of Nome, Alaska, is not the fault of the modern-day Godless Reds. The czars had an incredible imperialistic streak. Their greatest conquests in terms of territory (although not in terms of good beaches and luxury accommodations) came in the late 1500s and early 1600s, when Russians on horseback galloped across thinly peopled Siberia and the eastern steppe, eventually extending the empire to the Pacific.

The reason Russia got so much land was that no one else wanted it that much: There's a limited marketability to tundra and cold, nasty, unpretty mountains. Yes, there were good furs to be had, but the conquest was probably primarily ego-driven. Only with modern industrialization has the wasteland proven itself economically. The Soviets have dammed the rivers, cut down the forests, mined the minerals, and built cities in such places as Kamchatka and Irkutsk, previously known only for being difficult areas to defend in the board game Risk.

WHY DON'T CONSERVATIVE SOUTHERN DEMOCRATS CHANGE THEIR PARTY AFFILIATION TO REPUBLICAN, SINCE THEY VOTE THAT WAY ANYWAY?

"Most Reagan Democrats, as far as anybody can figure, are resentful rednecks willing to vote against their own interests because somebody black might get a break," the *Philadelphia Daily News* said in an editorial the day after the 1988 presidential election. That's hyperbolic but not without a streak of historical truth. Southern Democrats trace their roots to forebears who didn't like blacks and didn't want them to be able to vote or hold office.

You have to remember that Abe Lincoln was a Republican. After he was assassinated, radical Republicans, furious with the traitorous South, designed a system of martial law under which the former confederate states were occupied by Northern armies and governed by carpetbaggers, scalawags, and other people associated with the Republican North. For a decade blacks not only voted but also gained national elective office. Whites, loathing every minute of it, took up the Democratic banner, not to mention, in some cases, white hoods with eyeholes and pointy tops.

Reconstruction came to an end in 1877 in a political compromise in which U.S. troops were pulled out of the South in exchange for a few precious electoral votes that allowed Republican Rutherford B. Hayes to gain the presidency. Then the Democrats, gaining control of the state legislatures, established the Jim Crow laws, which established blacks as second-class citizens with no voting rights.

Suddenly there were no Republicans in the South. For decades afterward that made it impractical for anyone to register Republican, since most local, county, and state elections were decided by the Democratic primary, long before the November general election. Only in recent decades, with the boom in the Sun Belt, have enough Northern Republicans moved into the South to establish a nascent two-party system. Still, party affiliation is for some people as much a part of their identity as religion; that and sheer inertia keep many Democrats from changing over. In a couple of years Florida may become the first Deep South state with a Republican majority in its legislature, but the population will still be largely Democratic.

For fairness, and because we like to talk politics, we should note that Southern Democrats had plenty of nonracist reasons to vote against their party's candidate in the 1988 presidential election. Reason number one: He would have made bad TV. The president, as Norman Mailer has pointed out, is the nation's biggest television star. As uncharismatic as George Bush is—the mere sight of him triggers a twitching sensation in the thumb whether you're holding the remote control or not—he is not as bad as Michael Dukakis would have been. Dukakis, bless his heart, is an android. Americans don't really want a president who as a young man in the 1960s never smoked a joint. Dukakis supposedly once invited two burly union bosses to his house, asked if they wanted a beer, and when they said yes, returned from the kitchen with one beer and two glasses. He blew the election right there.

WHY DOES BRITAIN STILL BELIEVE IN KINGS AND QUEENS, INSTEAD OF GETTING RID OF THE RIDICULOUS ROYALS ONCE AND FOR ALL?

How can you wear a crown in the nineties with a straight face?

What your average royalty fan might not realize is how much power the monarch in England still retains, at least officially. The head of state is not the prime minister, but "Her Most Excellent Majesty Elizabeth the Second, by the Grace of God, of the United Kingdom of Great Britain and Northern Ireland and of Her Other Realms and Territories Queen, Head of the Commonwealth, Defender of the Faith, Sovereign of the British Orders of Knighthood." It is precisely this kind of crazy talk that incited *The New Statesman* to call the royal family "the plutocratic monarchist carbuncle on the face of the nation."

The military swears its loyalty to *her*, not the civil government. Theoretically she can fire the prime minister and reject any parliamentary edict that she dislikes. Britain has an "un-written constitution"; on paper it's still an old-fashioned monarchy. The queen doesn't pay any taxes, despite enormous private wealth. She doesn't have to get a driver's license. Her cars don't need tags. The one privilege she lacks is that she can't vote.

The monarchy, which dates to A.D. 829, costs taxpayers $40 million–plus annually. The money pays for the upkeep of Buckingham Palace and Windsor Castle and several other you-would-think redundant royal residences, for the yacht *Brittania*, for the royal retinue, and even for salaries for the royal family. And did we mention the queen pays no taxes?

Enough of the downside. Now to answer the question: The royals are a worthwhile expense. First, the royal family is an elite diplomatic corps. They work. You've seen those pictures of Charles doing crazy things like dancing in a grass skirt with primitive tribesmen. That's not a vacation to him.

Second, by unwritten agreement the queen turns over the income she gets from the vast properties owned by the Crown since the Middle Ages. See, although she's supposedly in-sanely rich, a lot of that isn't really hers. Take the crown jewels in the Tower of London, for instance. Or the big art collection. If she stepped down and dissolved the monarchy—she says she'd do it if Parliament asked her to—the Crown's riches would stay in state hands, and she'd keep only her private family property accumulated in the past couple of centuries (the exact accounting of which would be a headache).

Third, the queen doesn't use her power. Not since 1707 has a monarch scuttled an act of Parliament. To do anything so rude would incite a constitutional crisis, and then the royal jig would be up.

Fourth—here's the real answer—the royalty thing is one of England's top tourist attractions. It's pure fantasy that the whole family can enjoy! The royals are bigger than movie stars, bigger than the Beatles. Diana has personally jacked the glamour to a new level. When Charles and Diana were married, the government made $30 million on souvenirs alone. Royalty is the British version of Disney World.

WHY ARE SOME RULERS IN THE ARAB WORLD CALLED EMIRS, WHILE OTHERS ARE CALLED KINGS, AND STILL OTHERS ARE CALLED SULTANS?

Jordan, Morocco, and Saudi Arabia are kingdoms. Kuwait, Qatar, and Bahrain are emirates, as are five tiny states that make up the United Arab Emirates. The only sultanate left is Oman. Frankly we'd be sultans if we had the choice. We'd wear insanely baggy silk pants and play with sharp sabers. The title "king" seems pompous by contrast, too stuffy and inhibiting, and you'd probably have to wear a really embarrassing crown. An "emir" sounds like some kind of horned deerlike creature that roams the Serengeti Plain.

Fortunately we dug up an experienced Middle East foreign service officer who understood the true distinctions. A king is almost the same thing as a sultan, and both have more power than an emir.

First, there are real kings and fake kings. Fake kings are like the ones in England, who are rubber stamps for the real government, the parliament. Saudi Arabia has a real king. That's why the country is called Saudi Arabia, because it is run by the Saud family. King Fahd is picked by the family and has virtually absolute power. He gets to appoint everyone in the government. He's the final court of appeal. He doesn't mess around with democracy. But we Americans still love the guy, because he's got so much oil.

The sultan of Oman is also an absolute monarch. The only distinction is that when Oman was part of the Ottoman Empire—named after the cushioned seat, of course—there were many sultans ruling different lands, all answerable to the supreme leader, who controlled the empire and was so incredibly powerful he didn't really have a title; folks just called him by his name.

An emir is hamstrung by contrast. Emirs rule by the consent of the aristocracy. In this case being the ruler is more of a job than a hereditary privilege.

What about "sheikh"? That's a fairly generic title for an aristocrat in one of these emirates or sultanates or kingdoms. *Sheikh* means "prince." Our pronunciation advice is to treat it as a homonym of the word that means fashionable, rather than the word that means a frozen milk-based beverage that comes with burgers and fries.

WHY DO SOME PEOPLE BECOME "LEADERS"?

I nsincerity is crucial.

Our first source on this is *Strategy for Handling People*, by Ewing T. Webb and John B. Morgan, published in 1930, when no one was embarrassed about such things. They wrote, "One and all, great leaders are far more careful than most men in dealing with people. They take many precautions which lesser men neglect. They know that only through other people is it possible to succeed."

This is a polite, platitudinous way of saying: You need to learn to deceive and manipulate other people. Don't be candid, be careful. Take precautions. For example, lying is a good precaution. Why go through the day being yourself when you can be employing a *strategy* for handling people?

Our second source is *The Psychology of Dealing With People*, by Wendell White, 1936. He wrote, "Circuitous methods of acknowledging another person's worth are effective because they tend to keep him from questioning one's sincerity." Which, naturally, is highly questionable. White recommends certain surefire techniques for making another person feel good, such as asking for favors and "extolling the individual's occupation." Our favorite two strategies are listed consecutively:

1. Emphasizing the equality of man.
2. Implying that the one addressed is superior to others.

YOUR TAX DOLLARS

(In which the accursed Deficit, the seminally boring issue of our time, transmogrifies into a grotesque Polaroid of profligacy and prevarication in the nation's capital.)

There is a secret federal program that might be called Aid to Rich Foreigners. This is not a small program. Would you believe . . . $27 billion in one year? That's the 1988 figure for how much the United States government paid in interest on all the Treasury bills owned by foreigners.

Aid to Rich Foreigners in 1988 was twice the size of Aid to Families with Dependent Children. It was twice the size of the food stamps program. It was forty times what we spent on the Centers for Disease Control, the agency leading the fight against AIDS.

That's just one year. From 1981 to 1988 we gave foreign investors $165.4 billion.

What is more astonishing is that American taxpayers haven't stormed Capitol Hill with bayonets and bazookas to protest this boondoggle. No one cares. Where's the outrage? What does it take to get people riled? How much money down a rat hole before people wake up?

The net interest payments for fiscal 1990—the amount we paid to everyone who owned Treasury bills—was about $187 billion. That is $187 billion that could otherwise have been spent on something tangible, like roads, prisons, child care. At best it was a kind of "transfer payment," a way of redistributing money from a lot of various taxpayers to a lot of investors, a good many of them exceedingly affluent. Including those who live on other continents.

You could argue that $187 billion is a pittance. The annual gross national product, the combined sweat and strain of every American, is about $5 trillion. The wealth of the country, the accumulated capital, is about $15 trillion. So what's a measly $187 billion?

For starters it's more than any other expenditure in the budget except national defense and Social Security. That $187 billion is more than we spend on the National Cancer Institute, disadvantaged students, the National Park Service, land reclamation, solar system exploration, Aid to Families with Dependent Children, the CIA, the FBI, the Secret Service, the Environmental Protection Agency, alcohol and drug abuse prevention and treatment, the National Endowment for the Humanities, the Fish and Wildlife Service, crime-victims assistance, the Small Business Administration, job training for veterans, salaries for federal judges, and financial aid for students *combined*. It's *five times* that.

In 1985 Congress passed the famous Gramm-Rudman law, which promised a balanced budget by 1991. Later Congress switched the goal to 1993. Unfortunately just passing a law saying you will make the tough decision on whether to raise taxes or cut spending is not the same thing as actually making that tough decision. There is still no balanced budget in sight despite the much publicized budget deal between the President and Congress in the fall of 1990. Although the budget deal calls for some higher taxes and spending cuts, the government is not yet on a pay-as-you-go system, and a large proportion of the expected deficit reduction has been wiped out by the recent recession and the Persian Gulf War.

Everyone in Washington agrees that this situation is ter-rible, *terrible*, but it's too late to do anything about it, the pork has been doled from the barrel, the checks are in the mail. The alleged leaders want to make people happy, and that means not only buying more batplanes than anyone could possibly use, but also passing bills like the Mushroom Promotion, Research and Consumer Information Act. They have brought us such essential government triumphs as the Landing Craft Air Cushion Program, the Deepwater Port Li-ability Fund, the National Board for the Promotion of Rifle Practice, the Air Force General Gift Fund—a gift fund!—and the Railroad Retirement Board's ominously named Federal Windfall Subsidy.

Gramm-Rudman, meanwhile, has backfired. It encourages bookkeeping gimmicks. Congress and the president go through contortions every session to make the annual budget deficits— the yearly spasms of overspending that have ultimately added up to the $3 trillion national debt—look smaller and more be-nign than they are. There are innumerable ways of masking the deficit, including:

1. Taking items "off-budget." This means that we don't count them anymore. For example in April 1988 President Bush and Congress decided that the Postal Service would henceforth be off-budget, which has the convenient result of removing $1.7 billion in Postal Service red ink from the deficit calculations. Their motto is, A Billion Dollars Not Counted Is a Billion Dollars Earned. Worse, the president and Congress decided to ignore much of the cost of the savings-and-loan bail-out, which could reach $500 billion before it's all over.

2. Selling public property. In 1989 the government sold $5 billion in assets and thereby "reduced" the budget deficit slightly. You can picture the logical extension of this: We bal-ance the budget, but the Japanese own Yellowstone.

3. Attributing new expenses to fiscal years already gone by.

For example, those zany folks at the Pentagon switched a payday from October 1, the first day of fiscal 1990, to September 29, part of fiscal 1989. The Department of Agriculture also shifted some payments to farmers from the autumn to the summer. Although any person not currently housed in a long-term mental-health-care facility would realize that no money had actually been saved by either move, in the deficit calculations these actions saved $4 billion.

4. Counting Social Security as "surplus." This is the money that is supposedly being saved to pay for the Baby Boomers' retirement. There's nothing illogical about counting this as part of the government's annual revenue, but it's laughably hypocritical to try to have it both ways—pretending it's being saved when it's actually being spent. (More on this in a minute.)

The Republican presidents and the Democrats who control Congress have essentially conspired to keep the deficit intact, because they know that the people below them, the voters, just don't care. No one has ever marched against the deficit. There have been no sit-ins. No public official has ever been thrown out of office for deficit spending. When the Senate voted on November 7, 1990 to raise the debt above $3 trillion, it inspired only a couple of sentences on the eleven-o'clock news.

The fact is, people *like* the deficit. They tell pollsters they are worried by it, but on a day-to-day basis they like what the deficit gives them: a free lunch. They get the same old government largess, they get an economy hopped-up by borrowing, and meanwhile the tax rate has been lowered slightly, or dramatically in the case of the richest Americans.

Swearing off deficit-spending is like swearing off Häagen-Dazs. We are fully conscious of the fact that Häagen-Dazs isn't good for us; it's incredibly fattening. Eating a carton of Häagen-Dazs is like having a reverse liposuction. But it's so yummy! We may even try to convince ourselves that it's nutritious in its own way. We practice this same rationalization with deficits: Can they be so bad? After all, the eighties economy resurged from a recession at the same time that deficits rocketed upward. Maybe deficits are good!

Deficit apologists often use two false standards to downplay the significance of the red ink. The first is the standard of previous deficits. The apologists say we've had larger deficits in the past, when measured as a percentage of gross national product, such as in 1943. This reasoning is laughable. In 1943 we were in the middle of a global battle against fascist imperialism. Today we're merely in a war against our own bad judgment.

The second false standard is that of total economic collapse. In the early 1980s, when the shocking deficits came along, doomsayers said that this would destroy our country, sending it reeling into economic disintegration. That didn't happen, and it almost certainly won't. The economy will churn forward even if the deficits remain. If you compare the deficits with the overall national economy, they're not really that huge. So most economists have come to the conclusion that government debt, though a grave problem, is not catastrophic.

We have come to expect so little of our daffy government leaders that decisions that can be labeled Not Catastrophic are perfectly acceptable.

Countries don't die, they slowly waste away. Deficits rob from the future. The problem is not merely that we have a big debt that we must pay back; we'll probably never pay back that $3 trillion, because we can keep rolling it over indefinitely so long as the country remains intact. The real problem is that when the government borrows so much money from Americans (who buy most of the Treasury bills), it sucks up money that otherwise would be invested, to greater ends, in the private sector.

Look at it this way: The government is a plodding, inefficient, bureaucratic, complacent institution, the worst company that anyone could ever design. It is a giant version of the state Department of Motor Vehicles. This "company" pays a decent dividend to those who invest in it, but because it wastes so much of that invested money, the overall economy isn't helped much. The economy gets more of a boost if instead of buying savings bonds, we invest our money in, say, Spaceley Sprockets, which must operate efficiently in order to survive in the jungle of Free Enterprise.

Only through investment does a capitalist country get richer. But we don't invest much. For several decades this country had a savings rate of about 8 percent. In the last decade savings has dropped to 4 percent, far below any industrialized nation except Australia.

Because we don't save and invest, future generations will be poorer than they otherwise would be. That doesn't mean they'll be selling apples on the corner, however. As deficit apologists are quick to point out, even with this huge public debt, future generations are likely to make slightly more money, in real terms, than we do today. So you might ask, why the fuss? Why should we worry about those soft-bodied, snot-nosed future punks? Why should they get to drive Cadillacs if we're stuck with Chevys?

For starters the Robin Hood defense is questionable on moral grounds. No previous generation has countenanced a theft of wealth from its descendants. On a more practical level, our grandchildren may be driving Cadillacs, but Cadillacs might be a joke by that time, the equivalent of horse-and-buggy. The Japanese might be zipping around in, who knows, antigravitational devices.

Per capita GNP is also a phony measure of prosperity since it doesn't take into account environmental degradation and resource depletion, precisely the sort of problems the government could focus on if it wasn't wasting so much money on Rich Foreigners.

There is also a moral problem with the deficit: We are a rich country. We live nice lives. We have "leisure time." Some of us drive power boats that get two miles to the gallon. It is great to be an American. So why are we borrowing money from foreigners? Why are we using up capital that could be invested in poor countries where children starve to death? Do we have no shame?

We might fantasize about balancing the budget the easy way—by simply refusing to pay the $180 billion that we spend on interest on the federal debt. Unfortunately that's called default. That is bad.

There is one final way to pay off the mountain of debt that is our monument to the Häagen-Dazs Decade. We can print money. Just crank up the presses at the mint.

This is how they dealt with a similar problem in Bolivia. The only downside is that the more money you print, the less it's worth. The inflation rate in Bolivia got a little high—about 30,000 percent.

You could buy a Jag in the morning for what a moped would cost you in the afternoon.

Fortunately we will never have to learn what five-digit inflation is like. This is America, after all. The richest country. The smartest country. The bravest country.

This isn't Bolivia.

Yet.

At some point, Americans will have to decide how much they want to pay in taxes and who should get the money, because the current system—in which the hard choices are postponed—cannot last indefinitely. It is too late to simply cut discretionary spending. The government's major budget items are for what are called "entitlement programs," such as Medicare, Social Security, and government pensions. As the population gets older, and as medical costs increase, these programs will demand more and more of the federal budget pie. There's nothing in the 1990 budget deal between the president and Congress to suggest that anyone has figured out how this country can keep its promises to the elderly in, say, 2020. Spending on the elderly rose from 32 percent of the budget in 1965, discounting defense spending and interest payments on the debt, to 47 percent in 1990. Yet no one dares tamper with programs that affect the elderly.

"The great untold story of this year's budget debate is that it represents yet another step in turning the national government into a gigantic machine for taxing workers to support retirees," economist Robert J. Samuelson wrote in 1990. "The elderly are considered a group that deserves to be pampered and whose political power requires them to be pampered."

A little story about Social Security:

Robert Julius Myers is seventy-seven years old and lives with his wife, Rudy, in a brick Colonial house on a curving street in suburban Washington, D.C. They have been there fifty years. "The house cost $6,000, and it's worth $200,000 now," Myers says. He speaks in numbers. He's an actuary.

Inside, everything is clean and tidy and precious. The oak floors are covered with Persian rugs. The furniture is Old English. An '88 Mercedes is parked in the garage. The Myerses are not a modern couple with appalling bank loans and Visa balances. They do it the old-fashioned way: They own.

Mr. Myers works upstairs in his paper-strewn, diploma-heavy office. A white terrier prowls the house. Myers is a noted thinker, consultant, guest speaker, and source for journalists. He is Mr. Facts About Social Security. He and the Social Security Administration go back to 1934, when the agency was first being dreamed up by the Committee on Economic Security. Myers rose through the ranks to become chief actuary under five presidents, leaving in 1970. His income is substantial, he says.

Plus he has investments on the side.

Plus he gets $60,000 a year in a federal civil-service pension.

Plus he and his wife get another $18,000 or so a year, half

of that tax-free, from the United States Treasury. That's his Social Security.

The U.S. government—the one that is supposedly hurting for cash—is faithfully sending money to the Myerses. This does not mean that Bob and Rudy are doing anything wrong. They're lovely people—frugal, honest, without a trace of greed. You'd want them as neighbors. You'd want to *be* them.

"If the law says I'm entitled to benefits, I'll take them," Mr. Myers says. "As I see it, I'm legally entitled to the money. I didn't manipulate the system to get it."

The system is just quirky. Perhaps the biggest quirk being:

Rich people get Social Security checks.

And more specifically:

Rich people get bigger Social Security checks than poor people.

Supposedly there is a good reason for this. Ever since its inception during the Great Depression, Social Security has been promoted as an insurance program. Regardless of who you are, you get Social Security because it's *your money*. It's *saved* for you, tucked away for your retirement years. You work, you pay taxes, you reap the reward in the end. Social Security is not a handout, not—*ugh*—Welfare.

That's the myth at least. The fact that it is so universally believed underscores economist Milton Friedman's view of Social Security: "I know of no greater triumph of imaginative packaging and Madison Avenue advertising."

Social Security, in reality, has never been an insurance program. It has never been a contract that we make with ourselves to fund our own retirement. Our tax money is not set aside in a trust fund, as advertised. Nor are our benefits tied to how much we have paid in taxes. Most people get back many times what they put in, even after interest is accounted for.

To be precise, Social Security is an intergenerational transfer of money from workers to nonworkers. And that's fine! That's good! Social Security is popular because it's fundamentally a great idea, a government program that saves millions of people from the poorhouse. Without that check, many retirees would literally have to sell the farm to buy groceries.

The problem is that the government is quietly exploiting public ignorance of the way Social Security works to put the burden of the federal budget deficit unfairly on the shoulders of working Americans rather than on the affluent. The government has raised the Social Security tax five times since 1983. No one protested, since we were all told that this extra money would be set aside in a "trust fund" to pay for the retirement of Baby Boomers in about thirty years. What we were not told—this is the dirty little secret of the federal government—is that the trust fund is just an entry on a magnetic tape in a computer in Parkersburg, West Virginia. It's nothing more than a bookkeeping entry saying that the government owes *itself* money. The actual money we send the government goes straight into the Treasury and is spent on park rangers, speech writers, missile silos, and the Aid to Rich Foreigners program.

Worse, the Social Security tax is highly "regressive," a flat 7.65 percent of your paycheck, whether you work at Burger King or the Ritz-Carlton. (And let's not forget that the employer matches the tax, dollar for dollar. That's money that might otherwise go to the worker's salary, so the effective tax rate is 15.3 percent.) The really regressive part of the tax is that *it doesn't apply to any money that you make above $51,300 a year.*

Let's say you are a cop working overtime and moonlighting as a mechanic, and you manage—by never seeing your family—to put together an income of $51,300 a year. Your half of the Social Security tax, not including your employer's portion, is $3,924.45. No deductions or exemptions allowed. Meanwhile your old college roommate, a mergers-and-acquisitions lawyer, is making $2 million a year. His Social Security tax is . . . $3,924.45. He's chuckling all the way to the Ferrari dealership.

Now, let's say the guy next door is an "investor" who sits by the pool all day drinking daiquiris and patting his belly like a tom-tom. His income is in the form of interest on bonds and dividends from stock, sales of real estate, loan-sharking, and so forth. He pays NO Social Security tax.

Bill Cosby earns $100 million a year. His contribution to Social Security ends at about 3:00 A.M. on January 1.

The lower and middle classes are paying as much or more taxes than ever before. According to the Congressional Budget Office, the poorest fifth of the country—families of four making less than $18,692 a year—saw their taxes increase 16.1 percent between 1980 and 1990. That's because Social Security taxes went up, while most of the 1982 Reagan income tax cut went to the rich. Your average Americans, the people in what is known as the third quintile, midway between rich and poor, saw their taxes go from 20.0 percent in 1980 to 20.3 percent in 1990—not much of an increase, but disappointing in the age of tax cuts.

Compare their fate to that of the country's elite: The richest 5 percent of the nation—singles making more than $68,845, families of four making more than $134,206—enjoyed a tax cut of 9.5 percent. Income rose 46.1 percent. Nice going!

To be fair, the rich still pay a lot more money in taxes than the poor. The rich also tend to have a much higher overall tax rate, since the poor pay little income tax. Our tax system on the whole is still progressive. It's just not as progressive as it used to be.

Why didn't people complain when the government increased the Social Security tax? Maybe because they didn't know what the letters FICA meant on their paychecks. We all know that FICA has something to do with Social Security. We vaguely suspect that this is a special category of money that we'll get back someday. Indeed polls show that the majority of Americans don't mind paying money into that mystery fund. They assume FICA isn't a rat hole like regular income tax.

Federal Income Cash Assignation?

Fiduciary Interest Charge Amplitude?

Financial Investment Capital Application?

No, it's Federal Insurance Contributions Act. The money deleted from your check is a "contribution" in the same way that you'd pay a large stranger in a very bad neighborhood who asks if you want to contribute five bucks to him to "watch your car."

When we asked Phil Gambino, a spokesman for the Social Security Administration, if we could drop out of the system—eschewing benefits in exchange for not making any more "contributions"—he did not hesitate.

"No. Social Security is mandatory coverage for most workers."

If it's an insurance program, as Social Security claims, it's a funky one. This Q-and-A caught our eye in *Your* 1989/90 *Guide to Social Security Benefits*:

Question: "I never got married. What if I die the day before my Social Security payments are scheduled to start? Since I have no dependents, will I have lost everything?"

Answer: "Yes."

The biggest part of the Social Security myth is that you get your money back. You don't. It's a complicated, subtle matter that we didn't quite understand when we went to see Gwendolyn King, the boss of the Social Security Administration.

Stop fretting, she told us. Our money is going into "Special Obligation" government bonds. Safe, sure investments.

"When it's time to redeem those bonds, the U.S. government will make good on these bonds, as it has for the last fifty years," she said.

She said what we pay in FICA should not be considered a tax like what we pay to the IRS. "Don't add the two together. What you pay the IRS is totally different from what you pay in FICA. Try to get monthly benefits from the IRS!"

She was so reassuring. We've put our money in U.S. bonds

and not just ordinary bonds. *Special* bonds.

Now for the truth: Our future retirement benefits (or disability checks should we be unable to work) are based on our average salary, not on how much we paid into the kitty. This is an important distinction. As FICA *taxes go up, the benefits stay the same*. What we pay into the system doesn't matter. The FICA tax rose from 12.26 percent in 1980 to 15.3 percent in 1990, but that doesn't mean that any of us will get an extra cent when we retire.

Some quick history: Back in the Depression, Roosevelt wanted to help the elderly without stamping them with the stigma of the dole. He also wanted to avoid accusations of socialist leanings. So Social Security is supposed to be a compromise between an insurance plan and a welfare program. As with insurance, you build up "equity." Roosevelt knew that as long as people had to pay Social Security taxes, they'd feel they had a political and ethical right to receive the benefits decades later.

The equation by which preretirement income is "replaced" by Social Security is indeed progressive: A person earning minimum wage will get 57 percent of that income replaced every month by Social Security, while a person earning $51,300 will get only 24 percent replaced. Any extra income above $51,300 doesn't get replaced at all. So the benefit equations do favor the poor, if you look at the program purely as a pension. The only problem with this perspective is that in actual dollars the rich person still gets a much bigger monthly check than the poor person.

Is this fair? Obviously it has a certain appeal. It's the rarest of government programs, one that gives more money to people who pay a lot in taxes than to people who pay little.

But that's also the killer flaw with Social Security. It implies that the government owes benefits to citizens in some proportion to what each citizen pays in taxes. Need is, at most, irrelevant.

Not only that, the government gives people much more than what they paid in. The average retiree will get every tax dollar back in four years. Every dollar beyond that is gravy. The reason people get their money back so quickly is that many retirees worked during a time when Social Security taxes were extremely low—until 1950 they were 2 percent for employees and employers *combined*. If you factor in the interest that people would have earned had their tax dollars gone into an investment instead, the benefits may appear less generous, but people are still coming away with a lot of extra dough.

Still, the benefits don't make anyone rich. The average monthly check for someone retiring in 1990 was only $668. So the problem is not that the government is too generous. The problem is that the taxes are unfair and deceptive and do nothing to solve the long-term dilemma of Social Security.

Right now there are about 3.3 workers for every retiree. Between 2010 and 2030 the ratio will drop to about 2 to 1. The current forecast is that the mythical trust fund will show an incredible $12 trillion surplus by the year 2029, then rapidly be depleted in the decades after that. But in reality that $12 trillion will never be anything other than a bookkeeping entry. The actual cash must still come from the workers of the next century. This is precisely the situation that the mythical Social Security surplus is supposed to avoid.

When we think of the future, we tend to focus on how many dollars there will be. We forget that money is only paper. It has no intrinsic value except as tinder (as opposed to tender). What does matter is how many "goods and services" the country will be producing in 2025. That's worrisome. The Boomers will have stopped working. While they kick back in their recliners, drinking Dry Bud Lite Dark, there will be a shortage of workers at the recliner factory and in the fields where they grow the hops and barley. The only way of avoiding serious beer and recliner shortages in the future—which would in turn lead to higher prices and the erosion of the value of our Social Security checks—is to make investments today that will increase the efficiency and productivity of the average worker in 2025. Which means ending these big deficits. Ah, yes, the deficit! We knew we'd get back to that eventually.

At the heart of the Social Security scam is the use of the regressive FICA tax to whittle away at the budget deficit. There was never any possibility that the Social Security "surpluses" would be saved. As long as the government is running a deficit, it *can't* save money. It is impossible for the government to run a deficit in one account (the U.S. Treasury) and save money in another (the Social Security Trust Fund), because it's all part of the same pot, distinguished only by bookkeeping entries.

Consider your own finances. If, every month, you put $1,000 into a savings account but also borrow $3,000 to pay your bills, you are not saving money—even if you swear up and down that you are. And while you might even be accused of being an insane person, this is standard policy for the government.

The truth is, Congress must use the Social Security surplus to buy Treasury bills. It's the law. A smart law. T-bills, as Gwendolyn King said, are the safest investment in the country. Where else should that money go? In a mattress? In a safe under the floorboards? Junk bonds?

So the cash goes from the worker to the Treasury and is spent. Within a few decades the government will owe itself $12 trillion. The interest alone on that self-made debt will be hundreds of billions a year. It's all very frightening until you realize that the government of the United States can owe itself whatever it wants, without fear of bankruptcy or forfeiture. This is nothing but an accounting hassle.

Someone might argue that as long as the trust fund holds government IOUs, no politician can cut Social Security. That's not true. Congress can cut benefits any time it wants. The Supreme Court has ruled that we don't have a collective right to the money we pay in Social Security tax. It's not insurance, said the Court.

Now, then, let's suppose that the President and the Congress got their acts together and actually balanced the non–Social Security budget, and continued to take in more in FICA than is paid out in Social Security. Couldn't the surplus be saved then?

It would be hard. First, if the government ran a surplus, there'd be irresistible pressure to spend the dough. Federal budget surpluses are probably the stuff of science fiction.

Second, spending the money on anything other than Treasury bills would be risky and subject to political squabbling. One official might want to buy bank notes from Japan, another would want to invest in Disney, a third would want to buy the steel industry.

So the only viable option would be to do what President Bush has proposed: Buy Treasury bills from private investors, foreigners, banks, whoever holds them. That would reduce the national debt, which exceeds $3 trillion, and would sort of be like saving the money. Bush says he'd do this specifically with the Social Security surplus money, but he's exploiting public ignorance. You could just as easily say that we used Social Security taxes to run our national parks and that our national park budget was being used to buy back the government debt.

You see, money is "fungible." A great word! The dictionary says, rather obliquely, that *fungible* is an adjective that designates "movable goods, as grain, any unit or part of which can replace another unit, as discharging a debt." A better way of explaining the word is by anecdote. Eddie Cantor, the singer, was once criticized for accepting Social Security checks even though he was rich. His response: "I give that money to charity." A sophisticated person would see the flaw here: If he gives his Social Security money to charity, that means he keeps more of his other income. Money is fungible!

Let's think this out. There's no real difference between the use of Social Security taxes and income taxes. It all goes into the same pot and comes out of the same pot. So why does there have to be two categories of taxes?

Why is there a Social Security tax at all?

And why did *it* go up in the 1980s while income tax went down?

Because it's a tax that favors the rich?

Mighty suspicious.

Surveying the political realities of the day, it may not even be worth the effort to complain. A wedge is being nailed through the heart of the nation as economic losers and winners take their respective positions. Ignorance has formed an unholy and unbreachable alliance with greed.

For the individual trying to stay afloat in this sea of trouble— we are not, after all, mere statistics, mere numbers on a bar chart, mere means and medians and standard deviations—the proper course of action is clear:

Get rich, quick.

THE HUMAN BODY
(Yuck)

WHY DON'T CONTACT LENSES ACCIDENTALLY MIGRATE BEHIND YOUR EYEBALL AND WORK THEIR WAY INTO YOUR BRAIN?

There's a transparent layer of skin on your eyeball that runs about halfway back into your socket before it suddenly halts and folds up underneath your eyelid. In other words the slot between eyeball and eyelid ends before you get way back in the danger zone. Since there's a fair amount of room available, people have apparently "lost" their contact lenses in there for months or even years at a time. The white part of the eye is tough and insensitive, so you might not realize you've got something up there. Maybe you should check. (Or maybe not.)

WHY IS IT IMPOSSIBLE TO TICKLE YOURSELF?

Predictability. Tickling requires unexpected stimulation. If you try to tickle yourself, you get so much feedback from your fingertips and from the voluntary movement of your arm that the subsurface nerves don't get excited. When blindfolded, though, you are especially vulnerable to someone else's tickling maneuvers.

Tickling is a psychosexual phenomenon; it requires a certain frame of mind on the part of the victim. The tickle has to be perceived as a mock assault, not a real threat. There should be mild apprehension, not fear. Accordingly a child is more effectively tickled by a parent or a sibling than by a stranger. We are most easily tickled by those with whom we have an underlying sexual chemistry. This is even true for little kids: Boys are more ticklish when touched by girls than when touched by other boys. Sex is something we all fear and crave.

WHY ARE YAWNS CONTAGIOUS?

This'll wake you up: "Yawning is of medical importance because it is symptomatic of pathology such as brain lesions and tumors, hemorrhage, motion sickness, chorea, and encephalitis."

So says a 1987 University of Maryland report in the journal *Behavioral and Neural Biology*. So the next time you yawn, keep repeating to yourself: "Relax, there's only a small chance that it's cancer."

To understand this dreaded contagion, we should first dispense with the annoying notion among the true-fact crowd that yawning rapidly increases the amount of oxygen in your body and purges carbon dioxide. "It's absolutely not true," says Robert Provine, professor of psychology at the University of Maryland (Maryland seems to be a major yawn-research hotbed, for reasons that are obvious to anyone who's been there).

Provine gave pure oxygen to a number of test subjects. According to the Common Wisdom, they should have had no reason to yawn. They did anyway. Then he made them breathe air with one hundred times the normal level of carbon dioxide. They all died. Just kidding! But that would have been a great experiment. What happened actually is that nothing happened; they yawned the normal amount. Then Provine asked his students to yawn through clenched teeth, inhaling just as deeply as they would with mouths agape. Their yawns were briefer, frequently aborted in mid-yawn, and they reported that they hadn't satisfied their yearning for yawning.

So air isn't the point. The main respiratory benefit is that the deep breath expands tiny air passages called alveoli in the recesses of the lungs, helping to prevent them from collapsing. But the amount of oxygen taken in during a typical six-second yawn is actually less than the amount you get when you take several normal breaths in the same period of time. So when you yawn, you lose oxygen, not gain it, says Provine.

Another thing he discovered is that the big display of tonsils we associate with yawning is overrated as body language. Provine videotaped yawners, then altered the pictures so that some showed only the yawning mouths, others the rest of the face but not the mouth. Then he showed the videos to his students, to see which ones would spur the most yawning by power of suggestion. The mouths lost. Things like eyebrows are more important as visual inducements to yawning.

The yawn, you see, is actually an extremely complex "high amplitude" (that is, intense) process involving all parts of the body. The arms stretch, the face contracts, the eyebrows rise, the eyes narrow, the tongue retreats, the eustachian tubes open, the pressure in the middle ear reaches equilibrium with the outside world, the heartbeat speeds up, tears and saliva are excreted, steam shoots out of the ears as in cartoons, and so forth. So much is going on at once that it's impossible to say that one single thing is the cause or purpose.

We hate that attitude, so we'll offer this as the major reason why people yawn: It puts you on an even keel. Yawns make bored people more alert and (though this is not commonly realized) calm down people who are stressed out. People yawn not only when they're sleepy but also when they're anxious. A musician about to perform on stage is likely to go into a yawn spasm.

We still haven't explained why yawns are contagious. (Has anyone noticed how long it takes to get a straight answer around here?) There is, wouldn't you know it, an evolutionary explanation. Just once you'd think we could come up with something paranormal, like telekinesis, but no, it's always evolution, always science. Yawning synchronizes the behavior and physiology of each member of a larger pack. Each creature reaches that even keel—alertness, or calm, depending on the situation—simultaneously. Yawning is also a communicative signal: time to sleep. Large packs of animals need to synchronize their behavior because a group can be more efficient than individual creatures acting on their own schedule. Dogs and humans hunt better in packs. In fact yawning is common to all manner of creatures. Cats yawn. Chickens stand on their toes, flap their wings, and yawn. Fish yawn. Honest.

The biological explanation of the yawn contagion is trickier. It would be too simple to say it is merely the power of suggestion and too droolingly idiotic to think that there's some kind of microbe or aura that hops from person to person. You can be induced to yawn via television, by seeing a yawn or hearing one, by talking about it or merely thinking about it. There's some kind of yawn trigger in the brain. "You have a prewired yawn detector," says Provine. Exactly what this detector is, and where it is located in the brain, is something no one knows.

Admit it: You yawned while reading this.

You are forgiven.

WHY DO PEOPLE SLEEP?

Growth hormones are secreted in children only during sleep. If kids don't sleep, their growth is stunted. In people of all ages certain chemicals that enhance the immune system are released only during sleep. You may have noticed that you easily catch a cold if you haven't had much rest. Besides all that, sleep remains thoroughly mysterious. All animals sleep or rest, even though it seems on its face to be counter-evolutionary, a lowering of defenses. We don't just need sleep, we need dreams. In an experiment rats were allowed to sleep a normal amount, but were woken every time they lapsed into dream sleep (the equivalent of rapid-eye-movement sleep in humans). Within three months they were dead; strangely their bodies had lost the ability to retain heat. Incidentally, congenitally blind people have no visual dreams, but dream of tastes, smells, textures, sounds.

WHY ARE DREAMS METAPHORICAL AND SYMBOLIC, RATHER THAN LITERAL AND STRAIGHTFORWARD?

A recent example: A newspaper reporter is rapidly nearing deadline on a big story, and he fears he won't finish in time. One night he has a dream in which he is skydiving and his parachute won't open completely. He yanks on his cord frantically. He continues to rush groundward. He has only seconds left. . . . And he wakes up. Question: Why didn't he have a dream in which he was a newspaper reporter nearing a deadline on a big story? Why the elaborate and obviously metaphorical tale of skydiving?

And for you Freudians out there: Why are there so many snakes, clubs, gasoline hoses, knives, and asparagus spears, but so few actual, you know, *weenies*?

The answer is that the brain creates dreams through random electrical activity. *Random* is the key word here. About every ninety minutes the brain stem sends electrical impulses throughout the brain, in no particular order or fashion. The analytic portion of the brain—the forebrain—then desperately tries to make sense of these signals. It is like looking at a Rorschach test, a random splash of ink on paper. The only way of comprehending it is by viewing the dream (or the inkblot) met-aphorically, symbolically, since there's no literal message.

This doesn't mean that dreams are meaningless or should be ignored. How our forebrains choose to "analyze" the ran-dom and discontinuous images may tell us something about ourselves, just as what we see in an inkblot can be revelatory. And perhaps there is a purpose to the craziness: Our minds may be working on deep-seated problems through these cir-cuitous and less threatening metaphorical dreams.

The whole affair of sleeping is a bit weird. It seems a dan-gerous habit for any creature deemed delicious by another. It may be that sleep is a method of conserving energy, slowing down metabolism, getting through a long earth-day without needing that fourth square meal. In 1980 a Harvard scientist showed that we sleep because our body temperature drops; when people talk about their "body clock," they are referring to this internal thermostat, which operates (for reasons we can't figure) on a twenty-five-hour cycle. The bottlenose dolphin may be the only species to have figured out a way to get around the downside of sleeping: The hemispheres of its brain take turns sleeping; half now, the other half later.

Dreaming may be the brain's way of recharging itself. When you wake in the morning, your mind is fresh; you think better. What happened in the night? A theory developed by Francis Crick and Graeme Mitchison holds that dreams are a way of "unlearning," that the brain is sweeping up the neuronal dust, bagging it in the form of dreams, and throwing it out. Dreams are garbage.

This makes sense. Although we spend so much time trying to figure out what dreams mean and marveling at the connec-tions between our dreams and real life, the truth is that dreams are most remarkable for *not* being like real life, for being non-sense. Freud said that dreams are the "royal road" to the unconscious, but they are really more like a back alleyway, littered with trash.

WHY DOES EATING ASPARAGUS HAVE SUCH A MARKED EFFECT ON YOUR URINE?

First, a simple recipe. Take some medium-thick asparagus spears and briefly steam them so that they remain crunchy. Then quickly sauté the spears in butter, lemon, and freshly ground black pepper. Serve and enjoy.

An hour or two later you will notice something: Your pee smells funny.

Or maybe it won't. The production of odiferous urine after the ingestion of asparagus is a genetic trait found only in about half the population.

A 1987 study published in the British journal *Experientia* stated that of eight hundred volunteers who ate asparagus, 43 percent produced the mephitic emission. The remainder apparently have an enzyme in their bodies that breaks down a sulfuric compound called methanethiol that is present in the vegetable. Without this hereditary trait, the methanethiol isn't metabolized and comes out in your urine, causing the odor.

We should note that a 1975 study published in *Science* claimed that it is impossible to find this methanethiol in urine. In fact the real, unidentified culprit may become converted to methanethiol during experiments with asparagus. You fact checkers out there with access to data bases may also come across a 1980 Israeli study suggesting that everyone suffers from the asparagus effect but that only half the population can *smell* it. This view, however, does not enjoy popularity and credibility among most scientists.

The real mystery is why this phenomenon does not routinely

inspire projects at high school science fairs. Surely it's more interesting than cutting up toads.

WHY DO FINGERNAILS AND HAIR STILL GROW FOR A WHILE AFTER YOU DIE?

This is an old wives' tale. The tissue of a corpse, particularly the skin and the tips of the fingers and toes, shrinks as the body dries out. The result is an illusion of nail and hair growth.

Actually the drying out of a corpse—mummification—is only one of two options. If the body is kept in a cool, wet place, such as a basement, it may decompose more slowly and become what is known as *adipocere*. Dr. Humphrey Germaniuk, of the Dade County (Fla.) Medical Examiner's Office, describes *adipocere* as "a peculiar gray-white cheesy state."

"Like fine French Brie," he adds.

(We *knew* there was some reason we hated that stuff.)

WHY DO OUR BODIES FEEL MORE COMFORTABLE AT "ROOM TEMPERATURE" THAN AT OUR NORMAL BODY TEMPERATURE OF 98.6 DEGREES?

If we were all totally inert, indolent, stupefied human beings— vice-presidential material, in other words—we might be able to handle a room that was 98.6 degrees. But we'd have to be naked and prostrate. We couldn't get excited or emotional or even speak. And we'd still feel hot.

Our body wants to be at 98.6 degrees, and it ruthlessly maintains that temperature, no matter how hot or cold it is outside. Most mammals have similar body temperatures, probably because certain biochemical processes work best at that level. If our body gets too cold, our metabolism speeds up and burns more sugars and fats. If it's too hot, we sweat like swine, and as the moisture changes from liquid to gas, it sucks heat energy from our skin.

Now, let's say that we're in a room that's 98.6 degrees. Anything we do—walking, breathing, digesting food—requires energy, and thus another log on our internal furnace. Unless we can get rid of that extra heat, we'll burn up.

If the room is 80 degrees and we start doing calisthenics—that's what we had before aerobics, remember?—in short order the furnace will be blazing so ferociously inside that we'll once again be burning up, which is why we poop out and feel overheated. It's literally true.

The rate of conduction of heat between our body and the air around us is a direct function of the difference in temperature—that's a scientific way of saying what you already know, that it's easier to cool off in a cool room than in a hot one.

WHY CAN YOU ALWAYS TELL WHEN YOU'RE BEING STARED AT?

You know this feeling. You could be in a college lecture hall, having a typical daydream—lambs foraging through pastures, children frolicking in a sandbox, your mother going to the gallows—and suddenly you get the nagging, burning sensation that someone behind you is aiming eyebeams at the back of your head. You turn. Ah-hah! You are right. What is this, telepathy? Some kind of spider sense? Bat radar?

As it happens, there's a seminal study of the phenomenon, published in a 1917 book called Experiments in Psychical Research, by Stanford psychologist John Edgar Coover. In his chapter "The Feeling of Being Stared At" he shows that this peculiar sensation is universal around the world. Of his students, fully

77 percent said they could reliably know when someone was staring at them.

Then Coover proved them wrong.

The starees sat at a desk. Coover, behind them, rolled a die to decide whether to stare or not. Even number, he stared. Odd number, he closed his eyes and imagined a landscape. The students would then guess, during fifteen-second intervals, whether Coover was staring or not. Blind luck would make them correct about 50 percent of the time—in which case this would be just another example of the it-always-rains-when-you-wash-the-car syndrome, that nonphenomenon based on selective memory. But if the correct guesses significantly exceeded 50 percent, the sensation would suggest some paranormal or psychic perception.

There were 1,000 guesses total.

Correct: 502.

WHY DO WE SHED TEARS AND GET A RUNNY NOSE WHEN WE'RE UPSET?

It's bad enough being emotionally distraught, but then our face responds to the crisis by unleashing liquids of varying viscosities in a sudden and mortifying MucusFest. Is there some higher function being served here? Isn't there a better way of exhibiting distress? Like maybe having our eyeballs go *sproing* and fly out of their sockets on bedsprings?

First, let's describe as graphically as is editorially possible what happens when our nose "runs." Your basic mucus has suddenly been watered down, thinned out, so it flows. Where'd the water come from? Is there a secret water gland in the nasal cavity? Could it be cerebrospinal fluid leaking out of your brain? No. It's tears. The tears flow into your nose from your eyes, through a hidden passageway similar to the auxiliary drain that is supposed to keep a bathtub from overflowing. Here's the technical data from Dr. Phillip Waggoner, a professor of anatomy at the University of Miami:

"If you look real closely at the end of your eyelid nearest your nose, you'll see a tiny little hole. That's called the *puncta lacrimalia*. It drains into the *lacrimal canaliculi*."

Which any moron knows is the hidden passageway into the nose. This is for real.

So why are there tears in the first place? We should note that tears come in three varieties. "Basal tears" are secreted constantly and keep the eyeball lubricated. "Reflex tears" are what you get when you are poked in the eye, or when you cut up a gaseous onion. "Emotional tears" are provoked by messages from the brain stem, the command center of human emotion. The first two types have an obvious prophylactic/therapeutic function. Not the third type. Those sobs are still mysterious.

True, crying releases tension, but there's no reason tears have to be involved. A baby less than three months old will cry without tears.

It seems most likely that tears have evolved among humans as a communication technique. Social species, such as *Homo sapiens*, require and exploit all manner of signals. Gushing tears send a dramatic message that can, for example, break Dad's will and yield numerous exciting toys.

Still, it seems strange that humans are the only land animals, social or otherwise, that weep. To find another weeping creature, we have to look at the marine world, where seals and sea otters have been observed in crying jags when stressed out. Our nearest relatives, the apes, show signs of sadness and grief, but, like the Kennedys, they don't cry. Why not? Desmond Morris speculates, in *Bodywatching*, that apes don't cry because the tears would be largely invisible on their hairy cheeks. Only on the smooth-skinned human can the tears glisten and send their message. Not the most convincing argument we've ever heard, but it'll have to do for now.

So, kids, if your parents scold you for crying, here's your response: "Crying is an adaptive trait that separates humans from the apes."

That'll show 'em.

WHY ARE IDIOT SAVANTS SO SMART?

A utistic savants, as they are now called, can instantly and accurately multiply 6,427 by 4,234, or tell what day of the week July 4 fell upon in the year 1728, or play an entire sonata on the piano after hearing it only one time. But they are usually so mentally and socially retarded that they require institutionalization.

The phenomenon has been publicized by the movie *Rain Man*. The Dustin Hoffman character is no fiction. His talents are perhaps slightly exaggerated: Not many savants are so variously skilled at calculating square roots, memorizing the phone book, and winning thousands of dollars at blackjack. This guy does everything short of guiding the space shuttle back to earth. But all his feats are based on documented cases. For example he instantly perceives that 246 matches have spilled on the floor. The trick is based on a true incident (as opposed to an untrue incident) involving 103 matches.

Autism affects about five out of ten thousand children. They are withdrawn, emotionally aloof, silent. They manifest no love for their parents or other living things. About 10 percent have special abilities, but never any that involve any abstractions. They respond to stimuli such as music or math or calendars. The psychologist Bruno Bettelheim argued that children became autistic because of a disastrous relationship with a hostile, cold mother, though fortunately this view has joined the ranks of Funny Wrong Things That Scientists Used to Believe. The cause is now known to be purely physiological, a dysfunction of the brain, possibly caused by a virus or some other infection during pregnancy. One dramatic recent finding is that in many autistics the cerebellum—that cauliflower-looking thing at the base of the brain—is unusually small.

The question is: If the kid has brain damage or tiny brain parts, then how can he or she do those phenomenal calculations? There has been some talk of excess nerve growth in the brain. San Diego psychologist Dr. Bernard Rimland, who has an autistic son and has spent his life studying the phenomenon, contends that the only difference between autistics and normal people is in the power of concentration. "These individuals have a pathological capacity to concentrate on minute detail," he said. What that really means is they lack the capacity to process a multiplicity of stimuli. Theoretically any of us could do those *Rain Man* tricks if only we weren't distracted constantly.

Some of us might be autistic savants and not even know it. Bobby Fischer, the creepy chess player, was so absorbed by the game that during the award ceremonies for winning the world championship he continued to work out problems on a miniature chessboard.

WHY DID PRIMITIVE NEOLITHIC MEDICINE MEN THINK IT WAS A GOOD IDEA TO DRILL HOLES IN PEOPLE'S HEADS?

The migraine-inducing truth of the matter is that the first Stone Age trephinations of the human skull may have been for the sole purpose of obtaining discs of bone to use as amulets, or to compile bone powder that supposedly had magical properties. Worse, this may not have been what we call elective surgery. Srboljub Zivanovic, author of *Ancient Diseases*, says of the surgical patient (or victim), "Whether he did so voluntarily, watching while his fellow tribesman cut his scalp, groped for and cut the bone and opened the skull, or whether a number of men held him down, it is hard to say." (Though no harder to say, we might venture, than "Srboljub Zivanovic.")

Most paleopathologists reject this ritual explanation of early craniotomies and side with the "magico-therapeutic" theory that they were intended to allow evil spirits to escape. Epileptics, for example, were believed possessed; the hole-in-the-head therapy might have appeared to lessen or stop convulsions simply by coincidence. Trephinations have survived through the ages, even to the modern era in some primitive locales, as a surgical therapy for people with head injuries. Brutes, supposedly, get whonked on the head a lot, and brain surgery is a way of removing bone fragments from their brains. But even in Africa today people have their skulls divoted in order to get rid of—this is incredible—headaches.

More trephinated skulls have been found in Peru than in every other place on the planet combined. It's possible that the pre-Inca Peruvians took advantage of the narcotic coca plant as an anesthetic (though where they got the little spoons that dangled around their necks, scientists still don't know). The first discoveries of these holey skulls in the mid-1800s were greeted with disbelief by European surgeons. They said the primitives would certainly have died of infection. After all, your typical surgery in Europe was a germy affair with a singular unfortunate aftereffect: The patient died. And yet half of these barbarically mutilated Peruvian skulls showed clear signs of healing—those were living heads that had been drilled.

It turns out that Peruvian skull surgery was safer than the equivalent in the Victorian era. European hospitals were notoriously filthy and disease-ridden, and no one had yet figured out that it was important to wash one's hands *before* they got bloody. There was no anesthesia, thus the clinics were forced to employ "holders," cheery fellows of great heft whose sole function was to pin down screaming people all day.

Dr. Louis Bakay, a retired neurosurgeon and author of *Early History of Craniotomy* (yes, *all* the good book topics have already been taken), told us that until the mid-twentieth century, the essential technique for skull surgery hadn't changed in thousands of years.

"What they used was a drill. The same thing you can get at Black and Decker," he said. "You could also use a chisel and mallet."

Like, no thanks. We'll just take two leeches and call you in the morning.

WHY CAN'T SCIENTISTS KEEP SEVERED HEADS OR DISEMBODIED BRAINS ALIVE BY PERCOLATING FRESH BLOOD THROUGH THEM?

They can.

We were advised of this recently when we saw an advertisement for a book called *If We Can Keep a Severed Head Alive.* . . .

The pseudonymous author, Chet Fleming, is a Harvard Law School graduate who has made it his personal crusade to warn people about the new technologies in "discorporation."

"One of the most bizarre and disturbing developments in the history of medicine is approaching. In simple terms, it is possible to sever the head of a lab animal or even a human from the body and keep the head alive on blood processing equipment. Alive: conscious, alert, able to see and hear and think. And if it's a human head, able to talk," Fleming wrote in the *Harvard Law School Record.*

Fleming is distressed by the implications of this and in his book he asks, "What will the heads do after the operation? Would a severed head still be married? Or employed?"

Let us concede that this guy is perhaps the teensiest bit paranoid. He writes, ''I hope my fears about the possibility for evil misuse of this operation are exaggerated or unfounded. But in all candor, I'm genuinely frightened. The people whose lives might be prolonged by discorporation might be the Stalins and Hitlers of the next century. If used by bloodthirsty dictators or ruthlessly greedy people with enormous wealth and power, the ability to keep a severed head alive might lead to incredible suffering for millions of people.''

NO NO NO, we scream from our posts in the Why Things Are Technology Research Center and Snack Bar, that's not the scenario! The correct sequence of events—which we know from the plot of the 1944 horror thriller *Donovan's Brain*—is that the brain of a *successful businessman* is preserved in a vat, grows larger and larger, and then takes mental control over everyone who comes near it. When a hero tries to shoot the brain with a handgun, the brain forces the hero to shoot *himself*. The only way to kill it is to hope that lightning strikes and bakes the damn thing. Good movie.

The scientific expert in the field is supposedly Dr. Robert White, of Case Western Reserve in Cleveland, and frankly after talking to him for thirty minutes you have to wonder if he's not *out of his head* (humor). White said that brains can indeed be kept alive. Heads can be transplanted. White calls a head transplant a ''body transplant'' and gets really miffed if you keep using the term *head transplant*.

Most of the experiments in this area were done fifteen and twenty years ago, White said. He worked on monkeys. Others have had success with rats.

''The monkeys and rats have awakened and appeared to be monkeys and rats,'' he said.

But they don't last long. You're dealing with a major intensive-care situation. A brain, by itself, can only stay alive on machinery for a matter of hours or at the outside a day or two, just like a heart or kidney. So it's not practical to fool around with this sort of thing.

If spinal cord research ever comes up with a way of regenerating central nervous system tissue, then head transplants—whatever—might become attractive, White said.

"I believe that sometime in the twenty-first century a body transplant will be accomplished," he said.

Maybe we'll even be able to scan a catalog and pick a body we like. A weight-lifter frame. Olympic swimmer. The opposite sex! The possibilities are so exciting. The philosophers could debate whether a person with a man's head and a woman's body is a man or a woman. (We'll weigh in now with our pronouncement that it depends solely on what's in the pants.)

LOVE AND SEX

(Heartache, passion, orgasms, adultery, and other symptoms of glandular tyranny.)

WHY DO FOOLS FALL IN LOVE?

Let's skip the neurochemical explanations of love (it's located somewhere in the limbic system, not, as was once argued, in the hypothalamus) and the evolutionary explanations (love creates parental bonding that enables offspring to grow up in a healthy environment, and so on) and focus on plain old psychology, or science-by-couch. We will stipulate, for all you softies out there, that often people fall in love because they meet someone who is just so gosh-darn lovable. But here are some other explanations:

1. Personal failure. The "complementarity theory" of love is that a person falls in love with someone who has the characteristics that he/she desires but is unable to achieve. A 1985 study by the American Institute for Psychoanalysis theorized that people fall in love as a way of bolstering self-worth: "Someone may fall in love in order to magically acquire opposite traits that are idealized and glorified or to address a specific source of self-hate." (And you thought all along it was because he brought flowers.)

2. Re-creating the past. The bliss of falling in love is the result of the revival of the symbiotic feelings between the infant and mother, according to one psychoanalytic theory. A similar but

173

less Freudian view is that people fall in love with someone with whom they can reenact an earlier role, either from childhood or from a previous relationship. This is why some people repeatedly get involved in abusive relationships or marry alcoholics.

3. Make-believe. A Western Illinois University report stated, "The tendency to have mystical experiences, romantic love, and hypnotic susceptibility were positively intercorrelated, suggesting that they all involved the ability to suspend contact with objective reality." (Honey, I'll be working late at the office again tonight.)

4. Rebellion and revolution. Romeo and Juliet were challenging authority. Several theorists compare the act of falling in love with the joining of political, social, or religious movements. But perhaps love is just the body's way of protesting against:

5. Sexual repression. Studies clearly show that romantic love germinates most feverishly in sexually repressive social systems. Would Romeo and Juliet have been as urgent in their passion if their parents had said, "Here are the keys to the Jeep, why don't you two kids go up to the cabin this weekend and have some fun?"? The flip side to this is that a good way to bolster the love quotient in a relationship is to try to heighten sexual desire. Desire, of course, is only fun when you know there's fulfillment down the road.

Why Doesn't Passion Last?

Have you ever considered that maybe this is just your own personal problem? That while you poke at your TV dinner next to your silent, corpulent, pustule-pocked spouse, there are other married couples who right now are dashing gleefully into their bedrooms wearing elbow pads and crash helmets? Maybe it's just *you*.

Nah, it's everyone. Robert J. Sternberg, professor of psychology and education at Yale, has shown that in the vast majority of couples, not only passion but almost everything else declines over time: ability to communicate, physical attractiveness, sharing of interests, having good times, ability to listen, respect for each other, romantic love, and so on.

(Let's just go kill ourselves right now, okay?)

What does survive, frequently, is commitment. Commitment, in Sternberg's view, is one of the three essential components of love. The other two are passion and intimacy. If you have all three, that's consummate love. Commitment alone is "empty love." Intimacy alone is "liking." Passion alone is "infatuation." Intimacy and passion but no commitment is "romantic love." Passion and commitment but no intimacy is "fatuous love." Commitment and intimacy but no passion is "companionate love." We advise you to keep a chart with you at all times for handy reference in emergencies.

We still haven't answered our original question: Why doesn't passion last? Sternberg says it's like any addiction: You build up a tolerance.

"It's like with coffee, cigarettes, or alcohol," he told *Psychology Today*. "Addiction can be rapid, but once habituation sets in, even an increased amount of exposure to the person or substance no longer stimulates the motivational arousal that was once possible."

(Why does he talk that way? Because he's a scientist. He's *licensed* to speak like that.)

If you want to carry it to another level, you can look at passion in the context of the "opponent process theory of motivation," developed by psychologist Richard Solomon. There are two opposing forces. The first is positive: You have the hots for someone. It builds quickly and then levels off. The second is negative: The someone, you slowly realize, weighs 475 pounds and has to be towed behind the family car on a boat trailer. This negative motivational force is not only slow to develop but slow to fade.

We'll stop there and make up our own answer for why passion doesn't last: *Nobody's* that interesting.

Why Is a Heart Illustrated as a Neatly Symmetrical, Twin-Lobed Inverted Teardrop Even Though the Actual Human Heart Is Blobby and Pear-Shaped with Lots of Tubes Jutting Out of It?

In a funnier world Hallmark would sell Valentine's Day cards with graphic color photos of a human chest during open-heart surgery. Hilarious! And somehow more honest.

Where did that stylized heart, the one you see on the playing cards, the one on the bumper stickers between I and *New York*, the one so integral to the opening credits of I *Love Lucy*, come from? Is it really a frog heart or something like that, a bit of confusion from an old science lab project? Is there a deeper and perhaps more sinister symbolism at play?

The heart shape, we can now authoritatively report, is so ancient that it may predate the literacy of human beings. Richard Reichbart, a New Jersey psychologist, wrote his doctoral dissertation on the subject in 1983, concluding that there were innumerable origins of the heart configuration, many having nothing to do with sex. Once upon a time the "heart" configuration represented animals, for example. Primitive ceremonial masks from equatorial Africa that are "heart-shaped" represent the horns and snouts of certain creatures.

More significant to Western civilization is the fact that the ancient Greek cult of Dionysus worshiped the heart shape because that is the outline of the ivy leaf, many of which Dionysus purportedly wore on his head while he was engaging in his famed Dionysian rites, which were basically frenzied, drunken orgies.

Confusion within the cult may have given us the ivy shape as a symbol for the throbbing organ within our breasts. Dionysus was supposedly killed by the Titans, but his heart was saved and then fed back to his mother by Zeus. The mother reconceived Dionysus, and he became the twice-born god, symbolized by both ivy and the human heart. His worshipers tattoed the heart shape onto their bodies and apparently couldn't decide if it was a heart or an ivy leaf. (It's hard to keep these things straight when you party like the Dionysians. Supposedly the women became so frenzied they would tear animals apart and eat them raw. Then, according to Reichbart, they'd do the same trick with living human children. Another great Hallmark image!)

In the New World natives had their own heart images. The Aztecs, who were big on hearts, illustrated the organ as oblong, seedlike. And other Native Americans drew it as a blob, perhaps the most accurate illustration of them all.

Could the heart shape symbolize a more cosmic concept? Such as the union of two people? The philosopher Robert Nozick suggests in *The Examined Life*, "If we picture the individual self as a closed figure whose boundaries are continuous and solid, dividing what is inside from what is outside, then we might diagram the we [his term for a romantic couple] as two figures with the boundary line between them erased where they come together."

But that's too mushy. Maybe we should return to the simplest of all possibilities: The stylized heart is just a simplistic rendering of a real heart. The two are not so radically different. The actual organ is nearly symmetrical; if you pick up a heart and tilt it slightly, you can see a sort of tapering at the bottom and twin swellings at the top. We advise you not to do this without plenty of paper towels.

WHY DO WE THINK OF THE EMOTIONS AS BEING CENTERED IN THE HEART?

The emotions are centered in the brain of course. But when we experience a powerful emotion—fear, anger, grief, love— adrenaline pours into the blood, increases the blood pressure, and accelerates the heart. So it makes perfect sense to think the heart controls emotion. Otherwise when we say the Pledge of Allegiance, we'd have to put our hand on our forehead.

WHY DOES EVERYONE AGREE THAT CERTAIN CHARACTERISTICS MAKE A PERSON GOOD-LOOKING?

Sure, standards vary. Mick Jagger's swollen lips might seem a luscious masterpiece to one person and a repellent sack of giblets to another. As for Keith Richards, ugliness is part of the appeal. Who can figure? In general, though, there are certain features that we are drawn to, such as high cheekbones, symmetrical faces (heart-shaped?), smooth skin, large eyes, and Bodies by Jake.

How did these standards of beauty evolve? Is there anything inherently, objectively attractive about, say, Rob Lowe or Robin Givens, or is their attractiveness a purely arbitrary quality that is promulgated through television and advertisements? That little number Michelle Pfeiffer did on top of the piano in The Fabulous Baker Boys . . . we merely deluded ourselves into thinking she looked good, right?

The politically correct answer, of course, is that looks are entirely subjective. But once again the politically correct answer takes a stoning from the malicious truth.

A 1987 University of Texas study found that infants as young as two months old showed a preference for women's faces that had been rated attractive by young adults. The babies were shown pictures of good-looking and not-so-good-looking women side-by-side, and they lingered longer on the good-looking ones. Researcher Judith Langlois said her findings "seriously challenge the assumption that attractiveness is merely 'in the eye of the beholder.'"

Why would babies like the foxy faces? Maybe because good-looking people (in the eyes of adults) tend to have Fisher-Price faces: rounded and vertically symmetrical, shapes that babies show a fondness for.

How could babies develop a prejudice at such a young age? Certain behaviors are universal, regardless of environment, such as the human smile. All babies smile when they're happy. It's as true in Micronesia as it is in Minneapolis. Could this be nothing more than operant conditioning, with the babies learning to smile in order to receive affection? Researchers don't think so. Blind babies smile without provocation. And you can't train a child to smile when sad or to frown when glad. It is not so far a leap to think that our notions of attractiveness are as intrinsic as the smile.

Aren't there cultures where ugly people are considered the babes and hunks? Not so much as we used to assume. Beauty is fairly constant everywhere—even if in some places there are strange accessories such as Frisbee-size disks implanted in the lower lip and hair of purple and green cemented into six-inch spikes—and even if over time the ideas of beauty have been clearly influenced by cultural obsessions. (One example: The ideal of the beautiful female body ran to distinct plumpness during the Renaissance.) What is more significant is that given a big world and a long history, the ancient Egyptian concept of beauty does not differ much from ours today.

Perhaps beauty is merely an approximation of all the faces we see. Judith Langlois has suggested that attractive faces are in many ways *average*, a composite of other faces, without any large prominences or quirky features or mysterious bursts of hair. This explains why handsome or pretty people are often a whisper away from looking plain.

The really bad news, and no great shock, is that people assign all sorts of fantastic attributes to good-looking people. Beauty begets prejudice. This is especially true in the case of men judging women. In a study at San Diego State University, 140 male and female students were asked to give impressions of an essay and its author. All the students read the same essay, but they were given varying photographs of the purported author, showing a handsome man, an ugly man, a beautiful woman, and so forth. The female students showed no bias toward attractiveness. But the male students (those creeps) declared that the good-looking women were better writers.

The bias starts early. A study in 1977 showed that teachers give better grades to attractive children, even when achievement-test scores are identical.

Does this mean that good-looking people have it easy? Not at all. A 1982 study by the Carolina Population Center (it's incredible what you can yank off a data base here in the Information Age) tracked 1,300 males and females for fifteen years after they left high school. Each was rated on an attractiveness scale of 1 to 7, based on their high school yearbook photo (the rating was done by a panel of volunteers, with the scores averaged together). The results after fifteen years: Good looks will buy a woman a high-income, high-status husband but no gain in the professional world. For men, good looks are actually a hindrance. The better-looking guys were busts, and the ugliest little geeks were the most successful in life—the *ones*. They had the most education, the best jobs, and the highest overall status in life. The sixes were the biggest losers: less education, lower status, mediocre jobs. Only the sevens, the most magnificently handsome stud-muffins, were able to overcome the looks handicap and achieve at a high level.

"Attractive men get too many distracting heterosexual opportunities," says Richard Udry, coauthor of the report. The report showed that only four out of ten of the studious, homely boys engaged in adolescent premarital sex. Fully seven out of ten of the glamorous dudes did that stuff. "While they're chasing the girls, the ugly men are hitting the books."

WHY DO WOMEN WEAR MAKEUP?

We have found no support for our private suspicion that the origins of feminine makeup were in the bordello, where prostitutes simulated the flushed color of sexual passion with applications of rouge. But we'll spread the rumor anyway.

Lois Banner, a University of California history professor and author of *American Beauty*, gave us three succinct reasons why women wear makeup:

1. It's fun.
2. It's a disguise.
3. Women are objectified more than men.

The last strikes us as the central point: Women are decorative objects. Historically men have treated women as though they were fine, expensive possessions; for example, "He walked into the bar wearing a blonde on each arm." We don't mean to suggest that women shouldn't wear makeup. *Mirror Mirror*, by Elaine Hatfield and Susan Sprecher, contends that "good-looking" people are much more successful (a fact, as noted, that may extend solely into romance). As long as the society trains people to perceive painted-up women as "good-looking," it will be in their direct self-interest to keep doing it.

Centuries ago makeup was necessary to cover the severe scars of smallpox. Elizabeth I virtually troweled on the stuff. Men also wore makeup to achieve pale skin, an aristocratic touch that lost its impact after the French Revolution, when pale skin became a solely feminine trait. (Why do they call them bluebloods? Because rich people were so pale you could see the blue veins under their skin.)

WHY DO TEENAGERS GET SUCH POWERFUL CRUSHES?

To the extent that love is chemical, teenagers are more capable of love. That other version of love—a partnership in life, the fusion of two people into a single unit, inseparable even in those moments when She realizes that He is a disgusting, emotionally stunted moron with less interest in romance than in *Popular Mechanics*—is not the stuff of killer crushes.

The undiluted item makes you literally starve yourself in the name of love, choosing to forgo food and normal social contact in order to concentrate more fully on the wondrous perfection of the love object.

Why are such adolescent infatuations so powerful, yet so transient? Because they're new.

It's partly biology. Although teenagers have fewer hormones racing through their bodies, the hormones are a new phenomenon, and the body and mind aren't used to them. It's like drinking your first beer. You can't handle the sauce, so you get ludicrously, foolishly drunk.

Part of the explanation is psychological. Though we hate to quote a dinosaur like Sigmund Freud, he had a few memorable riffs, such as arguing that desire for sexual union is at the core of emotion. When this desire is impeded, or, in the case of teenagers, discouraged by parents and societal norms, we compensate by falling exaggeratedly in love, said Freud. Makes sense, no?

And let's not forget the sociologists:

"These attractions are more powerful in adolescence primarily because they're new. This is the first time that youngsters develop these relationships. . . . They really idealize them initially," says Dr. Anne C. Petersen, professor of health and human development at Penn State.

These first relationships are often imaginary; the primary goal is to impress your giggling pals. There is a secondary, subconscious purpose: For the first time you are transferring your affections from your parents to peers of the opposite sex.

Within a couple of years relationships get more serious, but the idealization continues, in part because of the invention in the eighteenth and nineteenth centuries in developed countries of the concept of "adolescence." Before then kids got married, and went to work when they hit puberty. Now we let them play for several more years, discover themselves, go to college, travel the world, listen to bad music, get disfiguring haircuts, and so on, before we suddenly throw them into the living hell that is the adult working world.

Since these kids are, like adults, capable of abstract reasoning, but lack the cynical experience of adults, they have what Swiss psychologist Jean Piaget called high idealism. The phrase could also describe what is so wonderful and yet so ridiculous about teenage crushes.

Adults get crushes, too, but they're rarer and more painful. Instead we tend to choose the longer version of romance, what is known as enduring love, which is love that we simply have to endure.

WHY IS THE LINE "ROMEO, ROMEO! WHEREFORE ART THOU ROMEO" SO FAMOUS?

I n Shakespeare's time men played both male and female roles on stage. So the greatest poet of all time actually is a bit short in the department of heavy-panting romance. Most of the impassioned love speeches are monologues, with the lovee out of sight. In all of Shakespeare's works the most romantic moment, and the most famous, and one of the few with two characters on stage, is the balcony scene in *Romeo and Juliet*. Why is the "Romeo, Romeo" line so memorized?

"I think the reason it's so famous is that it's the opening line in the balcony scene," guesses Michael Kahn, artistic director of the Shakespeare Theatre at the Folger in Washington, D.C. (Actually, it's not, but it is Juliet's first significant line as she stands on the balcony.)

But let's go beyond that, while noting that the words are nice music:

O Romeo, Romeo! wherefore art thou Romeo?
Deny thy father, and refuse thy name;
Or, if thou wilt not, be but sworn my love,
And I'll no longer be a Capulet.

Pay attention. Juliet does not want to know where Romeo is. (FYI: He's in the bushes!) A Shakespearean *wherefore* is not an inquiry as to location—it means *why*. The context is clear: Juliet is upset that Romeo (whom she just met in a moment of instant teenage infatuation) is a Montague, and thus a sworn enemy of the Capulet family. When she says, "Why are you Romeo?" she is cursing her cruel fate and articulating the central tension of the play.

WHY DO WOMEN HAVE ORGASMS, EVEN THOUGH, UNLIKE MALE ORGASMS, FEMALE ORGASMS ARE UNNECESSARY FOR REPRODUCTION?

It's debatable. But one side of the debate is a little stronger than the other.

Puzzle: Some women never have orgasms, and others do so infrequently and with difficulty. In the vast majority of cultures, say anthropologists, coitus is completed in terms of the man's satisfaction, with little regard for the woman. The anthropologist Margaret Mead found entire societies in which the female orgasm was virtually unknown. She concluded, "That whole societies can ignore climax as an aspect of female sexuality must be related to a very much lesser biological basis for such climax."

Some feminist scholars have argued that patriarchal "civilization" required the suppression of female sexuality and that in preagricultural times women were sexually insatiable.

Mocking this view is anthropologist Donald Symons, author of a sweeping book called *The Evolution of Human Sexuality*: "The sexually insatiable woman is to be found primarily, if not exclusively, in the ideology of feminism, the hopes of boys, and the fears of men."

Instead, he says, female orgasm is something akin to a vestigial characteristic, like nipples on a man's chest. Women have orgasms because, among men, orgasms are an evolutionary necessity. Remember, men and women aren't so different, and if natural selection dictates that a trait in one sex is advantageous, then it will often appear in the other sex as well, in slightly different form.

The male human orgasm has its counterpart in nonhuman primates and mammals. But it is unclear whether female animals have orgasms. Female dogs show some signs, but they are inconclusive. We do know that female primates, such as rhesus monkeys, can be manipulated to orgasm in a laboratory. But animals don't tend to linger at sex; the male takes care of business and gets out of there.

But wait: Why wouldn't female orgasm be to the evolutionary advantage of a species? Wouldn't female pleasure in sex make reproduction more likely?

Not necessarily. Females and males biologically have different game plans: Females need to be more discriminating than males, because they have a limited number of eggs they can produce in a lifetime, and once they are impregnated, they cannot conceive again for nearly a year. Males, by contrast, produce millions of seeds and could theoretically impregnate several women a day, every day. Females who engage in sex at a whim—failing to hold out for Mr. Right—would be less likely to have the choicest offspring. Symons quotes W. H. Auden: "Men are playboys, women realists."

Moreover, studies show that sex is enjoyable to women whether or not they have orgasm. While obviously a group of orgasmic men would proliferate more than a competing nonorgasmic group, the same cannot be said of women. Says Symons, "There is no compelling evidence that natural selection favored females that were capable of orgasm, either in the evolution of mammals or specifically in the human lineage; nor is there evidence that the female genitals of any mammalian species have been designed by natural selection for efficiency in orgasm production."

None of this demeans the female orgasm. Vestigial doesn't imply "second-rate." Quite the opposite: The female orgasm is at least as powerful as the male's and probably stronger. Unlike men, many women have multiple orgasms in rapid succession and don't enter into the period of exhaustion experienced by males immediately after orgasm.

Why Do Some Men Feel Compelled to Dress Up as Women? And Why Are Sexually Deviant Behaviors, Such as Voyeurism and Exhibitionism, Found Almost Exclusively Among Men?

Men who dress up as women used to be called perverts, then they became sexual deviants, and now they are merely a sexual minority.

There's definitely something interesting afoot in their brains: Many cross-dressers cannot become sexually aroused until they're dolled up. Others report that when dressed as women, they can finally relax, free of the pressures of being male. Cross-dressers range from the fetishists, who may focus on a specific item of women's clothing; to the game-playing transvestites, who only dress as women as a premasturbatory act; to the "transgenderists," who might spend days as women, thinking and believing and feeling that they are female. One of the remarkable things about transvestism is that it is found almost entirely among heterosexuals.

Researchers take radically different approaches to the issue, with some studying the temporal lobe of the brain to find a biological cause of gender confusion, others using old-fashioned Rorschach tests to seek out a psychological disturbance, and so forth. Transvestism is all the more peculiar because it's almost never found among women. True, some lesbians may wear men's clothing and seem masculine, but they are not trying to pass as men; they aren't compulsively adopting an alternate gender identity. Moreover women don't do other things that are considered perverse, such as peek in windows or show their privates to passing children. The only behavior among women that might be considered sexually deviant is prostitution, but there's an obvious economic, rather than psychological, motivation.

"Most perversions occur in the male," says Dr. Raphael

Good, a professor of psychology at the University of Miami. "It has to do with castration anxiety."

This would be the Freudian view: Little boys undergo a trauma that little girls do not. There comes a point where a child must separate his or her identity from the mother and develop a sense of individuality. Unlike little girls, little boys must also take on a new gender. Baby boys are essentially feminine, and when the relationship between mother and child is too close, the boy may not complete the transformation to "male." The requirements of being a male may always induce stress, and only by dressing as a woman can he relax.

The mother-son explanation may provide a clue to exhibitionism. Men who otherwise behave normally—hold a job, raise children, stay happily married—will be arrested outside a school for exposing themselves to girls of thirteen and fourteen years of age. These men don't want to have sex with the girls, they merely want to get a reaction—a shriek. Typically these are macho men who, beneath the swagger, suffer extreme anxiety about their manliness, including fears that their penises are inadequate, too small, too weak, or too insignificant. One way of dealing with this is to show it to someone. An exhibitionist prefers younger girls: They'll scream, confirming the significance of his masculinity.

The Freudian view is challenged by the biological view, which is gaining popularity. The Eve principle refers to the idea that fetuses are female until something happens to them to make them male—a biological process in the womb. If there is a glitch, however, the child may be predisposed toward gender confusion.

So you got your Freudian explanation, your biological explanation, and finally, because everything comes in threes, here is the learning/socialization explanation: People choose it. Any number of events in our lives channel us in a given direction, and we "decide" to become a transvestite in the same way that we decide to become a butcher or a baker or a candlestick maker. (Though, if you think about it, anyone who would decide to become a candlestick maker would have to be crazy.)

A transvestite in California gave the Why staff a final thought: Women's clothes feel better. He said, "I dressed up because I wanted to be closer to my Katharine Hepburnish mother; her clothes felt so much better than boys' clothes (satin is so much nicer on the skin than denim)."

THE BEATLES

(In which we reveal why geniuses have to get up early in the morning. And why they need interesting hair.)

Paul McCartney rolled out of bed one morning in 1965 with a melody on the brain. It was like a found object, so perfectly realized he figured he must have heard it somewhere. He fumbled with it on the piano. It had a classic melodic arc: a short phrase of three notes, answered by a longer phrase that soars to a high note before meandering back down the keyboard to another short phrase and a little jump at the end—all in all, a satisfying roller-coaster loop. Never much with words, he sang, ''Scrambled egg . . . da da da da da da scrambled egg . . .''

McCartney was just twenty-three, and his band, the Beatles, had conquered the world as surely as Alexander or Charlemagne. More than your average pop idols, they were angelic majesties, living gods, the acme of cool. They had achieved intensities of popularity that no one had known existed and probably weren't sanitary. Suddenly they were even bigger than Elvis, who was off in arrested animation. Legend has it that during the hour they first appeared on *The Ed Sullivan Show* in 1964, not a single crime in America was committed by a teenager.

The only asterisk by their name in 1965 was the stigma of teeny-bopperdom. This tune in McCartney's head would change that forever. "Scrambled egg" became "Yesterday," and at last count was the world's most popular song, recorded by more artists than any other in history. The critic Wilfrid Mellers tried to describe in technical terms why the song works so splendidly:

"The first bar, with its gentle sigh, seems separated, stranded, by the abrupt modulation; and although the troubles 'return to stay' with a descent to the tonic, the anticipated modulation sharpwards is counteracted when the B natural is flattened to make an irresolute plagal cadence."

An irresolute plagal cadence! To think that such a marvelous thing, whatever it was, might have popped into someone's head in a dream. Neither McCartney nor his songwriting partner John Lennon had had any musical training. They were musical savages, holy barbarians, proof that you can graduate summa cum laude from the University of Rock 'n' Roll without being able to decipher sheet music. They regarded with glee the labored exegesis of their music by highbrow types, as when William Mann, critic for *The Times* (London), swooned, "One gets the impression that they think simultaneously of harmony and melody, so firmly are the major tonic sevenths and ninths built into their tunes, and the flat submediant key switches, so natural in the Aeolian cadence at the end of 'Not a Second Time' (the chord progression that ends Mahler's 'Song of the Earth')."

Aeolian cadence? Sounds like a type of bird, said Lennon.

The Beatles lived out the glory and mystery of musical genius. That they would triumph as they did was improbable, fantastic, strange. There are thousands of musicians, but no one has ever approached the level of accolade and commercial success reached by the Liverpudlians. We ask: Why them? What was the secret?

That they were phenomenally talented cannot be doubted. Consider this story: In early 1964, when movie producer Walter Shenson was finishing a film about the Beatles, he realized that he needed another fast song to play during the opening credits;

to fit the movie title, it should be called "A Hard Day's Night." Late one night he told John Lennon that he wanted the extra song. The next day at 8:00 A.M., Shenson was summoned to the dressing room. Lennon and McCartney were there with two guitars. A pack of matches was propped up on the mirror with some tiny words written inside the cover. Lennon sang the first sixteen bars, McCartney the middle eight. The song went to number one on the charts.

If you diagram a Beatles song, it looks just like the songs of all those other bands that haven't sold a billion disks and tapes and aren't in *The Guinness Book of World Records*. They wrote upbeat, two-minute songs that, at least in the early years, rarely strayed from the pop-music convention of eight-bar strains, rigidly linked in an A-A-B-A-B-A construction. The Beatles were a standard four-instrument band: two guitars, a bass, and drums. So what is it that people heard in that sound? Was there genius in the mix? Who had it? Was it Lennon? Was it McCartney? Are the songs really superior, or were they just part of a marketing coup? How much of the band's continued popularity is nostalgia, the background radiation from the Beatlemania explosion?

And let us ask the most pertinent question: What's genius anyway?

Mozart is the prototype for the musical genius. Music came to him like an injection in the brain. "When I feel well and in a good humor, or when I am taking a drive or walking after a good meal, or in the night when I cannot sleep, thoughts crowd into my mind as easily as you could wish. Whence and how do they come? I do not know and I have nothing to do with it. Those that please me, I keep in my head and hum them," he wrote a friend.

Clearly he was gifted. It's well known that he was composing music at the age of five. What is less widely known is that it wasn't very good. Young Amadeus *was* precocious, but you wouldn't want to buy his records. He didn't write a great work until he was sixteen and had been playing music his entire life.

He was a prodigy partly because he had a prodding parent—the Brooke Shields syndrome. His father devoted himself to the boy's musical education, took him around Europe to hear all the great composers, and then demanded musical compositions from the little bugger.

This is the pattern of geniuses: obsessive, pushy parents. John Stuart Mill's father started him on a rigorous course of instruction when he was two years old. Michelangelo was also prepped for the job of genius. That doesn't mean they weren't naturally gifted; it just means that genius takes tending.

The fact is that genius is grotesquely overrated. Most "geniuses" are just talented people who get up really early in the morning. Thomas Edison wasn't being humble when he said that genius is only 1 percent inspiration and 99 percent perspiration. Research into how geniuses think has never shown any special cognitive shortcut; geniuses solve problems step-by-step like anyone else. They also do subgenius work, even truly awful stuff, which is why you can't simply assume that every painting or drawing by Picasso is a great piece of art. (If in doubt, hang it in the bathroom.)

John R. Hayes, of Carnegie-Mellon University, has shown that artists almost never produce their masterpieces until they've toiled for at least ten years. In Paul McCartney's case he started playing music at thirteen and wrote "Yesterday" at twenty-three.

Robert S. Albert, editor of the anthology *Genius and Eminence*, defines genius as "(1) the rare but radical *disruption* of preceding manners, attitudes, customs, or cognitive habits; and (2) the performance of complex tasks in manners and styles rarely observed." The Beatles fit that definition, for if you read the words closely, it is clear that genius is an achievement, not a predisposition. One cannot be born into genius; it must be earned.

Only McCartney came from a musical family; his father moonlighted as a jazz pianist. McCartney was a natural at the guitar. That's why Lennon hesitated to let McCartney join the

Quarry Men in 1957: This new kid was too good. Biographer Philip Norman, author of one of the best books on the Beatles, *Shout!*, told us in an interview that if McCartney hadn't joined the Beatles, he probably would have become "a very pleasant grammar school teacher organizing the end-of-term panto-mime. The mothers would have thought he was dishy." And John would have become an interesting, offbeat rock star with a band named, say, Johnny and the Moondogs.

John Lennon always claimed that the Beatles were great suc-cesses because they worked harder than anyone else. People figured this was just fake modesty. It was easier for them to believe that the Beatles were touched by God. But Lennon was right. The band played a thousand gigs before anyone had ever heard of them. In Hamburg, West Germany, they played eight hours straight, staggered at dawn to their beds behind a movie screen, and then were roused at noon by the matinee.

To ascribe the success of the Beatles to some kind of God-given gift possessed by John and Paul is to rob them of the full drama of their accomplishment. It's a much more remarkable story if you realize that two people who were not prodigies were able, through hard work and bountiful luck and ambition and great timing and not insignificant talent, to erect an edifice as towering—as full of genius—as the Beatles.

Plus there was the Hair Factor. The most immediately no-ticeable aspect about the Beatles upon their emergence was not their sound but their long, girlish hair, which in the conser-vative early sixties was a shocking sign of androgyny—and an indicator that the world was about to be turned upside down.

The fans were part of the Beatles phenomenon too.

"Creativity is not the property of a person," says Howard Gardner, a Harvard professor who studies creativity. "You can't just say a person is creative or noncreative per se. When you refer to creativity, it always refers to a dialectic between a person and what I call the field—basically, knowledgeable individuals who judge whether something is good or not.''

There were more teenagers alive in 1964 than ever before in history. Cheap transistor radios from Asia had flooded the market. Rock 'n' roll's great idea—a pounding backbeat that made you want to shake and shout—had been corporatized and denatured. The radio was starved for something other than Frankie Avalon. The scene craved a new sound. So many millions of kids were turned on to rock 'n' roll by Elvis that the odds dictated that Something New would happen.

Wrote Wilfrid Mellers, the critic, ''The Beatles, in common with other geniuses such as Bach, Mozart, and Beethoven, knew the right time and place to be born.''

The Beatles were just one of hundreds of bands hoping to fill that void. It's hard to know whether their triumph is a sign of superior musical talent, fate, hair, or what. Certainly they had ambition to spare. John was the one with the fire in the belly. He and manager Brian Epstein plotted to become bigger than Elvis as early as 1962, when they were still an obscure bar band. They were unapologetically commercial and would step on anyone who got in their way—as when they fired loyal drummer Pete Best and replaced him with one slightly better, Ringo Starr.

''Big bastards, that's what the Beatles were. You have to be a bastard to make it, that's a fact, and the Beatles are the biggest bastards on Earth,'' Lennon told Jann Wenner in a famous 1970 interview in *Rolling Stone* just after the band broke up.

No amount of ambition and luck could make up for lack of talent, though. The Beatles knew how to write a song. A track like ''I Want to Hold Your Hand'' seems, today, little more than a cheery, upbeat pop song whose main purpose is to produce nostalgia, but when it was written in 1963, it was a groundbreaking sound, not just in the tight harmonies and the driving rhythm known in Liverpool as the Mersey beat (after the Mersey River) but also in the way it changed textures. In the middle section the electric guitar disappears and is replaced by an acoustic guitar, softening the feel of the song momentarily and thereby heightening the intensity of the rhythm when the song goes electric again (". . . I can't hide, I can't hide, I can't hiiiiiiide!").

The song "She Loves You" had the same feature. At one point the snare drum gives way to tom-toms, producing a totally different feel. It may seem like a technicality, but these shifting textures—found in almost every Beatle song—were nonexistent in the popular music of the day. Whose idea was it to alternate the drumming on "She Loves You?" Beatle scholar Tim Riley thinks it was the drummer's idea. Yes—the secret genius of the Beatles was Ringo!

As for George Martin, the band's producer, he was probably more a technical help than a creative one, even if it was his idea to put a string quartet behind McCartney's guitar on "Yesterday." Martin writes in his memoir, "I have often been asked if I could have written any of the Beatles' tunes, and the answer is definitely no: for one basic reason. I didn't have their simple approach to music. I think that if Paul, for instance, had learned music 'properly'—not just the piano, but correct notation for writing and reading music, all the harmony and counterpoint that I had to go through, and the techniques of orchestration—it might have well inhibited him. . . . Once you start being taught things, your mind is channeled in a particular way. Paul didn't have that channeling, so he had freedom, and could think of things that I would have considered outrageous."

The secret of the Beatles was not, as many people seem to think, the collaboration of Lennon and McCartney. It was their rivalry, their intense mutual jealousy.

There are two kinds of people in the world: John fans and Paul fans. A John fan appreciates meaning in lyrics, avant-garde sounds, artistic daring. A Paul fan likes a nice tune. Whom you like defines what kind of person you are. Far from being illusory, this rivalry was solidly founded by John and Paul themselves as they carried on first a secret competition and then a public feud of pathetic, tragic dimensions. They didn't write songs together after 1965, other than to occasionally touch up each other's work.

John gets points for being the official leader of the band in the early days, but then Paul gets points for composing the first hit, "Love Me Do," a triumph quickly outstripped when John came up with the band's first number one in Britain, "Please Please Me." John expands his lead during most of Beatlemania, singing the bulk of the hits, publishing two books of acclaimed stories, and generally setting the tone for the band.

Then, just when John's championship belt seems most secure as he writes "Ticket to Ride" and "Help!," Paul wakes up with "Yesterday" and starts his charge. Paul gradually eclipses John with a series of monster hits like "Penny Lane" and "Paperback Writer" and "Eleanor Rigby" and "Hey Jude" and "Let It Be" and "Get Back" and "The Long and Winding Road," as well as conceiving the structure of two of the band's best albums, *Sergeant Pepper's Lonely Hearts Club Band* and *Abbey Road*. When the band finally breaks up, John edges back to parity with "Imagine," while Paul aggressively scores negative points with nauseating hit singles sung to such lyrics as "wo wo wo wo my love does it good."

Finally the balance of power irreversibly shifts in John's favor in 1980 when he brilliantly outfoxes Paul by getting murdered by a Nightmare Fan.

Paul now goes around trying to convince people that he, too, was in the band. His selling job is all the harder because the intelligentsia and the rock press have always been John-biased. John was the smart one. He gave awesome interviews and ridiculed authority, unlike nice-guy Paul. John labeled Paul conservative when that was like calling someone a Nazi.

Biographer Philip Norman claims that Lennon was three-fourths of the band, even though Paul was the superior tune-smith. How does that figure? Norman says, "Everything that the Beatles were in the beginning—funny, dry, charming, a little bit dangerous, offbeat, bohemian—was Lennon."

The person who is probably in the best position to judge the John-versus-Paul match is George Martin, their producer. Martin has said, "It's quite likely that, in terms of success, Paul's songs will last longer than John's, because they get more to the average man, to the heart strings, than John's did. That's being really commercial about it. But I couldn't put a cigarette paper between them." In other words, too close to call.

Martin does seem, on the whole, in the Paul camp. And Norman Smith, one of the engineers working for Martin, said, "There is no doubt at all that Paul was the main musical force. . . . Most of the ideas came from Paul."

Drugs fueled the band's creativity in the short run, but stamped it out over time. Their greatest creative work, *Sgt. Pepper*, is an LSD album. Simultaneously Lennon was eating so much acid he was destroying his ego. His music became less melodic. He gradually pulled himself together, but then hooked up with avant-garde artist Yoko Ono and craved an existence independent from the Beatle family. McCartney had to take over the band.

"Paul, like Yoko, was born to dominate. Behind his Robin Goodfellow mask of charm and insouciance beat the iron heart of the power tripper," Albert Goldman writes in his Lennon biography. "Is it any wonder that Paul got a little bossy, betraying his impatience with Ringo (who had gotten worse over the years) or with an uptight, crib-book guitarist like George, or a sullen, apathetic drug addict like John?"

The band broke up in 1970, a mere six years after Beatlemania had hit the United States. Alone, the four Beatles never seemed to measure up to their past greatness. The critic Lester Bangs wrote of the wreckage of the world's greatest pop band, "McCartney makes lovely boutique tapes, resolute upon being as inconsequential as the Carpenters. . . . Lennon will do *anything*, reach for any cheap trick, jump on any bandwagon, to make himself look like a Significant Artist. . . . Harrison belongs in a day care center for counterculture casualties. . . . Ringo is beneath contempt.''

Musical ability, like mathematical ability, often shows itself at an early age. Mathematicians do their best work by the age of twenty-five. If they haven't made a breakthrough by forty, it's hopeless. Less obvious is what happens to the musically gifted when they age. Researchers say there's no evidence that older people can't compose great works. Witness Beethoven. But then again, Beethoven was a plodding worker, never the type to create with the fall-out-of-bed method—like Paul McCartney.

Philip Norman says of McCartney, ''An enormous talent has just steadily declined over twenty years. It's really quite tragic. He started off like Picasso. And he ended up like Norman Rockwell.''

In fact all the greats of the sixties have slipped. Bob Dylan has done some fine work of late, but it doesn't compare with what he did in 1965. The Rolling Stones get by on skill more than inspiration. Bands like the Grateful Dead and the Who are museum pieces. The fresh, different, interesting music comes from a younger generation.

Howard Gardner, the Harvard creativity researcher, says that as people get older, they lose the ability to keep a great number of thoughts and ideas in their heads at once. Also, he says, ''One thing that happens to people is that they lose nerve at some point; they've been quite successful and they don't want to take risks anymore.''

Even if McCartney wrote another ''Yesterday,'' no one would care. It'd be a smallish hit on the Easy Listening stations. McCartney didn't change; the rest of us did. In the 1960s pop stars were taken seriously as spokesmen for their generation. People searched the grooves of a Beatles song for the coded messages, the secret instructions, the unspeakable insights. McCartney had the idea of putting a sound on the final note of "A Day in the Life" that only a dog could hear. People found out because their dogs howled when it came on.

If he did the same thing now, it would just be a nuisance.

There will never be another Beatles because rock will never be that young again. The great voyages of discovery have been completed. Never again will we be so innocent and so ready to be bad.

SPORTS

(In which we plunge into the world of grunts and perspiration and finally find out why Green Bay has a pro-football team.)

WHY IN CRUCIAL GOAL-LINE SITUATIONS, DON'T FOOTBALL TEAMS SIMPLY ALLEY-OOP A RUNNING BACK UP AND OVER THE DEFENDERS?

Lest anyone think the question absurd, remember that Bill Veeck once put a midget up to bat for the Chicago White Sox. He walked on four pitches.

Imagine this: Each pro team keeps a midget or two on its roster, in the position of "human projectile." Put some padding around the little guy, and heave. A team might even switch into a "two-midget offense," using one as a decoy.

Such a play would be nearly impossible to defend against: One big man could easily loft a seventy-pounder twelve feet into the air. The moment the midget crosses the plane of the goal, he's made six points.

Only one problem: It's against the rules.

Rule 17 section 6 of Official Football Rules, passed in 1910, states, "No player of the side in possession of the ball shall use his hands, arms or body to push, pull or hold upon his feet the player carrying the ball."

This and other rules were passed to eliminate "mass play," according to Joe Horrigan, curator and director of research at the Pro Football Hall of Fame in Canton, Ohio. At the turn of the century, football (then just a college sport) was not the graceful aerial show that it is today. The basic play in those days was the flying wedge, the blockers linking arms or gripping straps on their teammates' jerseys, charging ahead, grunting and biting and retching. When the pile collapsed to the ground, you'd try to lift or toss the runner farther, the way they pass students up the bleachers in the football stadium.

Because the sport was so brutal, the colleges in 1906 tried to open up the game by liberalizing pass rules. No one had ever passed before. Suddenly you could throw it ten, fifteen yards downfield at once! So the defensive safeties, who had always stood right behind the line of scrimmage, had to play farther back. The effect for football was the opposite of what had been intended: Instead of throwing, teams took advantage of the weaker, unsupported defensive line, firing the wedge down upon whoever looked like the wimpiest player. A horrible thing tended to happen to this kid: He would die! Or at least be horribly maimed.

The 1910 rules were the latest effort to eliminate mass play. Three years later Notre Dame threw the first bomb in football history, beating Army, and ever since the game has been, let's face it, sissified.

WHY DOES THE DINKY LITTLE CITY OF GREEN BAY, WISCONSIN, POPULATION 90,000, HAVE A PROFESSIONAL FOOTBALL TEAM?

The anomalous Packers of Green Bay are a holdover from a bygone era in which pro football teams were fielded by athletic clubs in midwestern industrial towns. Curly Lambeau, who worked for the Indian Packing Company, got his employer to pay for some uniforms in exchange for the nick-name. In 1920 the American Professional Football Conference was organized as a means of keeping richer teams from hiring away the best players with enticing salaries (a star could make as much as one hundred dollars a game!). Along with the Pack-ers the league featured such memorable teams as the Dayton Triangles, the Akron Pros, the Racine Legion, the Muncie Fly-ers, the Evansville Crimson Giants, the Rock Island Indepen-dents, and the Decatur Staleys (who can forget those classic Triangles-Staleys clashes?).

For an idea of what the early game was like, here's a de-scription from *The Official* NFL *Encyclopedia* of a contest between Canton and Massillon:

"Thorpe dropkicked two field goals and Canton led 6–0. . . . Massillon's passing attack began working, however, and an end named Briggs caught a pass on the 15-yard-line and raced across the end zone, disappearing in the surging crowd. Gid-eon (Charley) Smith, the first black player on the Canton team, followed Briggs in mad pursuit into the crowd. There, out of sight, a Canton trolley-car conductor kicked the ball out of Briggs's hands and into the arms of Smith, who emerged from the sea of humanity onto the playing field, the ball in his hands. It was a touchback and Canton's victory was preserved."

In 1922 the league expanded and became the National Foot-ball League. The powerhouse then was the Canton Bulldogs, which explains why they put the Pro Football Hall of Fame there. The franchises tended to lose money, and most of the smaller teams (the Pottsville Marroons, the Frankford Yellow Jackets, the Providence Steam Roller) eventually disbanded. The Packers survived because a group of local businessmen created the Green Bay Football Corporation, a publicly owned nonprofit organization. All other modern NFL teams are pri-vately owned by rich monopolists, who somehow skirt the anti-trust laws and charge twenty-eight dollars for even the cheap seats *and* prohibit the local telecast of home games that aren't sold out. Not that we care.

WHY DO THE SAME REFEREES APPEAR IN EVERY TELEVISED PRO FOOTBALL GAME?

W e were concerned that this was just our own personal misconception, as opposed to a universal misconception. But then we called up Jerry Markbreit, seemingly one of the most omnipresent football officials and author of the candidly titled memoir *Born to Referee*. Markbreit assured us he hears the question all the time.

"I have people say, 'You know, you're on every Monday night game.' In reality I've had two Monday night games," he said. "It's an optical illusion. I get that everywhere."

So what causes the illusion? Our initial guess was that one or two blue-chip crews work all the really big games, but a spokesman for the NFL officiating office said the league randomly assigns the officiating crew regardless of TV audience.

Naturally we assumed he was lying, and went to the agate listings in the sports section, where it names the officials in every game. Nope. He was right.

This leads to the next suspicion: There are many referees, but they are specially selected to look identical.

There is a seed of truth there. The NFL tends to pick people who are in a fairly narrow age bracket and then expects them to adhere to certain tonsorial codes, like no long hair, beards, or mustaches. Moreover they tend to be successful businessmen during the week, with all the straight-arrow bedrock-America features that stereotype that breed. Markbreit writes that officials are "reserved, disciplined, follow-orders men who are willing to place ourselves in a strictly regimented environment. All of a sudden, for a few days at a time over twenty weeks, we have to follow rules we didn't make—and we like it." They cannot take an alcoholic drink at any point while on the road for an NFL game. They cannot be one minute late to a meeting without being reprimanded. They must never swear.

More importantly (now we're getting to the answer), the zebras are meant to look the same by design. The uniforms are indistinct, and there are no names on the jerseys. Lastly referees are trained to behave like robots.

"If everybody is doing the same thing, how do you become distinctive?" Markbreit said. He has made a concerted effort to escape from the job's anonymity and has done it well enough to get a book contract. "I work very hard on my delivery and my diction. I don't know what the other guys do, but I make a special point to be very crisp and very positive and pronounce my words as best I can, so I can be distinctive."

But he can't be unusually demonstrative, like a baseball umpire. In baseball the umps and the managers are always screaming and spitting and kicking dirt at each other, but you never, never see this in football. Ed Marion, executive director of the NFL Referees Association, gives the reason: Baseball and basketball officials belong to a union. Football referees don't, so their jobs are not quite so secure. They can't get cranky and boisterous.

"The less we're seen, the more they like it," Marion said.

Our suggestion to Jerry Markbreit: Grow a beard. Put a dash of color in that outfit, maybe a nice red scarf around the neck. Get an endorsement contract for your cleats. And make up some new signals—say, an extended middle finger for when the coach becomes too abusive.

WHY ARE THERE SO MANY MORE NOVELS AND MOVIES ABOUT BASEBALL THAN ABOUT ANY OTHER SPORT?

For the Big Picture we go to W. P. Kinsella, author of *Shoeless Joe*, the basis of the movie *Field of Dreams*. In an interview with *Modern Fiction Studies*, a literary journal, he said, "On the true baseball field, the foul lines diverge forever, the field eventually encompassing a goodly portion of the world, and there is theoretically no distance that a great hitter couldn't hit the ball or a great fielder couldn't run to retrieve it. . . . This openness makes for larger than life characters, for mythology."

Of course. Diverging foul lines. No doubt if you polled the patrons of a sports bar during the World Series, they'd say they liked baseball because the field theoretically encompasses a quarter of the world's surface.

No other sport incites as much pomposity as baseball. The late baseball commissioner A. Bartlett Giamatti once said, "Baseball fits America so well because it embodies the interplay of individual and group that we so love, and because it expresses our longing for the rule of law while licensing our resentment of lawgivers."

Forget all that. There are two obvious answers to the question posed: (1) Baseball players don't wear helmets and bulky equipment that obscure their identities, and therefore are perceived as having more personality and accessibility; and (2) successful novelists and screenwriters tend to be of a relatively mature age, meaning they were children of the era when baseball was the undisputed pasttime of the nation.

WHY ARE THERE NO MORE .400 HITTERS?

N o one has hit .400 since Ted Williams hit .406 in 1941. The feat has been accomplished twenty-seven times in modern baseball history, but the twenty-sixth was in 1930. Does that mean people can't hit like they used to? Are modern players not as manly as the heroes of the past?

No. The decline of the .400 hitter is a sign of better athletes, and better play.

Proof of this is hampered by the fact that baseball has so many variables, but in every sport with a timer it is clear that today's professional athletes are superior. They have better nutrition and training, and there is a larger population from which to draw talent.

Then why, you ask with breathtaking foolishness, doesn't anyone hit .450 or .475?

The traditional answer is that defense has improved. Pitchers have stronger arms. Coaches use a new breed of relief specialists in late innings. Pitchers are now throwing a thing called a slider (though some old players contend they threw it for years). Night games cause averages to dip. Schedules are more grueling, the season longer. Fielding is much better.

This doesn't explain the absence of .400 hitters, because hitting has also improved. In fact batting averages today are not lower than the averages one hundred years ago: They're around .260 at the mean. In the interim, though, the mean average has fluctuated wildly. Averages jumped in 1893 when the pitcher's mound was moved back to sixty feet from slightly more than forty-five. Pitchers then came up with the radical notion of throwing the ball—get this—*overhand*. Averages dropped yet again in 1901 with the rule that a foul ball is a strike. The mound was lowered a few inches in 1968 to give pitchers less of an advantage. After each change the mean average settled back to about one hit in four at-bats (not including walks, sacrifice bunts, and so on).

If the average player can still hit .260 against better pitching and fielding, why can't a superstar like Wade Boggs hit .400 the way Ty Cobb or Rogers Hornsby did? Stephen Jay Gould, the biologist and baseball fanatic, has promoted a simple explanation: The range in talent has narrowed. As with all complex sports, there is a decline in variation over time. The distance from the worst players to the best players has shortened. Instead of averages fluctuating from .185 to .400, they fluctate from .200 to .360. The upper limit of genetic human ability stands fixed, a vertical wall that can be neared and maybe, if you are Ted Williams, touched, but never breached. Until significant genetic evolution comes along, no one is going to run a three-minute mile or hit a baseball one thousand feet. Ty Cobb and Rogers Hornsby stood close to the human limit, as does Boggs today. The difference is that Cobb and Hornsby hit 150 points higher than the mean batting average, and Boggs hits only 100 points higher, *because his colleagues are better*, even though they are still stuck at the "average" average of .260. So it is highly unlikely that we will ever again see a .400 hitter, unless they do something funky with the mound or the ball, or switch back to underhand.

WHY CAN'T PITCHERS HIT?

"Specialization. You don't want a guy who's a gall-bladder guy doing brain-surgeon stuff," the fabled University of Miami baseball coach Ron Fraser told us.

A few pitchers can swing a bat without too much embarrassment. Fernando Valenzuela of the Los Angeles Dodgers and Rick Sutcliffe of the Chicago Cubs, for example, have both managed a season with a .250 batting average—respectable if not spectacular. They pale in comparison, though, to some of the pitchers of yesteryear, such as Don Newcombe, who hit .359 with seven home runs in 117 at-bats in 1955, while also winning twenty games; and Don Drysdale, who hit .300 in 1965.

None of these guys played every day. Why not? Fear of injuries, Fraser said—which is the heart of the matter. Pitchers today are treated as though they have arms of glass. They don't just rear back and throw the ball like, say, a third baseman; a curveball requires an unnatural throwing motion, and with some pitchers wielding six different pitches, their arms are constantly going out of whack. No one wants them running the bases, sliding into home plate, and so on. It's like fine-tuned sports cars—you don't take 'em to the grocery store.

Compounding pitcher sissiness at the plate is the spread of the designated-hitter rule from the American League down into colleges and high schools. The DH rule allows someone else to hit for the pitcher, which means that many pitchers who reach the National League (which still doesn't have the DH rule) are asked to stand up at the plate for the first time since Little League.

As for the Babe   he was both a great pitcher and the greatest slugger of all time. In three seasons, from 1915 through 1917, he won sixty-five games on the mound for Boston, an extraordinary feat. But he was also showing awesome clout at the plate. His coach finally agreed, in 1918, to let Ruth play the outfield on some of the days when he wasn't pitching. "But after a few weeks of this experiment," says the biography *Babe Ruth: His Life and Legend*, by Kal Wagenheim, "Ruth wore a leather strap on his wrist and refused to pitch, claiming that his arm was weary."

Was this medical proof of the impossibility of doing both? Or was Ruth just being difficult? He was a famous pain in the neck: late-night boozer, woman-chaser, and so on. Maybe he was just hung over—not a condition you want to be in when you're the starting pitcher.

Toward the end of the 1918 season he agreed to pitch again, won two World Series pitching duels, and set a long-standing World Series record with 29 2/3 consecutive scoreless innings. The next season he broke the all-time home-run record with twenty-nine dingers, but pitched only occasionally. The next year he hit fifty-four home runs (more than all but one other *team*), and people forgot about his pitching prowess. On the last day of the 1933 season, as a gimmick, Ruth pitched a game for the Yankees. He went the distance, gave up twelve hits, but won, 6–5. Afterward, in extreme pain, he couldn't so much as raise his arm to tip his cap.

WHY CAN'T ANYONE BREAK ROGER MARIS'S RECORD OF SIXTY-ONE HOMERS IN A SEASON?

No one is likely ever to hit 61 again because no one can even seem to hit 50. Cecil Fielder managed to hit 51 homers in 1990, but it was the first time someone had reached that mark since George Foster hit 52 in 1977. The reason people think that Maris's record might be broken is that, because of statistical probability, someone always starts the year with a hot streak and bashes lots of homers and seems to be on pace to hit 70 or 80. Inevitably they cool down. George Bell of Toronto hit three home runs on opening day a couple of years ago but, sure enough, failed to hit 486 home runs during the season.

The real question is how, three decades ago, a player who is not even a Hall of Famer managed to hit sixty-one home runs and break one of the greatest records in the game. Why Roger Maris? There are many factors. Maris, a lefty, was the ultimate pull hitter, meaning he hit everything to right field, a convenient fact given that Yankee Stadium has a short porch in right, only 296 feet down the line. (Though, we should note, he did hit half his home runs when playing on the road.) Since then Yankee Stadium has been enlarged, and baseball rules dictate that every fence in the league must be at least 325 feet at the foul lines.

Another factor in Maris's favor was that it was an expansion year, with two new teams in the league and measurably weaker pitching. Everyone hit lots of homers.

Perhaps more importantly, Maris batted in front of the great Mickey Mantle. Pitchers had to throw strikes, lest they walk Maris and set up a two-run homer by Mantle. Mantle looked like *he* was going to break Ruth's record for much of the season and finished with fifty-four home runs. Maris hit loads of homers late in the season, precisely the opposite of what you see nowadays, when players like Mark McGwire and Kevin Mitchell get figured out by the opposing pitchers come August. The change may be due to a more scientific approach among coaches: They gather data on what kind of pitches a player has been hitting, in what part of the strike zone, with how many balls and strikes, and so on, rather than relying on the pitcher's and catcher's instincts.

In any case Maris had a truly great year, and the fact that he was never voted into the Hall of Fame may have been the final petty punishment for breaking the record of the game's most popular player.

WHY DO SO MANY PRO-BASKETBALL GAMES COME DOWN TO THE FINAL SHOT?

No one could accuse radical rationalists like us of being paranoid, but we do think it a touch peculiar, even suspicious, the way pro basketball has such narrow margins of victory. You think of that classic Chicago Bulls victory over Cleveland in the play-offs when Michael Jordan nailed a jumper with six seconds left to go up by a point, and then Chicago fell behind three seconds later when Cleveland made a quick lay-up, but then won the game anyway when Jordan made a dream-come-true shot at the buzzer. Great drama. True, there are last-second victories in baseball and football as well, but only in basketball can you be pretty confident of a tight game late in the fourth quarter, which raises the obvious question: Why not just start the game halfway through the fourth quarter? Save some time!

Now for the facts. A guy named Harvey Pollack is the statistician and historian for the Philadelphia 76ers and *the* recognized national authority on basketball scoring. Pollack's research shows that, prior to the 1988–89 season there had been 24,120 professional basketball games. The most common margin of victory: two points. Just under one-fifth of all games, 19 percent, were decided by three points or fewer. That doesn't include games that were tied at the end of regulation, went into overtime, and ended up with larger margins of victory.

You can read these numbers any way you want. Clearly a small minority of games are decided by the last shot. On the other hand, because scoring can be quickly accomplished in basketball, particularly with the advent of the three-point goal, games are exciting in the last two minutes even if a team is behind by six or seven points.

What is also arresting is that, according to Pollack's research, the *winning* team in an average NBA game gets *only 52 percent* of the total points scored. Why not more?

There are several obvious answers:

1. Scoring is easy. Unlike football and baseball, basketball has virtually outlawed defense. The "hand check" was abolished decades ago. Now you can block a shot or stand motionlessly in front of the opponent, but you can't hack him or take him down at the knees, which is the only way Michael Jordan, the Extraterrestrial, could possibly be stopped. What this means is that a team can stay competitive just by having a handful of guys who can run downcourt and shoot a jump shot. Which leads to:

2. There's plenty of talent to go around, because the rosters only allow twelve players. The twenty-five team league is therefore made up of the top three hundred basketball players in the country beyond college age. Almost all were stars in high school and college. This doesn't mean that all the teams are equally good. To the contrary, basketball has a larger gap between the best teams and the worst teams, as far as winning percentage is concerned, than football or baseball. The "parity" in the league only means that every team is going to be able to make enough shots to score upward of seventy-five points in forty-eight minutes of regulation play. The reason there aren't more blowouts is:

3. Basketball is physically exhausting, and players must play both offense and defense. In a long season with frequent games coaches must be careful to conserve the energies and bodies of their top players. So if a team gets up by twenty points, the stars will then head to the bench, and the margin between scores will be likely to contract.

WHY DO SOME BASKETBALL PLAYERS HAVE SUCH GREAT HANG TIME?

The greatest moment in the history of hang time, according to Tony Kornheiser in an article in *Sports Illustrated*, came late in game 4 of the 1980 NBA play-offs between the L.A. Lakers and the Philadelphia 76ers, with the Lakers up by five points. Julius "Dr. J" Erving, the Lindbergh of basketball flyers, drove along the right baseline and, about twelve feet from the basket, sprang into the air off his left foot. Laker Mark Landsberger quickly extended his right arm like a clothesline and blocked Erving's path to the basket, and Kareem Abdul-Jabbar filled in the only other route. "Erving seemingly had no place to go but off the court. So that's where he went, off the court, behind the basket. Dipsy-doodling the ball, ducking his head so he wouldn't slap it against the back of the backboard and tucking his legs for some extra hang time, he reentered the court on the other side of the basket, and just before touching down inside the left side of the foul lane, he extended his shooting arm like a hydraulic crane and underhanded a reverse topspin floater off the glass, kissing it off the front rim and in. A U-turn with a diameter the breadth of Guatemala."

Anyone who watches basketball knows that hang time is real. Elgin Baylor virtually invented hang time. Then came Connie Hawkins, Dr. J., and now Michael Jordan. They go up, and then, when you think they are going to come down, they just hang there, defying everything we know of Newtonian mechanics. Are they really tapping into some unknown antigravity force?

Don't be ridiculous. They're going up and down just like anyone else. But they are jumping farther on the horizontal plane, flattening out the arc of their leap, so they seem to hover above the ground, in comparison to the defenders, who tend to jump straight up and down. Elgin Baylor said, "For the most part I jumped horizontally, and the defenders jumped vertically; we were going in different directions." What's more, the great hangers have superior body control, and twist their limbs and torso to get around defenders in mid-leap, giving the appearance of changing directions. Dr. J would palm the ball off the dribble, wave it over his head, and take a final unseen (but legal) step before going into the air, prolonging the entire hang-move.

As for the greatest moment in hang-time history, someone timed it with a stopwatch: seven-tenths of a second.

NUMBERS

(In which we try to show that the world doesn't quite add up.)

WHY CAN'T MATHEMATICIANS USE ADVANCED FORMS OF DRAFTSMANSHIP TO FIGURE OUT THE EXACT VALUE OF π?

Last we heard, Columbia University research scientists had used computers to calculate π to a billion decimal places. We greeted this news with frustration. At some point they ought to figure the durn thing out exactly.

One would think the problem is just poor draftsmanship. Why, we wonder, can't they use advanced technology to draw an extremely precise circle with a diameter of one foot, and then use an unbelievably accurate tape measure to determine the circumference in feet, which would be π?

For those who don't know much about π, it is the circumference of a circle divided by its diameter. To be (fairly) precise, it's a little bit more than 3.14159, but a little bit less than 3.14160. Our imaginary experiment merely requires that the tape measure have enough little tiny lines along the edge so that the end of the circle falls on one of them.

Alas, no matter how well marked the tape measure, the termination of the circle would always fall between two of the lines, even if the tape measure included micro-whammo-micrometers and you used a science-fiction magnifying glass. The best you could hope for is a sorry approximation. Not even Columbia's computers can home in on the terminus.

This is because π is an "irrational" number, which means literally that it cannot be expressed as a ratio of two other numbers. The decimal expansion goes on forever, and then some, without ever falling into a pattern. It literally cannot be counted. It's inexpressible. Dunderheads will try to tell you that π is 22/7 but a little scribbling shows that 22/7 is 3.142857142857142857etc. Hah! Way too big! Do they take us for fools? More to the point, 22/7 is by definition a rational number (a ratio). To pass off π as a rational number is like describing Ted Bundy as a "noted felon."

Not only are irrational numbers annoying, they're ubiquitous. Geometry is shot through with them. If you draw a square that measures 1 unit on the side, the length of the diagonal will be the square root of 2—egad, another irrational number. When the fourth-century B.C. scholar Hippasus pointed this out to his colleagues, he got booted from the Pythagorean brotherhood. The world wasn't supposed to be so . . . indefinite. According to one story, the Pythagoreans drowned the heretic.

Mathematics: a dangerous job.

WHY DO MATHEMATICIANS ASSERT THAT .999999 REPEATED AD INFINITUM EQUALS EXACTLY 1.0?

You say you were just wondering this? Here's the serendipitous solution:

As we carry .99999etc. toward infinity, the number gets closer and closer to 1.0, right? But it never actually reaches 1.0, right? There's always a little space between the .999999etc. and 1.0, right?

Wrong. The equation proves the equivalency.

1.0

minus

.9999 ad infinitum
equals
.0000 ad infinitum.
Which is zero.
There is exactly zero difference. They are the same.

We have found that some people just refuse to accept this. Their problem is that they do not understand the concept of infinity. They realize that the .0000 stretches far out to the edge of the imagination, but they still think they can picture the 1 floating out there, somewhere, an exiled digit, but alive nonetheless. The mistake is thinking that Math exists independently of equations, that Math represents some kind of universal truth to which our equations aspire and inevitably fall short. The fact is that Math is a human invention, and if the equations say that 1.0 equals .99999etc., then it does.

Another way of limbering up the cortex to accept such a situation is to realize that the number of whole numbers (0,1,2,3,4 . . .) is equal to the number of even numbers (0,2,4,6,8 . . .), rather than being twice as many. In fact the number of whole numbers is equal to the number of "even numbers above one million," though common sense would tell you that the latter set of numbers is smaller. Do the equation: Every whole number can be paired with an even number above one million, forever. Zero is paired with 1,000,000; 1 is paired with 1,000,002; and so on, and on, and on.

WHY DO BOYS DO BETTER THAN GIRLS IN MATH?

We should preface the answer by repeating our absolute conviction that women, in general, are vastly superior to men. But the deficient male of the species appears to have a slight edge in math. (We realize that saying this is, among certain circles, the intellectual equivalent of scratching oneself in a rude place. Unfortunately that's where it itches.)

Without question, the fact that male high school seniors score about fifty points higher on the math portion of the Scholastic Aptitude Test is largely due to environmental factors—girls are still discouraged from achieving in such "male" pursuits as math, science, and engineering. (That doesn't mean that any and all observed differences between the sexes are the result of exclusively environmental pressures.)

Since 1972 a program at Iowa State University called the Study of Mathematically Precocious Youth has given the math part of the SAT to mathematically gifted seventh- and eighth-graders. The boys score about 35 points (out of 800) higher than the girls, year after year. Can the mathematics gap be environmentally explained? Probably not, says the program's director, Camilla Persson Benbow, writing in the June 1988 issue of *Behavioral and Brain Sciences*. These aren't your average kids—they're all math whizzes. The girls and boys have equal aptitude at computation, like multiplying and dividing. It is only when the test questions become more abstract, involving "math reasoning," that boys show an edge.

It doesn't make sense that environmental factors could be hindering one type of math skill (math reasoning) but not another (computing).

Interviews with the girls showed that, for the most part, they did not feel discouraged, did not lack confidence, and did not perceive societal obstacles. They had been singled out for their skill in math and they were proud of it.

Moreover the variance between boys and girls has remained about the same since 1972. If environmental pressures cause the gap between boys and girls, one would think that the gap would have narrowed since 1972 due to the larger societal change in attitudes toward gender roles.

This leaves us snooping around for a biological factor—that extra juice that puts the brainy boys over the top. Harvard neurologist Norman Geschwind (from the feminist gallery we hear boos and hisses) once came up with a hypothesis that high levels of testosterone in developing fetuses can do all sorts of strange things, such as hamper eyesight, screw up the immune system, and, on the plus side, help the development of the right hemisphere of the brain, which is associated with math reasoning.

Okay, it sounds idiotic, yet it would explain another mystery: Why does it seem as though every little kid who is really good in math has thick, Coke-bottle glasses and terrible allergies? It's true! Smart kids are four times as likely to be myopic than average kids. And kids who are extremely advanced in math are twice as likely as average kids to have hay fever. They are also twice as likely to be left-handed—which means they are right-brained. Left-handers are also better at spatial awareness and musical performance, areas that are controlled by the right hemisphere. There is, at the least, circumstantial evidence of a hormonal link among left-handers, bad vision, allergies, and math wizardry.

The Benbow report drew a lot of flak. Psychologist Lila Ghent Braine, of Barnard College, wrote, "I suggest that it is less attractive for many mathematically talented adolescent females to develop their skills intensively in mathematics than in fields where women are extensively rewarded, and which are more compatible with other cultural values for female adolescents."

Neurophysiologist Ruth Bleier argued that, even if there is a biological difference between seventh-grade boys and girls, it is still caused by environmental pressures: "Brain structure (biology) itself reflects and incorporates the environmental, cultural, and learning influence to which it is exposed before and after birth."

To which one is driven to respond: *before* birth? Like, are we sending our girls a bad message even when they're fetuses?

The Benbow report is nothing to panic about. A small statistical difference among a large population has no meaning when one deals with individuals. The Benbow study looks at children on an extreme end of the spectrum, and it is always at extremes that differences are most dramatic. The average height of men and women is only a few inches apart, but if you come across a shadowy figure that is six feet eight inches tall, it's *definitely* a man. Hopefully.

WHY IS THE CALENDAR SO SCREWY, WITH SOME MONTHS HAVING THIRTY-ONE DAYS, SOME THIRTY, AND ONE ONLY TWENTY-EIGHT? WHY IS SEPTEMBER THE NINTH MONTH INSTEAD OF THE SEVENTH? WHY IS JANUARY 1 WHEN IT IS, INSTEAD OF, SAY, AT THE WINTER SOLSTICE?

The calendar is like the white noise from a freeway: an annoyance that people take for granted. We regard the calendar as immutable, as though people never had a hand in it, as though February, for example, is allotted twenty-eight days because February really *does* have twenty-eight days in real life.

But if you take a few steps back and look again, the calendar takes on that character of grating absurdity that you associate with the scoring terminology in tennis. Thirty days hath September, April, June, and November—if you can discern a pattern there, you ought to be in a lab someplace, studying muons and quarks, or working on the Mordell Conjecture.

The most obvious calendar reform ("calendar reform" is a concept sort of like "Democrat president," something that people talk about even though it may never actually happen) would be to divide the year into 13 months of 28 days each. It would be convenient, because every month would have exactly four weeks and the first of the month would always begin on the same day of the week. You wouldn't need a calendar. Although 13 times 28 only equals 364, the last day of the year could be a holiday, or a double-holiday in leap years, assigned no month or day of the week. It could have its own name. Like maybe "Murray."

Instead we have confusion. The fundamental problem with calendars is that the astronomical indices of time—the rising of the sun, the lunar phases, and the seasons—don't match up neatly. There's a full moon every 29.53 days, and a year lasts 365.2422 days.

Early civilizations in the Near East built their calendars around the moon. Since a lunar month is about twenty-nine days, these ancient calendar months had either twenty-nine or thirty days. The Egyptians used a solar calendar, dividing the year into twelve months of thirty days each, with five or six extra days at the end of the year. The ancient Greeks, meanwhile, came up with a baffling system in which ten years of thirteen months each were interspersed among seventeen years of twelve months each. Come up with a rhyme for that, Plato.

In the year we would call 47 B.C., Julius Caesar threw out the moon-based Roman calendar and instituted what is, approximately, the calendar we use today, only more sensible. The first month, March, had thirty-one days. The second month, April, had thirty days. May had thirty-one. The number of days alternated between thirty and thirty-one. The final month, February, had thirty days only in the leap year; otherwise, twenty-nine.

Caesar decided that the calendar would go into effect on January 1 ("Ianuarius I"), which he decreed would be the day of the first new moon after the winter solstice. Bad move. New moons and solstices are in no way synchronous, so we now have a New Year's Day with no astronomical significance, stuck in the dead of winter.

After Brutus and his ilk murdered Caesar, the Roman Senate decreed that the fifth month, Quintilis, would thereafter be called Julius. Then, in 8 B.C., during the reign of Augustus Caesar, the Roman Senate had another fit of obsequiousness and decreed that the sixth month, Sextilis, would become Augustus. This, however, posed a potential embarrassment: Julius had thirty-one days, and Augustus only thirty. So the Senate stole the last day of the year, February 29, and affixed it to August. *Politics*.

The calendar still wasn't quite right. The astronomical year is about eleven minutes and fourteen seconds short of 365 days. Over the centuries this slight discrepancy caused the spring equinox, by which the date of Easter is determined, to drift inexorably toward February from its official date of March 21. By A.D. 1582 the real solar equinox was arriving on March 11. So Pope Gregory simply zapped ten days out of existence, and October 4, 1582, was followed by October 15. The Gregorian Adjustment included the proviso that, in the future, the leap year would not be observed at the century mark, unless the year is divisible by 400. Thus, there was no February 29, 1900, but there will be a February 29, 2000.

The Gregorian calendar isn't perfect. It'll be a day off in three thousand years. Our advice: Start planning now.

WHY IS VALENTINE'S DAY ON FEBRUARY 14?

Everyone agrees that the original Valentine was a priest in Rome during the third century. Whether he was a Christian or a pagan depends on what account you read. Supposedly he promoted the marriage of young lovers at a time when the mad emperor Claudius II had issued an edict against matrimony. Claudius thought it made men less willing to go off into battle. Valentine was jailed and then stoned, clubbed, and beheaded.

According to something we have here called *The Christian Book of Why*—yes, there's a why book for every faction—Valentine sent a note to the jailer's daughter on the night before his death. He signed it, "Your Valentine." He was supposedly executed on February 14, and we now celebrate this day by giving "valentines." Supposedly.

This sounds mighty apocryphal. And a little too—dare we say it?—romantic.

Another theory sticks to the birds-and-bees: The holiday denotes the mating season of birds. February 14 used to be closer to the spring equinox than it is today, so there were a lot of lovebirds in the air.

Hold on. Why would people celebrate the mating habits of birds? Isn't there something more down-to-earth underlying this thing . . . some pagan rite maybe?

Naturally.

Before there was ever a Saint Valentine, there was a pagan celebration among Romans called Lupercalia, in which each young man drew the name of a young woman in a lottery and then spent the next year fooling around with her. There was also much whipping of the women with strips of animal hide. The women thought this would make them more fertile.

Sick? Hey, we're taking this straight from the *World Book*. And if whips show up in the *World Book*, you know that's just the tip of this degenerate iceberg.

Lupercalia, named after the god Lupercus, was celebrated every February 15 for about eight hundred years, until the end of the fifth century A.D., when the Roman authorities apparently had enough of the whips-and-lottery nonsense and decided to reposition the holiday. They handed it off to some marketing genius, who dug through the files and came up with Saint Valentine.

WHY DO SO MANY PEOPLE CONSIDER THE NUMBER 13, AND THE DAY FRIDAY, TO BE BAD LUCK?

There is a consensus on the loose that claims that 13 is considered unlucky because there were thirteen people at the Last Supper. This consensus view is not to our liking. A single and rather obscure biblical citation seems a rather insecure foundation for so widespread a superstition.

We would tend to think that the real origin is in the study of numbers. Consider that the nearby number 12 is so useful—we employ it in clocks to count the hours, and in the calendar to count the months. The number 12 is well integrated into the world of integers, being divisible by 1, 2, 3, 4, and 6, and when multiplied by 5 gives you 60, another number that turns up frequently, to count seconds and minutes. The number 12 pops up in matters of dice and eggs. In contrast the loathsome 13 is ungainly, useless, an abomination. Among the low prime numbers—those that are indivisible except by 1—13 is the black sheep, lacking the evenness of the 2, the tectonic perfection of the 3, the handiness of the 5, the cheerfulness of the 7, and the symmetrical beauty of the 11. The 13 is bad luck because it's so damn ugly.

Friday is tainted because that is the day Jesus Christ was crucified. We aren't totally happy with this explanation either, but we can live with it. The real question is, If Friday is bad luck because of the Crucifixion, why do Christians commemorate the day as Good Friday?

Theologians say the *good* refers to the redemptive aspect of Christ's passion. Humanity was redeemed through Christ's death, forgiven for its sins and given the chance for salvation. Admittedly this is a complex theological point; one could argue that it doesn't even make the slightest bit of sense. If you want to know more, see a preacher.

This is as good a time as any to deal with yet another nagging biblical question: **Why does everyone seem to think that Jesus** was entombed *three days prior to the Resurrection, even though he died on a Friday afternoon and was out of the tomb by first thing Sunday morning?*

This is not nit-picking; any sensible person can see that from Friday afternoon to Sunday morning is, at most, two days. But from Sunday school on, you hear that three days passed between the Crucifixion and the Resurrection. Biblical scholars have a standard answer: Jesus said he would rise on the third day, and back in those days people calculated days differently than we do now. Friday was the first day, Saturday the second, and Sunday the third. But wait! This doesn't exactly jibe with the Gospels, which are inconsistent on this matter. While Matthew 16:21 does indeed paraphrase Jesus, saying that He will rise "on the third day," the Gospel of Mark 8:31 says He will rise "after three days." We take this from the Greek text, translated for us by Father Eugene LaVerdiere, editor of *Emmanuel* magazine, a publication for priests. To sample a more recent translation, the New King James Version quotes Jesus directly in Matthew saying, "After three days I will rise."

Did He jump the gun?

So confusing is this matter that some Christians consider Saturday night the time of the Resurrection and locate the Crucifixion on a Wednesday.

We need not be so literal. The Gospels are universally fuzzy on matters of time. They were written several decades after the fact. The reference to "three days" has a larger significance, harkening back to prophecies in the Old Testament, including references to a Messiah who would be killed and then rise again after three days. Three is sort of a magic number, a holy number, in the Bible. So when Jesus talked about three days, He might have been making a sly literary reference.

WHY IS 1 TIMES 1 EQUAL TO 1, WHEN 1 PLUS 1 IS 2?

We received this question by mail from a certain George W. in Miami. He went on to say, "I was taught early on that multiplication is a short form of addition, so things don't add up for me. At Fort Sill Artillery OCS, the chief gunnery instructor, supposedly a math whiz, tried to explain it to me but gave up—just accept it as gospel truth, he said. I didn't accept it then and don't now, but an Einstein I'm not."

George, you suffer from a conceptual disease that no doubt is epidemic. We've got the vaccine.

First, you shouldn't feel bad about having trouble with numbers. Einstein himself was famous for his poor math scores in school. What Einstein did brilliantly, though, was think abstractly, to perform "thought experiments," rather than bury his face in equations. Your error is to focus too much on the troubling equation—"1 times 1 equals 1"—rather than on the idea that the equation represents.

The phrase "times 1" is another way of saying "appearing only once." There is *no* multiplication whatsoever. There is essentially nothing to solve. You do not have to appeal to the Gospels to believe this. It's a statement that makes perfect common sense.

Unfortunately we are forced in grade school to take so many math tests that we tend to look at any equation as a mess of numbers and symbols that must be carefully manipulated, inverted, fused, and realigned in a certain precise pattern in order to get the official correct result. We did not learn to look at equations as *statements*. George looks at the phrase "1 times 1" and, quite logically, perceives two separate 1s. He is also quite correct in thinking that multiplication is a short form of addition. So he's wondering, in essence, where that second 1 disappears to. The trick is to understand that the second 1 never actually exists. "1 times 1" *means* 1.

Far trickier than the number 1 is the number 0. What is 5

divided by 0? Some people might say it's 0. Others might say it's "infinity." In truth, "5 divided by 0" is a nonsense phrase. It means "how many 0s are there in 5?" The reason the answer isn't "infinity" is that if you take an infinite number of 0s and stack them up, you're still at 0, going nowhere. So any equation that tries to divide by 0 is just gobbledygook, the equivalent of saying something like "the mome raths outgrabe."

Now let's go to an equation such as "10 times $\frac{1}{5}$ equals x." Most people will find x by going through all sorts of elaborate motions, first arriving at $\frac{10}{5}$ and then, through trial and error, reducing that to 2. A more conceptual thinker will look at the equation and say, "Okay, what's a fifth of 10?" and quickly come up with 2, not through scribbling on paper but through an instantaneous mental algorithm, the kind of abstract understanding of numbers that distinguishes the human mind from a computer.

So we say to you, George, learn to read the language of math. Stop crunching numbers. Be a person.

TIME

(In which we desperately attempt to understand why scientists keep trying to make the year one tick of the clock longer.)

The International Earth Rotation Service—an actual organization—decided to observe a "leap second" on New Year's Eve, 1989. The precise moment of this leap was at midnight Coordinated Universal Time, which is 7:00 P.M. on the East Coast of the United States. We were somehow supposed to adjust our watches so that, one second after 6:59:59, the time read 6:59:60 instead of 7:00:00.

Who has ever heard of the International Earth Rotation Service? Who appointed them to that job? Didn't the earth get along just fine before there ever *was* an International Earth Rotation Service?

In any case the group's official explanation for the needed leap second is that the earth is spinning too slowly. This is an outrageous lie. The earth is right on time; it is our clocks that have gone haywire. In fact there's a massive fraud afoot. Scientists in every technologically advanced country have created a monstrous concept called the Precise Measurement of Time, a crusade whose first casualty has been the earth, the moon, the sun, and the stars, those great referents for clocks since time immemorial. Time always was based on the movement of heavenly bodies. The earth is a type of clock. It set the standards for timekeeping. Now the standards are set by—the word sounds like some kind of disease—*cesium*.

Which is stuff no regular person ever comes into contact with, willingly.

Back in the good old days (actually until 1972), your basic shepherd tending a flock of sheep could tell what time it was by looking up in the sky. A second was very precisely and unambiguously defined as one-sixtieth of a minute, which was one-sixtieth of an hour, which was one-twenty-fourth of a day, which was how long it took for the earth to spin once. The people who had the job of determining the earth's spin worked at the Greenwich Observatory in England, and clocks were set in reference to Greenwich Mean Time.

That system has been discarded. Ditched. Flushed into the sewer.

Now only scientists can tell the time, because they're the only ones who know how to find cesium. A second is officially defined as 9 billion, 192 million, 631 thousand, 770 oscillations of a cesium atom.

Surely you have an innate feel for how long that is. (It's about how long it takes to say "one thousand one.")

Even distance is now based on cesium. Cesium defines not just time but space! For a long time there had been a rod stashed somewhere in Paris that set the standard for how long a meter is. In 1983 the meter was redefined as the distance that light travels in a vacuum in precisely 1/299,792,458 second. How long is a second? A second is 9,192,631,770 oscillations of a cesium atom.

It makes you long for the days when a cubit was the length of the king's forearm.

This slide from grace began in the 1930s. Astronomers who had studied the motion of the earth closely for many years finally concluded that the earth had lost some of its zip. The earth's rotation is slowing down because of tidal forces, atmosphere drag, meteor impacts, and assorted things like that. This is barely detectable. In a century the earth slows down by only about one second per 365 days. In other words each year—meaning, the amount of time it takes for the earth to spin 365 times—is a small fraction of a second longer than the one previous.

This sort of thing matters to the precision-minded. So by the late forties people were designing the first atomic clocks.

An atomic clock is based on the idea that atoms have an inherent vibration, or oscillation. They are energetic little suckers. They act like tiny pendulums. Anything that moves in a stable, repetitive cycle can function as a clock. Atomic clocks use high-frequency microwave currents to count the ticktock of these pendulums.

In 1972 Greenwich Mean Time was discarded in favor of what is now called Coordinated Universal Time. The second was officially redefined in terms of cesium vibrations. But to do this, obviously, there had to be a comparison to the conventional increments of time, based on the earth's rotation. But which rotation? Remember, the earth is slowing down. They needed to pick a year and say, this was when a second was really a second. They picked the year 1900.

But now you see an obvious problem: Because the standard for cesium time was fixed according to astronomical time in 1900, and because the earth has been slowing down since then, there is now a chronic gap between the cesium year and the earth year. This is why we have had leap seconds almost every year lately—a total of fifteen since 1972.

Newspaper accounts usually misreport this situation and say that the leap second puts the earth and the atomic clocks into sync. That's a vicious and despicable lie. On the night of December 31, 1989, the difference between the time determined by earth's rotation—called UT1 officially—and Coordinated Universal Time (UTC, based on the French translation) was about .58 seconds. The leap second only made that difference .42 seconds. The two time systems became precisely synchronous for just a fleeting instant sometime in October 1990.

The gap between a cesium second and an actual rotational second will grow. The earth will slow down at a faster and faster rate. In a century a typical earth year will be at least two seconds off the cesium year. Eventually there might be a need for leap seconds every month.

"Atomic clocks are much more accurate than the earth," explains Fred McGehan, spokesman for the National Institute of Standards and Technology in Boulder, Colorado. "The clock that we maintain here is off only one second every 300,000 years."

That's what he says now. But just wait 300,000 years and see if he's so smug.

The fact is, accuracy at the level he is boasting about is actually not so great, by today's standards. One second every 300,000 years? That's nothing! What does the thing run on, *springs*? What do they have to do—wind it up every morning? Now, the real monster clocks are called hydrogen masers. *Maser* is an acronym for *m*icrowave *a*mplification from the *s*timulated *e*mission of *r*adiation. Cesium can keep time to a billionth of a second, a nanosecond. But a hydrogen maser clock keeps time to a tenth of a billionth of a second—a hundred picoseconds.

And the next generation of timepieces will be the mercury-ion clocks, which are accurate to within femtoseconds, which are quadrillionths of a second.

At this point it gets almost absurd. This is like the quest for π. It's fascinating, challenging, but ultimately futile. Same with time. Time can never be nailed down precisely. In fact the more precise the clocks become, the less possible it is to make them in sync! No two of these clocks show the same time except in fleeting instants.

There are three things timekeepers worry about: accuracy, stability, and precision. Accuracy is the extent to which a time-keeping system can be replicated. One good clock isn't enough: You have to be able to make lots of them, and make them jibe. Stability is more important than accuracy: That's whether the clock is going to hum along nicely over a long period or start to speed up or lag. Precision is yet another matter: Does a second on this clock really equal a second?

Mihran Miranian, chief of the Time Scales Division at the U.S. Naval Observatory in Washington, points out, "A man with one clock knows what time it is; a man with two clocks never knows what time it is."

So why even bother?

"It's not a matter of just a bunch of pointy-headed scientists trying to divide up the second finer and finer," insists Dennis McCarthy, chief of the Earth Orientation Division at the Naval Observatory. The most important use for accurate clocks, one that goes back to the fifteenth century, is navigation. A sea captain looking at the stars through a sextant needs to know what time it is, or else his star charts are no help. It is not for nothing that each degree of arc in the sky is made up of sixty minutes. Nowadays navigation is even more demanding, because we have to steer planetary probes within a few thousand miles of large objects like Neptune without smashing things up, and we have to deliver our nuclear payloads directly on top of the enemy's missile silos. This requires a good sense of time.

This also requires that we keep track of the earth. Even though the earth is no longer the standard for the second, there is still an ongoing, and awesome, international effort to calculate the planet's rotation.

Just sighting the position of the sun won't cut it anymore—the sun wobbles and kvetches, suffering local gravitational quirks. Even looking at distant stars many light-years away isn't good enough—there's too much motion out there, everything shifting, spinning. You can't tell how fast the earth is turning if you compare it to things that are themselves moving around.

The trick is to look at quasars. Quasars are mysterious quasi-stellar objects some five to ten billion light-years away. They were formed near the beginning of the universe and emit powerful radio waves. They move, too, but they are so imponderably far away that they might as well be fixed in the sky. They have names like:

OJ 287

4C 39.25

OQ 208

0420 minus 014.

Kerry Kingham, an astronomer at the Naval Observatory, says, "We use radio telescopes all over the world and they all look at the same quasar at the same time, and they record observations on a very large magnetic tape—you might just say it's a high-speed recorder—and we also put an atomic clock signal on each tape from each station, and they ship the tapes here to Washington, usually, say, three tapes for a twenty-four-hour experiment, and we have a computing system we call a correlator, and we play the tapes back here."

That's how they compare UT1 (earth time) with UTC (cesium).

One day the Why staff traveled to Richmond Heights, a small

community south of Miami. Amid the pine trees and palmettos there is a fenced-off plot containing a small, nondescript, one-story building and a huge, towering, extremely descript hydraulic-powered dish that looks like it could pick up TV stations on Mars. It could in fact. This is a radio telescope. It is operated by the U.S. Naval Observatory under the direction of astronomer Alice Babcock. One wonders if people in the neighborhood realize that this thing isn't just looking at the moon and the rings of Saturn, but that it is part of some grand plan to figure out the time, of all things.

The day we visited, Dr. Babcock showed us a hydrogen maser clock. It was just a box, basically, with a red digital display. "It's probably off at about the nanosecond level, a billionth of a second," Babcock said. There was another one down the hall, and we insisted on shouting the times back and forth to see if they were in sync. This may have been the first such experiment ever conducted at the observatory and, though it had certain conceptual flaws involving response times and sound waves, we determined the clocks to be synchronous.

As luck would have it, this was the day that Gernot Winkler, the top time man at the Naval Observatory in Washington, chose to visit the Richmond Heights station. Winkler speaks in an Austrian accent and is as much a philosopher as a bureaucrat or metrologist. We asked him, Wasn't this quest for an exact knowledge of time ultimately futile? What's the point?

He said, "There is an aesthetic beauty in doing things precisely."

We noted that his $9.95 pocket watch is precisely in sync with Coordinated Universal Time. The ordinary clock on the wall was a couple of minutes fast. Dr. Babcock promised her visiting superior that this oversight would be swiftly corrected.

"The measurement of time has become the basis of modern technology," Winkler said. Even the clocks accurate to within a femtosecond may someday be of great practicality: "You cannot tell in advance when something that is discovered might have the most practical applications."

So finally we wanted to know: Where will it all end? Will Winkler and his minions ever figure out, beyond any correction or modification, the precise time, the exact time, the absolute Real Time?

"There is no time in nature," he answered. "I cannot consider time to be an objectively existing thing."

There it is: Time isn't real.

Or more precisely, time does not exist the way other things in the universe exist, like stars and galaxies and baseball mitts and James Brown, the Godfather of Soul. The only meaningful definition of time is that it is a dimension. Time is exactly like height or depth or breadth: It is a dimension by which to describe the movement and structure of things.

And just as we would all agree that "height" has no inherent existence, no tangible expression independent of existing objects, so, too, is time nonexistent.

Let's say, hypothetically, that for a few hours everything in the universe, including clocks, suddenly stopped—froze—then resumed without a hitch. Obviously we couldn't tell that this had happened—we'd have been in the deep freeze. So how do we know that this doesn't actually happen in real life? How do we know that last night, while we slept, there was not an interval of several hours when the entire cosmos was in suspended animation? Because, dang it, there is no time if the universe stops. There is no pendulum behind the scenes, there is no ticktock.

In deference to this relativistic universe, the time community has refrained from designating any particular clock as the keeper of absolute time. Instead the operators of atomic clocks around the globe, in the United States and Canada and Germany and Japan and France, continuously deliver their guesstimations of what Coordinated Universal Time should be to the master timekeepers in Paris. The numbers are lumped together to form an average.

So that's the official clock of the world: some numbers on a piece of paper.

BIG CRITTERS

(Dinosaurs. Zebras. Lemmings. And a solution to the mystery of why apes still can't talk worth a dang.)

WHY DON'T HUGE FEROCIOUS TYRANNOSAURUS-LIKE CREATURES ROAM THE EARTH ANYMORE?

Nature used to be exciting, as anyone knows who has seen that splendid documentary *One Million Years* B.C., starring Raquel Welch. The best scene is when a tyrannosaurus takes a horn in the gut from a fatally injured triceratops, while the cave people look on in fear. Or maybe it was a stegosaurus that won. Whatever.

Dinosaurs and humans didn't coexist, of course, but there is a small thread of accuracy in the Welch flick insofar as early humans did live alongside extremely large animals, collectively known as megafauna.

There were woolly mammoths, mastodons, giant thirty-foot lizards, and ground sloths a dozen feet high at the shoulder. All became extinct, for mysterious reasons, within the Pleistocene era, between 1.8 million and 10,000 years ago. In geologic time that's like yesterday.

The disappearance of this megafauna has been the focus of a long-running scientific debate. One camp has a simple explanation: We killed them. Humans systematically hunted down large, sluggish creatures and wiped them out. This is called the Pleistocene Overkill Hypothesis.

The other theory is that climatic changes, associated with the various ice ages, affected large animals more than smaller ones. Defenders of this theory point out that humans never killed off all the big creatures in Africa, such as the elephants.

We are partial to the first theory, because we like the term Pleistocene Overkill Hypothesis on aesthetic grounds and because it seems suspicious that all these big creatures vanished at the same time that humans were spreading across the planet. Mammoths and giant bison and horses abruptly disappeared in North America about ten thousand years ago, soon after the first humans crossed the land bridge from Asia and spread southward.

The implication is that early Native Americans were not the serene ecologists that we like to imagine.

"If you believe the Pleistocene Overkill Hypothesis, then you must accept that early humans in North America did not manage their resources effectively," says paleontologist Bruce McFadden of the Florida State Museum in Gainesville. This doesn't mean that Native Americans were willfully raping the environment; they might have simply been hungry. At least *they* didn't build smokestacks or strip mines.

Speaking of big creatures, the tyrannosaurus may not have been so ferocious after all. Paul Colinvaux, an Ohio State zoologist and author of *Why Big Fierce Animals Are Rare* (great title!), argues that the limited number of calories in the food chain makes it difficult to be really big and fierce and heat-radiating. Thus the tyrannosaurus may have been "a waddling, slow-moving beast. . . . Most of its days were spent lying on its belly, a prostration that conserved energy."

Gosh, sounds almost boring. Fortunately there has arisen yet another revisionist hypothesis: Dinosaurs were warm-blooded, meaning they were probably faster and wilder and just a lot more fun than anyone realized. That's more like it.

WHY CAN'T YOU RIDE ZEBRAS?

Zebras are more difficult to tame than other members of the genus *Equus* (sorry to dash the zebra-riding fantasies of children worldwide). Sometimes you see circus performers riding zebras, but these are the rarest and most broken-down of creatures, the moral equivalent of bearded ladies and dog-boys. As a rule zebras are a pain to deal with and get skittish and mean around the monochromatic species of *Homo sapiens*.

The real message here is that the "wild horses" of today truly aren't wild. The next time you see a Hollywood Western with some cowboy "busting" a wild bronco, just remember that he's trying to break an animal that is descended from domesticated, tame, specially bred horses brought to America by Spaniards in the sixteenth century—and not a truly wild animal. Horses were first domesticated a couple of thousand years before Christ, in the Eurasian steppe. They provided a major source of meat, just as they do today in the tragic cafeteria of the Why Things Are World Headquarters.

Selective breeding has given us the modern horse. Meanwhile the progenitor of the modern horse, a subspecies called Przhevalski's horse, hasn't been seen in the wild since one was spotted on the Mongolian steppe in 1968.

In fact the ancient African tribes never tried to domesticate the zebra. But in an environment teeming with food and potential beasts of burden, Africans may not have needed zebras the way the Eurasian-steppe people needed horses. So they didn't tamper with them or manipulate their genetic stock, leaving zebras to remain wild, nasty, animalistic.

Incidentally we have an answer to the ancient question of whether zebras are white with black stripes or black with white stripes. They're white with black stripes. That is the word from Bill Xanten of the Department of Mammals at the National Zoo in Washington. His proof is that, among zebras, the white stripes are uniformly white but the black stripes vary in inten-

246 ■ WHY THINGS ARE

sity from zebra to zebra, just as you'd expect from a pigment on a white background.

WHY ARE THERE SO MANY BIZARRE NAMES FOR A COLLECTION OF ANIMALS, SUCH AS A "PRIDE" OF LIONS AND A "POD" OF SEALS?

O ur favorite is "a parliament of owls," because you can imagine them in powdered wigs.

According to James Lipton, author of An Exaltation of Larks, the English nobility had nothing better to do in the fifteenth century than sit around and think up funny names for groups of animals. This was called the "venereal game," after the word venery, an archaic term for hunting. Terms became widely circulated by word of mouth, then established through the publication of "books of courtesy," which instructed a gentleman how to behave in proper society and, among other things, use the right name for a bunch of foxes ("skulk").

Many of the terms are conspicuously cute, like "a cowardice of curs," or "a murder of crows." Others sound cuter than they are meant to be: A "school of fish" is a corruption of "shoal of fish," which is an appropriate image.

Some others:

A hover of trout, a husk of hares, a labor of moles, an unkindness of ravens, a murmuration of starlings, a knot of toads, a gang of elk, a fall of woodcocks, a rafter of turkeys, a kindle of kittens, a pitying of turtledoves, a crash of rhinos, a congregation of plovers, a bevy of roebucks.

Now if only someone would tell us what plovers and roebucks are. (We will just assume a woodcock is a rooster that lives in the forest.)

WHY DO SOME FISH PREFER TO LIVE IN THE ABYSS OF THE OCEAN, FIVE OR SIX MILES BELOW THE SURFACE, RATHER THAN SOMEPLACE MORE PLEASANT?

The answer, of course, is that they don't find it unpleasant down there at all; they are perfectly adapted for the environment and would perish anywhere else. Darwinian mechanics dictate that environmental niches will always get filled. Since it's a low-energy environment, the fish (and eels and whatnot) move very slowly. They are like slugs; their bodies are soft and weak, scant of muscle. Even those frightening fish with oversized fanglike teeth that you may have seen in *National Geographic* do not use their cuspids to chomp on prey but, rather, to form a cage in which small fish become trapped.

One of the remarkable things about low-energy deepwater environments is that there is enough food to keep the food chain humming. Some marine biologists say there is enough bacteria even at the bottom of places like the Mariana Trench—seven miles deep—to supply the base of the food chain. But Dr. Dick Robins, marine biologist at the University of Miami, tells us that the key source of food is the flotsam and jetsam that rain down from the surface, where life is teeming. Dead fish sink. Scavengers await in the abyss. Think about this the next time you hear that we are dumping trash and radioactive waste into deep water. Good plot material here for a horror film.

WHY DO FISH HANG AROUND UNDER BRIDGES EVEN THOUGH THEY SEE THEIR FRIENDS GETTING YANKED OUT OF THE WATER WITH BARBED HOOKS IN THEIR LIPS?

Let's be brutally honest: Fish are not rocket scientists.

"They don't know they're being fished," says Dr. Arthur Myrberg, professor of marine science at the University of Miami.

Fish hang out at bridges because bridges provide good shade and darkness. A bridge has lots of plankton hanging off it, perfect for snacking. Also, bridges usually span the narrowest portion of a bay or river, so there is a good current of water, making it easier for fish to swill water through their gills.

When a fish sees another fish thrashing around wildly and then flying vertically out of the world, its pathetic little fish brain tells it that something dangerous may be happening, and it darts for cover. But after about thirty seconds it calms down and resumes its normal life, which is dedicated to mindless feeding and reproduction, sort of like the Why staff on a Friday night. A shark that has been hooked, reeled in, unhooked, and thrown back in the water may chomp down on a fishing line within a couple of hours. Fish are not totally lacking in memory, but they lack good judgment.

WHY IS CORAL OFFICIALLY CONSIDERED AN ANIMAL EVEN THOUGH IT OBVIOUSLY ISN'T?

What people don't realize about coral is that it's a nocturnal animal. So when you go snorkeling or scuba diving in the daytime, all you see is this hard, pitted, rocklike thing, or in the case of the soft corals, you see what appears to be a plant, with lots of branches and twiggy extensions. But if you dove at night, you'd see innumerable polyps erupting from the coral as they wake up and start eating. Wouldn't that be exciting!

WHY DON'T SHARKS CONSTANTLY FEAST ON HUMANS AT THE BEACH?

You would think they'd chow down like there's no tomorrow. Go to any major urban beach and the shallows will be filled with slow, helpless, meat-falling-off-the-bone humans. It looks like a shark picnic as far as the eye can see. So why don't they start gorging?

Sam Gruber, the legendary shark man of the University of Miami's Rosenstiel School of Marine and Atmospheric Science, gives a couple of reasons:

1. We're too big to swallow. "A human represents a big, unwieldy, unreasonable prey item, something they wouldn't even consider. Basically a shark swims up to the prey and sucks it in, doesn't even bite it."

2. Beachloads of humans are a new phenomenon and sharks haven't had a chance to adapt to eating us. The human population of earth was paltry until the last few hundred years, and there weren't enough swimmers to represent a major food source. Theoretically sharks could gradually learn to eat us, but we wouldn't stand for it. We'd stay on dry land or swim in lakes and rivers.

We should note, though, that even lakes and rivers aren't totally safe. Sharks live in landlocked Lake Nicaragua. Bull sharks have been found one thousand miles up the Orinoco River in South America. They swim way up the Mississippi. They eat human carcasses in the Ganges River. But don't worry; it probably won't happen to you.

Which is just what everyone thinks seconds before they are

turned to ground chuck in the maw of a Great White.

About twenty-five people die in shark attacks worldwide each year. That compares to about two thousand people being devoured by alligators and crocodiles. Fewer than half of shark attacks are spurred by hunger; the rest are just plain aggression—a very persuasive type of social message. The way scientists can determine whether the shark bit a person out of hunger or some other reason is quite brilliant: If the person loses a big chunk of flesh in the attack, or, say, a leg or two, then the shark was probably hungry. Science marches on.

WHY DOES A CAT PLAY WITH ITS PREY BEFORE KILLING IT?

Only domesticated, pampered cats do this. In the wild they don't fool around; they simply kill and eat. The hunting instincts of your average suburban cat are so rarely indulged that when the cat finally finds a little mouse or a bird, it can't stand to see the hunt end. The cat overreacts. It invents games, like Catch 'n' Release. Pin 'n' Hold. Swat 'n' Claw. Disfigure 'n' Disembowel. You know what we're talking about. There is one exception according to Desmond Morris in his book *Catwatching*: farm cats, who get plenty of chances to hunt, will play Catch 'n' Release, but only mothers. Mama cat takes the maimed mouse back to the litter and, as the little fur balls watch in admiration, shows them how to seize and kill live meat.

WHY ARE DOGS SO LOYAL?

Compared with cats, we mean. Even the diehard feline apologist has to admit that few cats can muster the kind of mindless, slobbering enthusiasm for their owners that seems to come naturally to dogs.

Both the dog's amiability and the cat's relative aloofness can be traced to a time before either species knew the sound of a can opener, as Desmond Morris has written in his fine volumes on both animals. In the wild, cats are solitary hunters who rely on stealth and speed to trap their prey. Wolves, however, are team players, and dogs are descended from wolves. They accept their master as the leader of the pack, but only if you get to the puppy prior to about the eighth week. Otherwise it'll always be wild and there's nothing you can do about it.

Why Do Lemmings Commit Suicide by Marching Into the Sea?

They don't. Lemming suicide is an old myth perpetuated by writers needing an analog for humankind's self-destructive tendency in the nuclear age. Also there's a big lie told by Disney, as we shall explain.

A lemming is a rodent that lives in the Arctic. It is cuddlier than your average rat. Downright cute.

Every four or five years there is a "lemming year" in which the creatures propagate so dramatically that they swarm the countryside by the hundreds of millions. In the lemming year of 1974 the normal lemming population of 22,000 in the district of Hardanger, Norway, swelled to 125 million. There are distasteful consequences to these population explosions. It is impossible to travel by car or train: The roads and rails are too slippery with squashed lemming viscera to permit traction.

With that many lemmings scuttling about, accidents happen, particularly along the steep fjords of Norway. They fall in the water—sometimes in batches. "When you have thousands and thousands of small animals running together, they just don't see the water or the cliff," zoologist and lemming expert Arne Semb-Johansson of Oslo University told the Reuters news agency in 1987.

Why does their population explode? In the Arctic, where the food chain is extremely simple, wild fluctuations in population are found in the few species that can actually survive in such a climate. Lemmings breed much more rapidly than any of their predators, such as weasels and foxes. They are baby factories. They hit puberty in about two weeks. The mating itself takes only a couple of seconds, but they do it repeatedly, many times in an hour, and twenty-one days later the female drops a litter. Within another couple of hours—hours!—she's ready to mate again. Soon the babies have babies. The numbers increase exponentially.

There's something in the grass that makes the critters libidinous, says University of Utah biologist Norman Negus. The chemical is 6-methoxybenzoxa zolinone, and it is found in new, green grass shoots. It jazzes up the endocrine system of the rodents.

Most people probably would not know about lemming suicide were it not for the 1958 Disney film *White Wilderness*. It shows lemmings hurling themselves off a cliff to their deaths. Great footage! But faked, apparently.

Negus says a friend of his, a biologist named Tom McHugh, was a photographer for the film and he admitted that the lemming scene was staged. The creatures were captured in northern Canada, shipped to a filming site far away, and herded off a cliff to their deaths, as the cameras rolled. Only later did McHugh learn that lemming suicide is a myth. He was dreadfully sorry for what he had done, Negus says.

The photographer is deceased, so we couldn't ask him directly if the story is true. We did check with the Disney film archives in Burbank. Tom McHugh is indeed listed as a photographer for *White Wilderness*. A publicity book for the movie states, "The dramatic pageant reveals the greatest mystery of the northland: the 'suicidal' migration of the lemming. Countless multitudes of the little furry creatures go headlong into the sea, over every obstacle, in a blind and pitiable frenzy induced by overcrowding."

And by documentary filmmakers.

WHY DON'T APES EVOLVE INTO HUMANS ANYMORE?

This is a distant cousin to the question, How come scientists can't find the missing link? There really isn't a missing link, as the "creature" is traditionally imagined. That's because apes did not evolve into humans. Humans and apes are genetically quite similar—in fact humans are genetically closer to the chimpanzee than the chimp is to the gorilla—but *we* did not come from *them*. Humans and apes evolved from a common apelike ancestor who lived about five million years ago or so.

Why don't we have any fossils of that original ancestor? The bones may have rotted on the jungle floor. The creature was akin to the pygmy chimpanzee and lived in the trees of the rain forest, an environment poorly suited to the fossilization of bones. The alkaline soils of central East Africa are much kinder, and so that's why we can find early ape-man bones.

The excellent fossil record that traces the rise of *Homo sapiens* makes the reluctance of so many people to accept evolution all the more bewildering. Millions of Americans think evolution is a Big Lie perpetrated by godless scientists. Perhaps this intransigence is forgivable: Evolution posits the nearly absurd notion that single-celled smudges of green slime gradually transformed themselves into large, complex creatures capable of playing rugby (and later, into human beings). But the validity of the theory has been proven beyond a doubt.

Even the Catholic church accepts evolution—and has since shortly after Darwin published *The Origin of Species* in 1859. The Church sees God as the moving force behind the process of evolution.

If evolution is true, then why is it called the "theory" of evolution? Because of habit. And because, more importantly, no one is sure precisely how evolution works. The theory is in constant revision.

High school textbooks have always described evolution as painfully slow, gradual, operating only in geological time scales. They taught us that evolution is progressive, that modern human beings are the final synthesis of eons of modification. You see the March of Human Progress illustrated again and again, from monkeyhood through the Neanderthal phase, until finally you end up with someone who looks like a TV anchorman, only he's naked.

All this is a gross distortion of what really goes on.

Creatures evolve the same way that character in *The Sun Also Rises* goes broke: gradually and then suddenly. Evolution is often quirky and sometimes ensures the survival not of the fittest but of the luckiest.

Humans are perhaps an unlikely species, but *intelligence* may be inevitable. Life-forms tend toward greater complexity, with few exceptions. But if that's true, then—finally, back to the question!—why don't apes evolve into humans anymore?

Why don't they get smart like us? Why don't they stop lolling around all day in the woods and learn to use rocks as tools, build simple clay pots, and eventually assemble vast planet-destroying nuclear arsenals that permit the signing of arms-control treaties?

Because they don't need to. They do just fine as apes. They have virtually no natural predators. Food is plentiful. They can hang out. There's no impetus to mutate into a creature who goes to discos.

Apes have evolved only slightly compared with man's rapid transformation. If anything, they have become better apes, with longer limbs for climbing.

Humans evolved because millions of years ago much of the rain forests of East Africa dried up. Surrounded by a radically altered environment, tree-dwelling apes faced a dilemma: adapt or die. Many died. The survivors employed two strategies for survival. *Australopithecus* developed huge jaw muscles that allowed him to chew anything he found (grass, leaves, a tire tread by the side of the road, and so on). *Homo erectus* developed stone tools that allowed him to cut into carcasses and eat meat. Meat is a much better source of protein than tree leaves, so the hardy, technological *Homo erectus* thrived while the *Australopithecus* died out (there may have been some homicides in there). The genes encoding intelligence were able to survive better than those encoding big jaw muscles.

What would happen if all the humans on earth were systematically killed? Would apes eventually evolve into humans?

Maybe. Evolution is convergent in many ways—humans and octopi have similar eyeballs, even though we're only distantly related. But evolution is opportunistic, and another version of *Homo sapiens* might never come along. Humanlike creatures never came close to evolving in the New World, which had innumerable varieties of species and climatic conditions that might conceivably have spawned intelligent bipedal primates.

If we all died, a new, highly intelligent, technological species might not even emerge from the ape family. Dolphins and whales already possess great intelligence. Something could emerge from the cat family. Or possibly, because they have such nimble hands, raccoons, squirrels, or rats could evolve into the Masters of the World. There could even be a struggle for domination between the Squirrel People and the Ratmen. This is the honest truth.

We asked Ashley Montagu, the venerable anthropologist, if he thought apes might ever evolve into humanlike creatures. He did not hesitate: 'I think they have enough sense, to take a look at human beings . . . and say 'no thank you, we don't want to be like them.' "

|MAGES

(In which we try to show why fiction is sometimes the highest form of truth.)

WHY DO VILLAINS, AFTER THEY CAPTURE THE HERO, THINK OF SOME ELABORATE AND CHANCY MEANS OF SLOWLY KILLING HIM RATHER THAN JUST DISPATCHING HIM WITH A BULLET TO THE BACK OF THE HEAD?

There are the obvious answers, and then there are the deep and obscure ones. Clearly James Bond and Captain Kirk owe their lives to the innumerable foolhardy death rituals concocted by their sadistic foes. The Obligatory Elaborate Death is always preceded by the Obligatory Spilling of the Beans, also known as the Recognition Scene, where the villain explains his diabolical plot to rule the world, a moment of braggadocio that will lead to his downfall once the hero escapes.

Just the other day we caught Captain Kirk trying to connive his way out of certain death by appealing to an evil alien despot's instinct for elaborate homicide. Kirk said disingenuously, "Where's the sport in a simple hanging? The terror, the intrigue, the *fun*?"

The evil alien despot, seeing the logic of this, decided that he would conduct a "royal hunt," in which Kirk would be tracked and killed like a wild animal. "Again?" is what we were praying Kirk would say, but instead he went through the motions and eventually the evil alien despot saw his vile ambitions

257

shattered and the *Enterprise* continued on its poorly defined and no doubt federal-budget-breaking mission.

In addition to the Obligatory Elaborate Death, the Bond and *Star Trek* series also invariably feature a minor character (typically another 00 agent or a crewman aboard the *Enterprise*) whose life expectancy can be measured with a stopwatch. Let's say Kirk and Spock beam down to a planet of violent man-eating plants, taking with them an obscure crewman. You know instantly: He's meat. His chances of surviving the next sixty seconds are exactly zero. This is the phenomenon of the Obligatory Sacrificial Lamb.

We know why movies and TV shows and books and comics do this: It's more dramatic. But within the context of the story, why are the villains so obsessed with elaborate death?

We found our villain expert in the person of James Combs, who teaches a course in politics and popular culture at Valparaiso University in Indiana. He explains villainy not in terms of pure evil or sadism or drama-lust, but as a rejection of Western values of individual liberty. The point of the Obligatory Elaborate Death is not to kill or even physically torture the hero but to rob him of his freedom, of his right to control his own life.

"Villains want to subjugate and control people, while heroes want to liberate and free people," Combs says.

As long as there is totalitarianism in this world, there will be villains who want to kill their victims slowly.

WHY DO PEOPLE LIKE PROFESSIONAL WRESTLING SO MUCH EVEN THOUGH IT'S OBVIOUSLY FAKE?

People aren't as gullible as you think. Perverse, yes. Willing to abandon their last vestige of dignity and cheer large sweating men in underwear engaged in a lurid quasi-sodomitic ritual, yes. Gullible, no. Wrestling fans know it's fake.

They just pretend it's real. The fans are acting, same as the wrestlers. It is their job, for example, to taunt Brutus Beefcake and prevent him from noticing that Tito (the Burrito) Santana has suddenly recovered consciousness and is about to take the Link's head to the canvas in a crushing scissors-hold.

This is participatory theater at its best. If the fans didn't show up, or if the TV cameras didn't work, the match would be canceled.

So why do people enjoy this nonsense? According to *Business Week*, four million people regularly attend wrestling matches, and four of the top ten cable TV programs in 1988 were wrestling shows. What's the appeal? The answer must be that the wrestling match is an allegory for the larger society, for life itself.

Yes, it's that heavy. Think for a moment: There is always a clean, polite, neatly groomed Good wrestler who plays by the rules, and an Evil wrestler, usually dressed in black or wearing some kind of hideous mask, who employs illegal holds, backbreaker knee-drops, and "foreign objects" that are readily apparent to the crowd and to the appalled TV announcer but that somehow escape the notice of the beleaguered, hapless referee. Bad guys tend to have heavy Russian or Slavic characteristics, like Nikolai Volkoffs; one is a supposed South African named Colonel De Beers; another is a faux Iranian named the Iron Sheik.

"It presents a very clear-cut ethical system, what's good and what's not. You don't have to think about it," says William Coleman, a theater professor at Mount Union College in Alliance, Ohio, who has written about this purported sport. In a 1984 article for the journal *Etc.*, he wrote, "All of this might be interpreted as a reaction to a world (from the fans' vantage points) where individuals are powerless, where justice is not administered fairly, and where the good guys and bad guys are not known for certain."

In wrestling there is no such ambiguity: Good always triumphs over Evil. Whenever Evil does manage to win (for instance by banging a chair over the good guy's head when the referee isn't looking), it is merely the penultimate act in the drama, setting up the revenge of Good.

The referee represents, perhaps, the legal system and the civil government, which people think of as witless, inept, and fundamentally unfair. The announcer is akin to the press—deluded, imperceptive. Only through the spunk of the individual can justice be meted out.

That said, the traditional Good-Evil wrestling has given way in the late eighties to a hybrid form of wrestling that more consciously aspires to comic absurdity amid a rock 'n' roll MTV atmosphere. Wrestling promoters have tried to grab a more upscale crowd, and that requires using celebrities like Mr. T and rock stars like Cyndi Lauper, who, in the eyes of the serious wrestling purist, mock the sport.

Bedrock wrestling fans are not likely to admit to subtler sociological or psychological motivations. They are more apt to say they like the violence, the celebration of brute force, the physical intensity of Kamala the Ugandan Giant or the hirsute Missing Link. If challenged on the authenticity of the fights by sneering outsiders, they'll often deny it's faked. That people would invent these false gladiator duels is a sign of both the untapped reservoir of hostility in society and the desire to create a system of beliefs that is bizarre enough to allow exclusive membership.

WHY DO WE DECEIVE OUR CHILDREN EACH CHRISTMAS ABOUT SANTA CLAUS?

There are five reasons.

One: Because as parents we enjoy the ruse as much as our children do. In a world of doubt and pain and well-founded cynicism we can, for a moment, vicariously experience the rapture of believing that somewhere there is a being who cares for us so much and so selflessly that he will personally deliver sacks of gifts to our home on Christmas Eve, asking nothing in return but that we be good.

Two: Because we fear our own mortality and thus do not want our children to grow up too rapidly. We want to keep them in an innocent state of Santa-belief. So obvious is our desire that often our kids will pretend to still believe in order that they not disappoint us.

Three: Because as parents we have a hard enough time getting kids to behave properly and therefore employ Santa, an omniscient and personable God-like figure, as an extension of our authority.

Four: Because we intuitively understand what has been verified by *Hippocrates* magazine in a poll of two hundred child psychiatrists, and also supported by academic research at the University of Texas, the University of Chicago, and Cornell: It is good for young children to believe the world is filled with fantastic, benign, caring beings; that parents are not taking advantage of the child's gullibility as long as we do not lie outright when questioned directly; that the discovery of the Santa Claus deception is actually a positive revelation for about two in three children, who can feel pride in their acquired wisdom and can bond with their parents when upholding the myth for younger siblings.

Five: Because through ritual and tradition we try to transcend our temporal limits, straining to connect with past generations (in this case all the way back to the fourth century, when a bishop named Nicholas in the town of Myra in Asia Minor purportedly saved three impoverished girls from a life of prostitution by anonymously throwing purses of gold coins through the open window of their house) and to generations future. Though our own time is short, we can collectively breathe eternal life into our surrogate, Santa Claus, who will nobly represent our culture, carry on our good works, and offer comfort and the possibility of miracles to the little children who must inherit the earth.

WHY WOULD ANYBODY PAY $40 MILLION-PLUS FOR A SINGLE PAINTING BY PICASSO OR VAN GOGH?

People will pay huge sums for paintings because there are other people bidding in the same price range, creating a "market." Van Gogh's *Irises* is "worth" $53.9 million only because that's what someone paid for it. Similarly if people were to pay tens of millions of dollars for a single head of cabbage, then *cabbage* would be "worth" tens of millions of dollars a head. The Japanese corporation that bought Van Gogh's *Sunflowers* for $40 million had to *compete* for it against other high rollers. The Old Masters are now like any other financial instrument, worth no more nor less than whatever someone will pay for them. Paintings are commodities.

The rich got very much richer in the eighties, and they are now nervous about holding on to paper money. Richard Feigen, the New York art dealer, said to us, "Why is a painting not worth forty million pieces of green paper? The green paper is worth fifty cents in the paper market." And certainly a Picasso is more fun than a debenture.

Admittedly the market-value analysis isn't satisfactory by itself. Something peculiar underlies the art craze. We have detected several potential X-factors:

1. The new godzillionaires don't have a lot of what used to be called breeding. They realize that art is the new secular religion and they, too, want to be blessed. Relatively few great artworks ever hit the market, and when they do, there is a mad scramble. Van Gogh's *Irises* was bought by too-rich-to-think conglomerateur Alan Bond, who supposedly once asked a friend, "This Picasso, now, is he worth having?"

2. Buyers like Bond employ the eighties trick of heavy borrowing. A bank loaned Bond half the $53.9 million for the painting, and the auction house, Sotheby's, put up the rest. Obviously Sotheby's has a vested interest in getting billionaires to jack up the art market.

3. Auctions are the discos of the eighties. Studio 54 and Xenon have been replaced by Sotheby's and Christie's, where people dress up and make a display of their absurd wealth. In the frenzy of the moment they outbid one another in increments of a million dollars. This is the mating cry of the very rich.

Still, you have to wonder why the market doesn't collapse, why the collective consciousness doesn't wake up one day realizing that a head of cabbage is really only worth thirty-five cents. The market did decline slightly in 1990 but is still outrageous. One fantasizes that these rich investors will end up on the sidewalk outside the Whitney, offering to trade their original Van Goghs for someone's watch. (In the fantasy the someone in question refuses to trade because the paintings are, he says, "too blurry.")

Art appears to be a sounder investment for the nineties than stocks—baffling, given that with a stock you at least get a chunk of real capital, a piece of the company, dibs on the inventory, the steel and mortar of the headquarters. With art you get nothing but an image.

But perhaps that is the answer to this mystery. Art is so ethereal, so vague, it cannot be undermined by financial analysis. The stock market, on the other hand, is tethered to the value of the companies that issue stock. You can do a little math and tell if the stock market is overvalued. For example when the stock market peaked in the summer of 1987, just before the October crash, the combined value of all stocks was absurdly higher than the combined assets and income of all the companies selling stock.

The art market, however, operates entirely on subjective values, free from the constraints of objective accounting and quarterly earnings reports. The foundation of the market is something vague called Art History—that and vanity.

For the rest of us who still think an art purchase means buying a Rolling Stones poster, there is the solace of knowing that your average rich owner of a pricey Picasso is no doubt secretly disappointed by the painting. In the frenzy of the auction house he never realized that there was something about the painting that was dreadfully wrong. The woman's eyeball . . . *it's on the wrong side of her head.*

WHY ARE MODERN ARTISTS LIKE PICASSO CONSIDERED SO GOOD EVEN THOUGH THEIR STUFF IS UGLY AND UNREALISTIC AND LOOKS LIKE A CHILD DID IT?

Picasso and his ilk helped liberate art from the tyranny of "single perspective." Painters had always depicted things the way they supposedly looked, but in truth this was an abstraction and distortion of reality, because it turned the viewer into a remote, stationary, singular eyeball.

In real life we regard objects from multiple perspectives in multiple time frames; instead of being passive observers we interact with what we see, we change and destroy. Picasso, trained in the classical style (yes, you dumb goobers, he could paint a horse that looked like a horse), was one of the first artists to say we need not paint things even remotely as they appear to be, that we need only relay their hidden essences.

WHY IS CONTEMPORARY ART NOW CALLED POSTMODERN?

You can't help but feel old and crotchety when you see a book with a title like A *History of Postmodern Architecture*. That's an actual book. The modern era? Over. Even postmodernism already has a "history."

Of course *modern* still has the generic meaning of "recent," of "hap'nin' right now." Modern art and architecture are usually considered synonymous with twentieth-century art and architecture, but that's a fairly arbitrary cutoff point. People have used the term *modern* to refer to their own period ever since the Renaissance. Among academics, "modern history" still refers to the period since A.D. 1500.

Semantics aside, there has been a distinct change in art and architecture that signals the demise of what we all consider modernism. Modernism was infested with The Theory: The past was execrable, the domain of ignorance and despots, and had to be rejected.

Ornamental architecture, for example, was deemed to be bourgeois, undemocratic. Begone, Corinthian columns! Buildings were of steel and glass, endlessly repeated units and pods that revealed their function and internal structure in order to better reflect the prospect of a new egalitarian world. Painting abandoned the pretense of trying to accurately reproduce the real world. Artists concentrated on the media themselves: the paint, the colors, the shapes, until finally you had Jackson Pollock just hurling the stuff onto a giant canvas.

Modernism officially ended (a few experts somehow decided) at 3:32 P.M. on July 15, 1972, when dynamite mercifully brought down the highly modern, nearly windowless Pruitt-Igoe housing project in St. Louis. It was hideous. That was one of the trademarks of modernism: At a cocktail party, buzzing on a little white wine, it was easy to be seduced by The Theory, but in the harsh light of a coyote morning you'd chew your arm off to get out of bed without waking it.

In contrast postmodern art and architecture is a Romper Room of giddy excess, nostalgia, melodrama, camp—all the things that weren't allowed before. No longer is the past or popular culture rejected: Postmodernism takes inspiration from the Jetsons and Caesars Palace, as well as from the Parthenon. Let's put some really cool Greek temple ruins in the middle of the new civic center! Let's stick rhinestones on a piano and call it art! That's postmodernism.

WHY IS THE MONA LISA CONSIDERED THE WORLD'S GREATEST PAINTING EVEN THOUGH THERE'S NOT MUCH TO IT?

What makes the Mona Lisa the world's finest example of human artistic aspirations is that, no matter where you are in the room, her eyes follow you.

Simple! Now we can go to the next item!

Except that the roving-eyes phenomenon, long associated with the Mona Lisa, is a commonplace optical illusion found in innumerable paintings and photographs. So, get that out of your head. If you need one decent cocktail-party remark, use the Italian name of the painting, and say, "Maybe if someone had the nerve to clean La Gioconda, she wouldn't look so blue, so horribly submarine. But of course the last time they cleaned her, they took off the eyebrows."

It's true. No eyebrows anymore. Freakish.

Art historians cringe when asked why Mona Lisa is the greatest painting on earth. They hate to rank things like that; such questions strike them as horribly lowbrow. Nonetheless we'll plunge forward and tell you a few reasons why the Mona Lisa is not just hype, but is a genuine masterpiece among masterpieces:

1. The artist. Leonardo da Vinci (1452–1519), had so awesome a range of talents that anything he touched is virtually

priceless. His sketches and drawings are themselves master-pieces. He was a painter, architect, engineer, cartographer, botanist, geologist, zoologist, musician, and physiologist. Perhaps no one else has ever had such a mind. And only seventeen of his paintings survive.

2. The rendering of Mona Lisa, the verisimilitude, surpassed anything else in its day. Leonardo studied human anatomy like no other artist. He perfected a technique he called *sfumato*, in which the tones are smoothly blended, light gracefully becomes shadow, the outlines are soft. Mona is a triumph of naturalism at a time when other art remained flat, painterly, two-dimensional. "The nose, with its beautiful nostrils, rosy and tender, seemed to be alive. The opening of the mouth, united by the red of the lips to the flesh tones of the face, seemed not to be colored but to be living flesh," artist Giorgio Vasari wrote in the mid-1500s, when the painting was still brightly colored and clean.

3. There is a psychological mystery to the painting that engages the viewer centuries later and demands interpretation. Leonardo no doubt intended to create a timeless work. The woman with the enigmatic smile is of obscure identity. She's a work of invention, of fiction, at a time when artists and writers were expected to stick to standard religious and historical narratives. What is she thinking? Art historian Walter Pater marveled at the "beauty wrought out from within upon the flesh, the deposit, little cell by little cell, of strange thoughts and fantastic reveries and exquisite passions." Kenneth Clark later wrote, "The Mona Lisa's smile is the supreme example of that complex inner life, caught and fixed in durable material, which Leonardo in all his notes on the subject claims as one of the chief aims of art."

You might argue that these are merely historical virtues, that the Mona Lisa is simply outdated. But a work of art cannot be separated from its place in history; there is no objective instrument that can register the absolute quality of art. There have been plenty of adept forgers who have produced convincing replicas of the Mona Lisa. Are they as talented as Leonardo? Of course not. Nor are the smattering of painters who have painted derivative works in the style of the High Renaissance. Without the genius of imagination, a painting is just a craft work.

That said, the Mona Lisa would probably not be the world's most famous painting were it not for some self-sustaining hype. Napoleon kept it in his bedroom. It was stolen from the Louvre in 1911 and presumed disappeared forever before the thief turned it over in 1913. It was kept in a cave during the Second World War. It is easily parodied. Its celebrity is so distracting that for a lot of people it is just an icon, a symbol, and has no more artistic impact than the picture of George Washington on a dollar bill.

The painting is probably not Leonardo's greatest work. To judge from the literature, that spot is reserved for *The Last Supper*. Brilliant in both design and emotion, the mural captures in freeze frame the complex psychological reactions of the disciples to the announcement by Jesus that one of them will betray him that night.

Unfortunately Leonardo painted on a slightly damp wall, using an experimental technique, and the mural disintegrated during his own lifetime. What we know as *The Last Supper* is the work of subsequent lesser artists, who painted over the original. A "restoration" has been under way for many years, to strip off the non-Leonardo paint. The art historians are in a purist mode. The problem is, so far the restored *Last Supper* looks like someone splashed acid over it. Leonardo would be appalled.

At this writing they have yet to restore Jesus; whether he keeps his eyebrows is anyone's guess.

WHY AREN'T SATURDAY MORNING CARTOONS AS GOOD AS THEY USED TO BE?

The old cartoons were never intended for television. They were short, animated films, destined for theaters, so they had relatively high budgets considering their length—a mere six minutes.

Bugs Bunny was invented in the late thirties as a preview for movies in the theater. Bugs didn't make it to TV until 1957. About that time the demand for new cartoons dried up when theater owners started to realize that the public would pay to see a movie even without a cartoon at the start. In 1963 Warner Bros. closed down its animation department and fired everyone on the staff. That the old episodes still play on TV is a testament to their timeless quality.

Chuck Jones, an early animator of Bugs Bunny and the inventor of Road Runner, told us by telephone that a typical Bugs Bunny cartoon would have from twelve to fifteen different drawings per second (there are twenty-four frames per second in film). For a six-minute episode that meant upward of five thousand drawings. But a Transformers-style cartoon today may have only three or four drawings per second, and the characters never do anything subtle like recede into the distance. Often only the jaw moves.

"I call it illustrated radio," Jones said. "They start out with a soundtrack and then put as few drawings to it as they can get away with. The soundtrack is so explicit that you can turn the picture off and still tell what's happening."

In his day he said, "Our characters acted. They were defined by the way they acted, just like any other actor."

Obviously full animation costs big money—about $100,000 a minute for Disney quality—and no one is going to sink that into a Saturday-morning cartoon. But even a relatively low-budget made-for-TV cartoon like Johnny Quest in the late sixties was at least well drawn, if poorly animated. And one of the most poorly animated shows was also one of the best: Bullwinkle. It was funny, erudite, goofy.

Cartoons today have become advertisements for products—Transformers, G.I. Joe, Rambo, Smurfs, Care Bears. They all have their own shows. The toy companies pay for the programs and order scripts with specific instructions to highlight the latest Action Figure or Maiming Device that coincidentally is about to arrive at Toys "R" Us.

Incidentally a lot of people keep asking us, "Why do Mickey Mouse and all other animated characters have only four fingers?" We got the answer from animator Frank Gladstone: "The hand is easier to animate when you only have four fingers."

WHY DOESN'T LOIS LANE EVER REALIZE THAT CLARK KENT AND SUPERMAN ARE THE SAME PERSON, CONSIDERING THAT THEY'RE ALWAYS IN THE SAME GENERAL AREA BUT ARE NEVER SEEN TOGETHER, AND THE "DISGUISE" IS JUST A PAIR OF EYEGLASSES?

In the comic book the closest that Lois has ever gotten to the secret was when she dragged Clark to a Superman cartoon playing at a movie house in Metropolis. Clark was freaking, because he knew that every Superman cartoon showed him, Clark, stepping into phone booths and popping out as the Man of Steel. So, during the crucial moments of the cartoon he distracted Lois by coughing and kicking her purse. Whew!

In the movie *Superman* II Lois did learn that Clark and Superman are the same, but Superman later zapped her brain with a dose of amnesia (the all-purpose disease for comic book writers) and she went back to being a dupe. Why is she so dumb? Do the glasses really fool her? Or is it that inevitable lock of hair that drops down onto Clark's forehead the moment he bursts out of the phone booth?

The disguise, we learned, has two extra dimensions.

First, Clark and Superman have different voices. Starting with the first radio broadcasts in the early forties, Clark had a wimpy tenor. "This is a job . . ." he would start to say, then his voice would drop several octaves to baritone level, "FOR SUPERMAN." Second, in the comic books Clark has facial characteristics that are markedly different from Superman's. Clark's jawline is softer. Curt Swan, who drew Superman for nearly thirty years, intentionally made Clark appear less angular than Superman. "I wanted him to appear more meek. Just sort of a good Joe," Swan has written. Do the extraordinary powers of the son of Jor-El include the ability to alter facial morphology? This would seem the best explanation, except that no one connected with the Superman character has ever offered it.

A more puzzling question is, **Which of Clark/Superman's voices is the real one?** And which face? Perhaps even he doesn't know. The Kryptonian-American, like many hyphenated citizens, feels torn apart by conflicting existences—he is both a cringing, sexually inert, white-bread newsman and a costumed, cosmos-traveling superhero. Both identities are, in essence, an act, which is why Superman must retire so often to his Fortress of Solitude. Lois remains unable to discern the real man because there is not one there.

WHY DOES NO ONE EVER REMEMBER WHO DIRECTED THE MOVIES *THE WIZARD OF OZ* AND *GONE WITH THE WIND*?

ight up front we want to say that we're still peeved that W. C. Fields turned down the role of the Wizard.

As for our question: Most movie aficionados know who directed such American classics as *Citizen Kane*, *It's a Wonderful Life*, *Psycho*, *Dr. Strangelove*, and *The Godfather*. *Casablanca* is a bit trickier. But nobody, absolutely nobody (we've checked), remembers who directed *The Wizard of Oz* and *Gone With the Wind*.

The incredible thing is, it was the same man. He also directed *Captains Courageous*, *Dr. Jekyll and Mr. Hyde*, *Treasure Island*, and other fine films. Nobody remembers him.

He even won an academy award for Best Director for *Gone With the Wind*, yet everyone thinks of that as David O. Selznick's picture, because Selznick was the producer and put his name in big letters on the marquee.

The reason we don't remember his name—we'll provide it eventually—is because he wasn't an "auteur," as a film critic would put it. Since the early 1960s it has been fashionable to think of the director as the author of the movie. This is a simple enough idea when you look at the films of such people as Frank Capra, Alfred Hitchcock, Woody Allen, or Martin Scorsese, because they have an identifiable touch and usually work on their own scripts. But the man who directed *The Wizard of Oz* and *Gone With the Wind* in the same year was just a technician, a craftsman in the service of the real auteur—the Metro-Goldwyn-Mayer studio.

In a recent issue of *Premiere* magazine, *E.T.* director Stephen Spielberg says that the director of Oz, along with fellow human trivia-answer Michael Curtiz (*Casablanca*), were "the unsung heroes and the workhorses of the '30s and '40s. They were upstaged by great filmmakers like Hitchcock and Capra and Sturges, who had their own personal signatures. These directors didn't have signatures; they were chameleons. They could adapt to any story, in any period, with any premise."

Which, you could argue, is not necessarily a good thing. In fact that sounds a lot like a description of a hired gun, a mercenary, a cinematic soldier of fortune. A work of art demands a guiding moral, intellectual, and aesthetic vision. Perhaps it is somewhat egomaniacal to insist that a movie bear one's personal signature. The Europeans, imprisoned by their intellectual conceits, have always had a secret fondness for the old-fashioned American studio films, with their unshamed artlessness. American films were sentimental, grand, and crafty in the sense of technical proficiency.

Oz was just one of forty-one films spewed out by MGM in 1939; their goal was to make a movie a week. Oz, according to Aljean Harmetz in *The Making of the Wizard of Oz*, was intended as a prestige picture, a money loser that would maintain the studio's status as the Tiffany of the industry. But no one figured they were making an American classic.

The $2.8 million movie lost money. Most critics dismissed it.

"I sat cringing before MGM's Technicolor production of *The Wizard of Oz*, which displays no trace of imagination, good taste, or ingenuity," critic Russel Maloney wrote in *The New Yorker*.

Only after its 1956 debut on television, the first of what would become a record thirty-one broadcasts as of 1989, did the movie catch on. How come?

"It looks a little better on television than it does on the big screen," explains Andrew Sarris, former film critic for the *Village Voice*. "On the big screen it looks a little fake and stylish and Broadwayish."

It must be more than that. The movie taps into the soul of every child, and it is probably not so much because of the obvious intended message—"There's no place like home"—as it is because of the witch. Margaret Hamilton, though on the screen for a total of only twelve minutes, represents every child's fear of the dark side of Mother. There is that one unbelievably scary moment when Dorothy, trapped in the witch's castle, looks in a crystal ball and sees Auntie Em calling her name in distress—only to transform into the visage of the cackling witch. Good Mom, Bad Mom. For a second there they are fused. Gosh, that gives us chills even now!

Oh, yeah. Victor Fleming.

Why Is That Giant Fetus Hovering Over the Earth at the End of 2001: A Space Odyssey?

The movie was made in 1968. Our wild guess: The filmmakers may have been experimenting with controlled substances. Not that we'd want to defend this statement in court! Just a hunch.

The Star-Child, as coscreenwriter Arthur C. Clarke called it, is obviously the reincarnation of astronaut David Bowman, who had undergone a rough time of it lately, including getting sucked into space and transported at superluminal speed through a Stargate, ending up in a very clean, empty hotel, where he suddenly got old.

Bowman is last seen reaching out to touch the mysterious rectangular black monolith that keeps popping up in the film and that, a few million years earlier, had inspired apes to use tools and whack their rivals to death. Bowman and the monolith merge in a flash of light, and suddenly the fetus is there, with wide-open eyes.

So that's the easy answer: The fetus is Bowman, evolved to another level.

But what does that mean? Why is it floating above the earth? What's it doing up there?

We should note that Clarke and director Stanley Kubrick were making things up as they went along. For the last two decades Kubrick, the genius behind the movie, has been resolutely silent on his intended meaning, preferring enigma; Clarke has spoken through a novelization of the movie. In the novel the Star-Child sets off global panic as he circles the earth, from a thousand miles below. Apparently the earthlings have noticed the babe up in the heavens. "The alarms would be flashing across the radar screens, the great tracking telescopes would be searching the skies—and history as men knew it would be drawing to a close." The Star-Child somehow wills the detonation of the nuclear bombs floating around the earth's atmosphere. This is your basic apocalyptic sci-fi ending. Kubrick, however, couldn't use the holocaust ending in the film, because it would have been too much like his movie *Dr. Strangelove*.

The significance of the Star-Child is that he is the next level of humankind. In many of Kubrick's films, mankind is a repellent, murderous, ill-fated, technology-imprisoned species. Knowledge is sinister. Our tools are more advanced than our souls. The 2001 astronauts are dull, bored people, confined to their life-sustaining, life-benumbing machines. Death comes instantly, silently, with exposure to space. The only truly human, spiritual death in the movie comes when Bowman slowly shuts down the homicidal computer HAL 9000.

Here is where the Star-Child enters: It is able to survive in space without the protection of technology. It is beyond human. It is . . . the Superman.

Miami University of Ohio English professor Richard Erlich, a sci-fi expert, notes that the dramatic soundtrack music is Richard Strauss's tone poem *Also Sprach Zarathustra*, named after the book by Friederich Nietzsche, who postulated the rise of the superman, creator of a new heroic morality. The Star-Child is Nietzsche's Superman. (Though the baby is not as powerful as the creators of the monolith, who are perhaps several stages yet more advanced.)

What is that dang monolith, anyway? A teaching device. Maybe an angel. Legend says that when the film came out in San Francisco, one man in the audience was so overcome by the monolith he ran into the screen shouting "It's God! It's God!" Behind the screen was a brick wall.

WHY ARE SOME ADVERTISEMENTS SO OBSCURE AND AVANT-GARDE THAT YOU CAN'T FIGURE OUT WHAT'S BEING SOLD?

If you see an advertisement and you don't understand it, you should immediately realize that the ad is not directed at you. They don't want to sell *you* anything. You're not cool enough to be in the target audience. The point is to build an image for the product among people who, due to their innate hipness, "get" the ad. One Miami ad person told us, "The people who are going to buy it already know what it is, so all you're trying to do is establish an image."

The most obvious example is perfume ads. What can you say about perfume? What ad copy could you write? Not anything worth much. Thus the ad shows naked people writhing around in the sensational attitudes of ecstasy, usually in numbers not divisible by 2. Get it?

Now even car ads have succumbed to the avante-garde. They no longer show the car! Take this new car Infiniti. The first ads showed pictures of nature—swirling water at the beach, for instance. No chrome in sight. Madison Avenue has taken no-words ads a step farther—now you don't even get to see the product.

Kenneth Cole shoes are another example. In the ads there are no shoes. Instead there are political statements. We talked to Richard Kirshenbaum, of Kirshenbaum and Bond, which produces the Kenneth Cole ads, and he said, "It's a good way to appeal to a very trendy market." He wants Kenneth Cole shoes to be perceived as politically correct. Woe to the hapless sole—er, soul—who would be caught in a pair of wrong-headed shoes. Friends would sneer: "You fascist."

As for other obscure ads, Kirshenbaum says, "You don't have to understand the ad, you just have to know it's cool."

That there is perhaps the slightest, weensiest overemphasis on style in the advertising industry may have something to do with the personnel: The business is full of frustrated writers and artists. They want to *express* themselves. They are literally called creatives, as in, "Let's let the creatives handle this." True success for the creatives would require that they get out of the ad business altogether and write a great novel or paint a great painting or shoot a great photograph, at which point they would no longer be a creative—they'd be "talent."

But in the meantime how can a young, creative person send a neat message? "How about we show half a dozen stark-naked men and women slouching on the roof of a tall building, looking utterly bored." This really happened. It was an ad for perfume.

Or maybe a car.

THE STORE

(Fruitcakes. Coke. Beer. French fries. A quick glance at the world of products, in which we figure out why Super Glue doesn't stick to the inside of the tube.)

WHY DO PEOPLE GIVE FRUITCAKES FOR CHRISTMAS EVEN THOUGH EVERYONE HATES FRUITCAKE?

According to USA *Today*—yes, our research department is on vacation—a MasterCard survey showed that three-fourths of those polled listed fruitcake as the present they dislike the most. An American Express survey had similar results. Yet people keep on giving fruitcake, causing our funny friend Dave Barry to theorize that there is actually only one fruitcake in the world, constantly circulating.

We called the Claxton Bakery in Claxton, Georgia, the world's fruitcake capital.

"The surveys are incorrect. My dad's been in the business over fifty years, and he's made over 160 million pounds," said the bakery scion and co-owner, Mid Parker. If you lined up that many fruitcakes, he said, "They'd stretch almost all the way around the equator."

Parker's theory is that people really do like fruitcake and that fruitcake-bashing is a new thing. "I never heard any negative publicity about fruitcake until a couple of years ago. Johnny Carson [who stole the joke from Dave Barry] made some negative jokes about fruitcake on his show."

279

So, who are his customers? It turns out that Claxton Bakery sells mostly to Civitan clubs, who sell the fruitcakes to raise money for community-service projects, such as helping the mentally retarded. No doubt that's how so many get into circulation: People want to be charitable, so they buy the cakes, and soon the country is flooded with hard, impermeable loaves of sucrose-saturated matter impregnated by nuts and orange peel and frighteningly dyed green and red lumps of pineapple. (Such nuggets may hint at the relationship between fruitcake and Christmas: Fruitcake is similar to the age-old mince pie, which supposedly was baked in the shape of a manger—nice trick!—and filled with spices that symbolized the gifts of the Magi. Nowadays, of course, it's hard to find a Magus, much less frankincense and myrrh, so we settle for dyed pineapple bits.)

Why do the Civitan clubs sell fruitcake, instead of chocolate cheesecake or oatmeal cookies or whatnot? According to Civitan International's Dorothy Wellborn, editor of the *Civitan* magazine, the fruitcake campaign began in the fifties when a Civitan member from the Tampa area, Earl "Catfish" Carver, visited the Claxton Bakery and liked the fruitcake so much he took a couple hundred pounds of it back home. At regional meetings, he suggested that fruitcake be sold at fundraisers. Fruitcake went national.

Why did he like fruitcake so much? Possibly because Claxton makes a fine fruitcake, reputably the best, but there is also the significant fact that fruitcake is the Samsonite luggage of foodstuffs. It is indestructible. It can weather intense fund-raising. The shelf life of a Claxton fruitcake is 120 to 150 days. In the refrigerator "it's indefinite," says baker and co-owner W. Dale Parker. "It lives right on."

Just like, for example, plutonium.

WHY DID THE COCA-COLA COMPANY CHANGE THE FORMULA OF COKE?

In a frenzy of greed they forgot that in the soda business taste doesn't matter. What's important is style, not substance.

See, they really *did* make Coke better, according to every taste test. To this day blindfolded people, including those who swear by Old Coke, prefer the taste of New Coke to the classic concoction. And yet New Coke dwindled to 1.7 percent of the market within two years of its introduction, with Classic bolting up to 19.8. The lesson here is one that the Coke executives should have already known: The soda pop industry is constructed entirely on image.

Pepsi didn't start to challenge Coke for soda pop supremacy until the sixties, when it began the feel-good, informationless "Pepsi Generation" advertising campaign, showing young people cavorting and frolicking and exulting with all that excess animal vigor that comes from too much sugar and caffeine. Coke later answered with the "Coke is It!" campaign, though we wonder if that wasn't actually just a bit *too* vague. By 1980 Pepsi had nearly caught up to Coke; taste tests showed people preferred the sweeter Pepsi. So the Coke execs decided to change the formula to make it more Pepsi-like, sweeter and smoother, without Old Coke's bite. (We have always thought that the Coca-Cola Company secretly fantasized about making Coke more like Gatorade, something you could chug in huge bottles, but there's no documentary evidence of that.) New Coke, though rejected by consumers, got the Americana reactionaries into such an uproar that Classic Coke surpassed Pepsi, and the two Cokes together have widened the Coke-Pepsi gap. Coke remains a great success story: People all over the world drink the stuff at any meal except breakfast.

That's where Coke's new ad campaign comes in: Coke in the Morning.

Mark Preisinger, manager of media relations for the Coca-Cola Company, told us, "We're targeting people who drive to work and stop off for fast-food breakfast."

Coke and a McMuffin. Yum.

WHY IS CHICKEN SOUP MORE LIKELY TO BURN YOUR MOUTH THAN ANY OTHER KIND?

To be painfully frank, we have here an explanation for a phenomenon that we can't actually prove. See, someone here in the office scorched his mouth the other day on some chicken soup, after which a storm of anecdotal evidence began to accumulate, resulting in a trend.

We called Campbell's Soup in Camden, New Jersey, and spoke to Bob Walter, food technologist for red-and-white condensed soups (he swears that is his official title). He could not confirm that chicken soup is more likely to burn, but he said that if it is so, it is because of the fat. In a beef-broth-based soup, the fat is evenly dispersed, but in chicken soup, it rises to the surface. Fat clings. When you sip the soup, the chicken fat gloms onto your tongue and palate, coating, clinging, scorching like mad, unlike the watery broth, which clears the area expeditiously.

WHY DO WOMEN'S SHIRTS COST MORE TO DRY-CLEAN THAN MEN'S?

It used to make a lot more sense: Women tended to wear frilly, puffy, dainty blouses with lots of grommets and piping and twitters and wheezers. Now, though their shirts are cut more like men's (sometimes identically), dry cleaners will still charge three times as much for women's shirts as for men's. The official, startling explanation is that women have to pay more because their shirts are *smaller*. They're harder to fit onto the pressing machine. More likely the cleaners are merely exploiting distaff vanity—women, being more concerned about appearance (you know it's true!), place a higher value on a dry-cleaned, pressed shirt, so are willing to pay more. No one ever said that market forces were *fair*.

WHY ARE MCDONALD'S FRENCH FRIES BETTER THAN ANY OTHER FAST-FOOD FRIES?

Where we come from, it is simply *known* that McDonald's has the best fries. Just to make sure, we conducted a highly scientific poll of the first twenty people we ran into. Fifteen said McDonald's has the best fries. Five voted for Wendy's, though this staggered us so greatly we had to assume they were thinking hamburgers. None sided with Burger King. (We should hastily note for the sake of journalistic balance that in our opinion McDonald's hamburgers are aggressively insipid, supplying the sensation of having just consumed McMatter.)

Jerry Randklev, McDonald's quality-assurance manager for potato products, said McFries are the best with "better mouth feel" and "a more natural baked-potato taste" because, number one, the company *cares* about fries more intensely than anyone else. "It is," he said soberly, "our flagship product." His counterpart at Burger King, Chuck Baddley, declined to match Randklev's claim of market superiority, saying instead that Burger King's fries are more "consistent."

McDonald's has two secrets to its fries:

1. Most fast-food companies, including Burger King, blanch the raw sliced potatoes in hot water for, say, thirty minutes. Blanching is a precooking technique that helps control texture, color, and flavor. Burger King claims that a water blanch is best if you want every fry to be like every other fry, day after day. But the water also leaches out some of the natural sugars that make a fry taste so good. McDonald's, however, blanches its raw fries with quick blasts of steam rather than water. The patented process supposedly keeps more of the sugar inside.

2. A potato is 80 percent water. McDonald's uses a patented process that more vigorously removes the moisture from the fry. Burger King contends that too little moisture makes a fry taste mealy, which to us sounds like a lame attempt to defend fries that have the consistency and tensile strength of earthworms.

WHY CAN'T YOU PUT A PHOTOCOPY OF A DOLLAR BILL INTO A COIN CHANGER OR VENDING MACHINE?

The bill "validators" inside the machines have thirteen ways of recognizing a genuine U.S. buck, says Jim Douglass, vice president of marketing for the St. Louis–based Coinco, Inc. The cross-hatching around Washington's head is particularly hard to replicate on a photocopier, because the lines are so small. But let's say you did make an elaborate duplicate. It still wouldn't work: The primary characteristic the validator is searching for is magnetism. On a genuine dollar bill some of the ink is magnetic. Some ain't.

Incidentally we've also discovered why, when you put a perfectly good quarter into a soda machine, it so often falls uselessly into the coin return. The industry standard is that a machine should accept 95 percent of good coins on the first try and the other 5 percent on the second try. John Cunningham, vice president of sales for Mars Electronics, said there is great variation in the diameter, thickness, and metal content of supposedly identical coins. In an electronic coin mechanism, the coin rolls through a narrow gap through which a current passes, and as it does, the frequency of the current changes. A quarter will alter the frequency much differently than will a nickel.

But this "inductive sensing" gets confused when a coin is structurally aberrant, or even if it happens to roll through the mechanism quirkily. The same goes for mechanical—nonelectronic—coin units. Unless the coin rolls down the rail just so, it'll get bounced down into the coin return. What throws both systems off is dirt: Coins are filthy. The grime throws off the calibration. Remember this the next time you're at a vending machine with someone you're trying to impress—particularly the word *calibration*.

WHY DOESN'T SUPER GLUE STICK TO THE INSIDE OF THE TUBE?

What makes Super Glue turn from a liquid to a solid is not, as all you nerds reflexively shouted out, air. That's for other glues. They just dry. But alphacyanoacrylate—that's Super Glue—is triggered by minute traces of moisture. Your basic humidity will do the trick. Super Glue works better in Miami than in Phoenix. When exposed to moisture, the glue molecules start crystallizing, linking up like a daisy chain. That's why you can't swallow it like ordinary classroom paste; Super Glue solidifies before it reaches the throat. ("But Super Glue is already wet!" our puerile friends tell us, thinking that anything liquid must necessarily contain H_2O. Not true.) Because of this moisture sensitivity, the people at Super Glue headquarters, the Loctite Corporation, have to assemble the tubes as though handling the deep-space virus from *The Andromeda Strain*. Water molecules are rigidly policed. Loctite wouldn't give details of this process except to say that years ago some of the human workers were found to be contaminating the tubes and had to be replaced by robots.

Bonus medical fact: If you accidentally Super Glue your eye-lids shut (note use of trademarked name as a verb), wash with warm water, apply a gauze patch, and sit tight. Don't try to pry it. The eyelid will open in one to four days, undamaged. According to the Loctite Corporation.

WHY DOES FRANCE HAVE THE BEST WINES?

"The soil?" was the first guess of the imbeciles we are forced to work with (which is, come to think of it, a generous reference, considering that in the old days it was widely understood that an imbecile, while mentally deficient, was more advanced than a moron, who was more advanced than an idiot; the hierarchy is no longer used, for sensitivity reasons). Dirt has nothing to do with it. Nor does the climate. France is actually kind of cold for growing grapes.

France's secret is . . . the law. Government regulation. Forget Free Enterprise. To make a bad wine in France would not only be low-class, it would be, under certain circumstances, illegal. Vintners in France get jailed for wine fraud. They hurl them-selves out of windows when they get accused. The fussiness is rooted in history: The French were major wine producers as far back as the Dark Ages, and they take this culture-of-the-grape thing seriously.

Only in recent years have Italy and California started strictly regulating the production of wines, and neither approach the compulsiveness of the French. In California you can pick grapes any time you want. In France you must wait until a committee in town votes to pick, lest the quality decline and hurt the town's reputation.

The first serious French vintners were monks. Wine was both a sacrament and a great way of catching a buzz. The great monastery of Cluny is in the center of Burgundy. When the ascetic Cistercian faction of monks decided that life in Cluny was too fancy and devil-may-care, they fled to other parts of France and Europe, bringing with them the culture of the vine.

In the year 1395 Philip the Bold of Burgundy (you just know a more accurate name would have been Philip the Insufferable Bonehead) passed laws to maintain the quality of his wines and forbade the use of the inferior Gamay grape. So began a history of tough standards.

By the turn of the twentieth century, the introduction of American vines in Europe brought a plague of the root louse phylloxera. The vineyards became graveyards of dead vines. French wine was saved from extinction by the discovery that the European vines could be grown on phylloxera-resistant American rootstock.

In 1905 France passed the first of the modern point-of-origin laws. Take a bottle of French wine—yeah, yeah, you usually drink it out of the jug, but let's just try to be high-class for a second—and look for the words "appellation contrôlée." They will probably be next to, or sandwiched around, a place-name. For example, a wine labeled Bordeaux simply means that it comes from the famous region by that name. Haut-Medoc is a specific district within the Bordeaux region. Pauillac is still a smaller spot within Haut-Medoc. The more specific the label gets—down to an individual château with perhaps only two or three acres of vines—the more layers of quality control are applied.

There's obviously one major problem here for anyone who

is not a registered Wine Weenie. Who the heck knows whether Pauillac is smaller than Haut-Medoc? Are we supposed to carry maps with us? Isn't it good enough to know where France is? (You go to England, take a right.)

Why Does Procter and Gamble Make So Many Brands of Laundry Detergent—Bold, Cheer, Lemon Dash, Dreft, Gain, Oxydol, Tide, Era, Solo, Liquid Tide, and so on?

Evidently our confused little question has come up before, because after we called Procter and Gamble, the company sent us a handsome monograph entitled, *Why So Many Different Detergents?* The answer, of course, is that they're all incredibly different and special and diversified and generally wondrous beyond belief.

"All our detergents are designed to provide good, overall performance. However, just as consumers' needs/preferences differ in respect to the type of car they drive, or the type of movies they prefer to see, so our market research has shown consumers look for different features in their detergents," the monograph states. Our guess: Everyone who liked *Rambo* and drives a Dodge Charger buys either Bold or Gain; BMW-driving fans of obscure Truffaut films buy Liquid Tide, but would switch brands "if something more expensive came along."

Procter and Gamble is famous for doing more market research and product testing than any other company in the world. It controls more than half the U.S. detergent market, dwarfing Lever Brothers and Colgate-Palmolive. The P&G monograph details the many subleties of the detergent brands. For example, Gain "leaves a clean, fresh scent on clothing and is economically priced," while Tide "was the first laundry detergent developed to handle the whole family's laundry—from lightly soiled lingerie to heavily soiled work clothes.''

It says nothing about what we should use on lightly soiled work clothes and heavily soiled lingerie. Figures.

Now let's take a closer look. We came across a consultant's report showing that 60 percent of consumers buy laundry detergents and other household cleaners by brand name. That's high. A smaller percentage, for example, give a hoot about the brand of their cat food. Or the brand of their sneakers. Or socks. But more than 60 percent care about the brand of their TV and of their coffee.

This brand-name consciousness reflects the underlying fact that detergent is a ''high involvement'' product that people are really particular about. They demand all sorts of variations, both real and imagined. A low-involvement product would be something like sugar: People buy whatever brand of sugar is cheapest. Another is solid vegetable shortening—there's only one national brand, Crisco. The highest involvement product is diapers, because if they don't work, your life is utter misery. Deodorants are also high-involvement.

Thus P&G can't market a single monster brand named Boffo. There must also be Boffo with Bleach, Liquid Boffo, Liquid Boffo with Fabric Softener, Lemon Boffo, Boffo Lite, Boffo Dark, Boffo Dry, and so forth. At the same time there can't be too many brands, because supermarkets charge money for shelf space, a practice some companies see as outright blackmail. So P&G will test-market a product for a couple of years before going nationwide.

How do people decide which detergent to buy? Either they are easily manipulated by advertising or by familial lore to believe that one detergent is superior to another, or they are such canny consumers they really can tell which detergent will be best at removing Junior's nosebleeds, which best alleviates the water hardness from the ground well, which removes those peculiar odors that Pa picks up down at the slaughterhouse, and so on. If you look at the brands closely, there really are differences. Some claim to be good in cold water. Also, there's different smells and colors: Many have different-colored granules speckling the standard white flakes. It may seem like Procter and Gamble has a lot of different detergents, but really they've just got one for every major color.

Ultimately the answer to the question must be: because they make more money that way. As long as the market is segmented, it makes sense to own as many of the segments as you can—the whole supermarket aisle if possible.

WHY IS AMERICAN BEER SO INSIPID?

We ask this question at some personal risk. Americans have a scary intensity when it comes to brand loyalties. There's that classic scene in the movie *Blue Velvet* when evil Frank asks the young, yuppacious hero what his favorite beer is. "Heineken," the hero answers timidly. Frank explodes: "Heineken? (gross expletive) that (gross expletive)! Pabst Blue Ribbon!" Frank and his psychotic pals torment the poor boy the rest of the night.

In Germany, the serious beer drinker's paradise, the law requires that brewers use only four ingredients in their beer: barley malt, water, yeast, and hops. The malt gives beer its fullness; the hops adds the crucial bitterness. But American breweries cut the malt with rice and corn and use much less hops. They also use more carbonation. Some breweries may even add preservatives and artificial coloring.

Why would American brewers do this to us? Why would they dare to make something like Schlitz?

Because we want it. The free market is rational, usually (for exceptions, see the special report on Wall Street, page 295).

Price is only a small factor: We drink a lot of beer and want something cheap. But the truth is, your average Joe *likes* the taste of Schlitz. Despite the proliferation of imported beers in supermarkets and pubs, American beer still accounts for 95 percent of domestic consumption. "Over a long period of time Americans have developed a taste for beer that's very light and very carbonated," said Jeff Mendel, assistant director of the Institute for Brewing Studies in Boulder, Colorado.

Okay. So why is that? Why do we like carbonated water with a little yeast action thrown in? Why do Europeans view beer as a fine spirit that should be carefully selected to go along with a particular dish, while Americans view it as something to chug by the kegful at frat parties?

Because we've been trained by Big Business to like our beer weak and chuggable.

In Europe even small towns are likely to boast a local brewery, or maybe even more than one. But America, more than any other country, has seen a consolidation of industry since World War II into larger and larger companies. Before Prohibition there were hundreds of breweries in America. But the big companies drove the smaller regional competition out of business. In recent years, only six giants—Anheuser-Busch, Coors, Stroh's, Pabst, G. Heileman, and Miller—controlled about four-fifths of the market. That number went to five in 1989, when Coors bought Stroh's. Miller, by the way, is owned by an even bigger company, Philip Morris Companies, Inc.

To maximize profits, beer companies need to maximize market share, shoot for the center of the bell curve, seize the middle ground. To sell a lot of beer, you need beer with great "drinkability." The substance in nature with the highest drinkability is probably water. The lowest is probably Guinness Stout. It's mud.

Beer companies that need to train sixteen-year-olds to drink their product aren't going to make it all the harder by producing a full-bodied ale or a Russian imperial stout.

Being quick-minded, you're now thinking: Why doesn't Anheuser-Busch, for example, make one token full-bodied heavily hopped beer to compete with Heineken? Because the demand is too small, and these are mass-market companies. "You can't build a Rolls-Royce on an assembly line," said Joseph Owades, director of the Center for Brewing Studies in San Francisco (there are a lot of these institutes and centers; it beats breaking rocks for a living).

Yet, on the contrary, American beers are getting lighter even as the demand for heavier foreign beers has increased. During the seventies, as Americans became more health- and weight-conscious, breweries gradually weakened their flagship brands. A 1970 Budweiser was markedly harsher and heavier than a 1980 Budweiser. The recent success of "lite" brands has eased the pressure to make flagship brands weaker still.

We're bracing ourselves for the day when Miller comes out with a new product: Lite Light.

WHY DOES THE CAMPBELL'S SOUP COMPANY ADVERTISE ITS V-8 JUICE AS "100 PERCENT VEGETABLE JUICE" EVEN THOUGH THE MAIN INGREDIENT IS JUICE FROM A TOMATO, WHICH IS A FRUIT?

The *New Columbia Encyclopedia* says, "The name fruit is often applied loosely to all edible plant products and specifically to the fleshy fruits, some of which (eggplant, tomatoes, and squash) are commonly called vegetables." It also says, "There is no clear distinction between the vegetables and the fruits." Webster's states that a tomato is a fruit, specifically a berry, but that it is "used" as a vegetable. And what's a vegetable? Well, we're reminded of an old story about when Ron and

Nancy Reagan went to a fancy restaurant. Nancy told the waiter she wanted the filet mignon and a baked potato. "And for the vegetable?" asked the waiter. "He'll have the same," Nancy said.

WALL STREET

(In which we take a savage journey into the heart of capitalism.)

Gloom pervaded Wall Street. The streets were soaked with black rain.

Thirty-eight floors up a financier sipped decaf and tried his best to shed no light on his secret world. We were in one of the lovely breakfast rooms of a major investment house. The financier had gray hair, a gray suit, a gray demeanor. It was our first interview of a three-day exploratory safari through the world of High Finance, and it was not going well. The financier spoke cautiously, opaquely, the diffidence no doubt a reflex in an industry in which information is absolutely essential and sometimes criminal.

He permitted the use of only two quotes, to be unattributed: "The ability to buy and sell securities is the ability to provide liquidity to the transfer of ownership."

and

"Wall Street exists to try to determine what is value and to try to provide capital to companies so they can grow."

He was not a live wire.

The intruding reporter foundered on the jargon of Finance. Could you have talked to this man? Could you have talked intelligently, soberly, to a man who speaks the Securities Language, whose lexicon strays not far beyond the safe ground of "mortgage-backed securities" and "asset-backed securi-

ties," "corporate bonds" and "commercial paper," "debt capital" and "equity capital"?

We only wanted to ask a few basic, naive questions:

Why do you people make so much money?

What do you do all day, exactly?

Why does the stock market suddenly crash every so often?
Could it happen again?

Is greed destroying America?

Why did this Michael Milken person make $550 million in
one year?

Where did that money come from? From *us*?

Is Wall Street a malignancy in the heart of the American
body just when we were feeling grand about winning the Cold
War?

What about the selling of America to the Japanese? Does
"the United States" still exist as an economic entity?

Are we doomed?

It is hard to take a panicked, untutored tongue into the
sweatless executive dining rooms of Wall Street, where any
pointed question can be deflected with counterquestions, definitional squabbles, disdain for the brand of crass ignorance
that demands a simple synthesis in a complex world . . . and
so the breakfast interview yielded only that fine gargoyle's-eye
view of the skyscrapers in downtown Manhattan and a momentary glimpse of the Wall Street aesthetic when, early on,
our private waitress walked in and said, "Our special today is
a zucchini-and-Brie omelet." In the private dining rooms of
Wall Street you can't order a sticky bun.

Afterward, at 9:30 in the morning—witching hour for the New
York Stock Exchange—the intruding reporter was walking up
Broad Street when along came a young man protected by an
umbrella that said:

Integrated Resources
Because There's Money to Be Made

Finally a straightforward message! This guy was just what we were looking for, a prototypical Symbolic Analyst. Symbolic Analysis is a phrase economist Robert Reich uses for work that involves the manipulation of information: investment banking, law, research science, public relations, journalism—the kind of work in which you are not likely to build up calluses. Educated work. It's the only way to make real money these days. In the new economy if you fix cars, cut hair, deliver meals to the elderly, teach children, baby-sit, hammer boards together, pour concrete, string electrical wire, or pick crops, you'll be lucky to make enough money to buy a decent little home. You need to get into symbols, talking on the phone, tapping keyboards, jotting memos, work that lets you walk out at the end of the day with a fat paycheck and baby-smooth hands. Work that sometimes is hard to explain.

You can figure that the kings of symbolic analysis are these Wall Street types, so we followed the man with the umbrella into an office building that looked like every other office building in New York, only more indistinguishable. Ambushed outside the elevator, the man agreed to show us around. His name is John Riso, and he was thirty-two years old.

On the fourth floor we entered a crowded office with long banks of desks, each desk holding one or two computer screens. It might have been a newsroom; half the offices on Wall Street look like newsrooms, only more crowded, louder, with narrower desks, more computer terminals, and a greater intellectual intensity. Something had enraptured these people.

"We're a quiet company. Nobody really knows who we are," John said. He pointed: "New Account area, Settlements area, Customer Service area." The last was his turf; he said he was supervisor of West Coast Customer Services. He patted his computer terminal and said, "That's the bread-and-butter right there. Everything we need to do is on our terminal. The mainframe is over in Jersey. Automatic Data Processing."

The workers manipulated their keyboards.

"Our Aggressive Growth mutual fund was number one for the first quarter this year. We're so diversified. We do limited partnerships, we do private placement"—and so on, lots of finance terms. Wall Street, it quickly becomes apparent, is a more variegated place than one might suppose, with countless types of money-making and money-moving schemes. Never before have there been so many people manipulating so much money in so many ways. Stocks and bonds are just for starters.

The flip side is that not everyone is soaking in riches. John Riso is a case in point: He said he makes less than $40,000 a year. Can't afford to live in Manhattan. That's what he gets for not working for percentages, for not committing himself to a life of pure moneysucking.

Yet he still has the Wall Street edge. He's wired in to the big game; he's got his Quotron monitor, flashing the latest stock prices, rolling out the late-breaking financial news. Watching the Quotron is like watching a game show on TV; you see the money being made—not by geniuses but by any Joe willing to be a player.

A friend walked up and said, "Get it up?"

"LA?" John asked.

"Please."

John stroked a key on his computer and his Quotron monitor flashed the latest price for L.A. Gear, the company that makes running shoes. Up 3¾. That came after a $4 rise the day before. Several other colleagues crowded around. The numbers bespoke lost opportunities. Somewhere out there in America people were buying L.A. Gear stock, watching it rise in price, then selling it again for instant profit. So easy. Make a phone call, take a risk, jam free money into your wallet. Money for nothing! No calluses required. John and his colleagues had thought of buying L.A. Gear yesterday, when the company projected high first-half profits and the stock jumped through the roof (though in fact it had already been jumping, a sure sign of insider information leaking out). They had been chicken.

"We coulda made big bucks," John said. "We can't buy it now. Too expensive. It's all timing. You have to be in the right place at the right time."

John didn't have the answers we wanted to the big questions—the greed factor, yea or nay on malignancy, U.S.-as-illusion, and so on—but he provided the first insight: Before there is greed, there is wanting. Wanting is the foundation upon which Wall Street cultivates outright greed. The allure of easy money is riveting—one could stare at the Quotron all day. The rules are so simple: Buy low, sell high. The mystery is that so many Americans don't even play the game, like people who haven't discovered the joys of bridge.

John stopped for a moment and said, "There's so much money out there, you can't believe it. There's so much money, these money managers, they—it's just incredible."

He was reverently speechless.

"I love the industry," he said, "because it's such a challenge to try to figure out what the hell's going on."

(And . . . Because There's Money to Be Made.)

Greed is a mortal sin. In Dante's *Inferno* the avaricious and the prodigal share the fourth circle of Hell, endlessly pushing stones in imitation of Sisyphus, going around and around, bumping into one another, having a fruitless and lamentable existence. Avarice made a comeback in the eighties; not only is it nothing to be ashamed of, it is something to flaunt.

For Wall Street the sluice opened wide: incredible streams of money. Play the game! Master the technique! In 1986, during the halcyon pre-Crash days, a finance executive at Drexel Burnham Lambert facing a $9 million personal bonus summed up the securities industry: "This is Disneyland for adults."

In the movie *Wall Street*, Michael Douglas plays an odious financier named Gordon Gekko. At one point he tells a throng of stockholders why he is attempting to wrest control of their company from its current managers:

"Greed, for lack of a better word, is good. Greed is right.

Greed works. Greed clarifies, cuts through and captures the essence of the evolutionary spirit. Greed, in all of its forms, greed for life, for money, for love, knowledge, has marked the upward surge of mankind, and greed, you mark my words, will not only save Teldar Paper, but that other malfunctioning corporation called the USA.''

The film is a polemic against greed, and Gekko's machinations are rendered in monochrome, but the painful truth is that he's almost right.

This requires an economics lesson. Let's go to the textbooks. First, Adam Smith. We're going way back, to the eighteenth century. Smith was a quiet, bookish Scot who in 1776 published the landmark text *The Wealth of Nations*. One of his central messages is that the marketplace—it was not yet called capitalism—allows the betterment of society even though everyone is running around being selfish. Common sense would tell you that such a society would be as disciplined and as orderly and as fair as a bread riot. Salvation, Smith says, comes from the competition factor. No one can be too greedy or he will lose his business to competitors. The marketplace militates against gluttons, usurers, and con artists.

The genius of a marketplace economy is that it allows personal freedom while simultaneously encouraging the improvement of society. Who guides the marketplace? No one. But our individual efforts, taken together, create a kind of autopilot for society—the Invisible Hand, in Smith's words. The Invisible Hand is sort of like God; you can't see it but you know it's there, a benign master—logical, progressive, fair.

Not so, said Karl Marx, the superstar economist of the 1800s. Marx predicted that capitalism would destroy itself: that profit rates would decline, the exploited proletariat would be driven to revolutionary fervor, and a new system of socialism and then communism would rise.

He was wrong of course. Capitalism has proven to be a better way of organizing an economy and seems more likely to foster political freedom. Here's just one of the analytic errors made by Marxist economists: They predicted that private industries would gradually fill up the society with all the wares and products that anyone would want, and then the factories would have to shut down. What they underestimated was the voraciousness of Western society and its ability to invent ever-higher standards of living and demands for consumer goods. They did not anticipate the Walkman or the VCR, much less tanning salons, Post-It brand yellow sticky notepaper, floating pool butlers, phony car-phone antennas to make you look rich, and other essentials of modern-day Having.

Marx did give us an enduring concept: Capitalism is an evolving system, prone to excess, or permanently adolescent if you will. And the Invisible Hand clearly is not so far-reaching and benign as Adam Smith believed. The marketplace has little incentive to deal with long-term problems, which is why there is a hole in the ozone over Antarctica and why tropical reef fish are infested with tumors from toxic waste. Capitalism needs protection from its own vices.

Earlier this century the world's third great economist, John Maynard Keynes, gave us the antidote in the form of the "mixed economy," in which the government regulates the marketplace—outlawing monopolies, controlling the money supply, jailing greedheads, and so forth. It's sort of a synthesis of free enterprise and socialism.

But how far should we go? Are these greedheads a menace to society? Should we tie their hands? Cut off their fingers? Rip off their eyelids and tie them face-up in the hot sun?

The ceiling of the bond trading floor at Salomon Brothers is two stories high, as though the individual traders in their individual pods might someday sell air rights. Their narrow desks are stocked with two or more green diode computer screens, and a telephone with dozens of lines, number charts, scratch pads. The density of the operation allows the most primitive of internal communication: direct shouting. No need for intercoms. The language, like all tongues on Wall Street, is exotic to the uneducated ear: a cacophonous Creole of codes and numbers and place-names, shouting, shouting, screaming, punctuated by curses, jock language, thunderous high-fives, hoots. It all comes together in what Tom Wolfe, in his novel *The Bonfire of the Vanities*, called ''the sound of well-educated young white men baying for money on the bond market.''

Reality imitates fiction. The first salesman we met announced, ''I am the Master of the Universe!''—mimicking Sherman Mc-Coy, the protagonist of Wolfe's novel.

The real-life Master of the Universe is Hal Cohen, the oldest guy in sight, at forty-nine still selling bonds next to kids half his age. He sat in front of three green screens, pitching bonds to clients who are linked to Cohen via dedicated phone lines. All his lines were ringing at once. The Province of Newfoundland had sold some bonds to Salomon Brothers, and now Cohen screamed into the phone:

''No way! C'mon! We can do better than 40!''

He punched another line, said only seven words before hanging up: ''How ya doin'? Ricky? You're the best!''

Another trader walked up: ''Twelve million 250.''

''You want to do 8¾?'' asked Cohen.

''Eight and three-quarters plus 18.''

It's the Securities Language. Occasionally a semicoherent sentence escapes, as when the second trader said, ''I got another trade so good I don't want to tell you about it. Check this out. F—— P—— Group. You know that piece-of-shit holding group. . . .''

An adjacent trader, Jeffrey Coley, realized that a reporter was interviewing Cohen. He said—there's a lot of adrenaline in the world of high finance—''He may be the best salesman in the world. What was that book? He makes that guy''—thinking of Sherman McCoy—''look like an odd lot.''

(Wall Street humor.)

Most working human beings on the planet earth perform a

function of some type and, in return, are paid money by someone else. Money is the reward, after the fact. Wall Street operatives cut out most of the middle step. They focus directly on making money. Making money is both the end and the means. Making money is the function itself, not just the reward.

They love their jobs.

Most, anyway. Several years ago a Princeton graduate named Michael Lewis entered Salomon Brothers as a trainee and made $45,000 his first year. He performed well, sold a lot of bonds, and the second year he made $90,000, including bonuses. His third year he made $275,000. He was twenty-six.

The next year he would have been eligible to start making commissions, in addition to bonuses and salary. He figured he would have made $350,000, then $425,000 his fifth year, and at least $550,000 his sixth—though he was on a fast track and might have been made a managing director, in which case he would have made $1 million a year, all before the age of thirty. But he quit. Three years was enough. He became a writer and wrote the best-selling book Liar's Poker.

"It was a very ruthless sort of environment," Lewis told us. "It reminded me of the eighth or ninth grade, when the big people got their way, and if you did something they didn't like, they beat you up. There was a lot of bullying going on. It was a very crude environment."

Sudden wealth swells the head. The young male traders hassle their female colleagues, Lewis said. Customers become objects of ridicule and abuse, if not subjects of outright rip-offs. The work would become utterly monotonous were it not for the intoxicating pay. It's like poker: You can play it all night.

"It got to be easy. The job is not that complicated. You get a group of large institutional investors, people who have in excess of $500 million to play with, and you train them to do what you want them to do," Lewis said. "You're entertained by just the community of gambling at your table."

What exactly do they do?

One answer Wall Streeters give is that they, and they alone, are able to create a large, viable market for certain things that others want to sell (like the anonymous financier said, they provide "liquidity"). If the city of Miami wants to build a bunch of new schools, it borrows the money by issuing bonds. You can't sell bonds on a street corner, so the city calls up Salomon Brothers, which handles the deal, sometimes buying the bonds itself before reselling them. Salomon Brothers doesn't build the schools, but it does help rich investors move their money around.

In one of these deals Salomon may make only the narrowest of profit margins—but it adds up. One bond salesman (not at Salomon) told us that in a typical bond sale he might make only 3.2 cents per hundred dollars in bonds sold. A skimpy profit. Buy low, sell a wee bit higher. That would come to $320 per million dollars of bonds sold. Of that he would keep about $120, and the rest would go to the firm.

But there's good news! In his best day this young bond salesman might move $100 million in bonds. That would mean $12,000 in one day—all for talking on the phone.

Hal Cohen said on his average day—his *average*—he sells $100 million in bonds. On his best day he sold $2 billion. He said he lives in a nice home in the best part of New Jersey.

Let's get another of our original questions out of the way: Why do they make so much money?

Because the client can afford it. Even the enormous fees charged on Wall Street are minuscule compared with the totality of a major deal. Any percentage of a billion dollars adds up to a lot of money.

Still, why can't a cut-rate company come along and take away all the business from these pricey Wall Street operations? Why is anyone willing to pay the huge commission to Morgan Stanley or Goldman Sachs when there must be a cheaper store in town?

The main reason is that most huge financial deals—say, a

merger, or a stock offering, or a takeover—are rare events for the businesspeople out in Duluth or Tucson and they want to be sure their deal is being handled by an extremely reputable firm. It's like being charged with a crime: You get the best lawyer available. And a rich investor in Memphis feels more comfortable in the soft, padded mitts of these patrician financial institutions, with their grand foyers, mahogany bookshelves, panoramic views of New York, zucchini-and-brie omelets, and promises of great fortune, because money attracts money.

Several Wall Street traders told us, somewhat defensively, that the economy would grind to a halt without them—that if they weren't laboring away, "providing liquidity," the money couldn't move as easily. But most don't even try to justify the pay. They smile a wide coyote's grin. What's wrong with a little greed?

If a Wall Street operative does ever feel a wince of guilt, he can always remind himself that it is quite expensive to live in New York properly. Keeping up with the Joneses is murder.

What exactly is a bond? Is that like a stock? On television the government used to run commercials saying, "Take stock in America, buy U.S. Savings Bonds." Are they interchangeable?

No. Stockholders literally own the company. The company pays them "dividends." Bondholders are owed money by the company. The company pays them interest on that debt.

The prices used to fluctuate much more dramatically in stocks than in bonds. That changed when the federal government deregulated interest rates in 1979; suddenly, bonds acted like stocks going precipitously up and down in price.

Now for "junk bonds." The official term for these is high-yield bonds. These are bonds issued by new, unproven, small, or troubled companies—which means, most companies. MCI, the long-distance carrier, was a junk company. Most airlines are junk companies. All *junk* means is that these companies are not (to use another term) "investment grade," that they have not been rated AAA or AA or A or BBB by the investment rating analysts. To get anyone to buy their bonds, the companies have to pay higher interest rates—say, 15 percent. Junk bonds have been around for decades, but until a few years ago relatively few were sold, because the chance of default seemed too high.

Enter Michael Milken—one of the most astounding characters of the eighties, Finance's answer to Alexander the Great.

Milken, known for his ill-fitting toupee and his past habit of wearing a miner's lamp on his head so that he could read balance sheets in his predawn bus ride to work, rose to fame as the head of the Beverly Hills–based junk-bond department at Drexel Burnham Lambert. The geographical distance from the center of Wall Street reflects Milken's beyond-the-mainstream strategy. He single-handedly transformed the junk-bond market from the tiny sneered-at stepchild of Wall Street to the bone-crushing behemoth of the late eighties. In 1982 only $30 billion in junk bonds was outstanding. By the middle of 1989 there was close to $190 billion.

Milken succeeded by realizing that Wall Street had been overly snobby. There were thousands of companies that could make good on their debts, but couldn't find anyone to lend them money. Milken found people. He cultivated a network of aggressive, deep-pocketed operators like Ivan Boesky (who later went to prison for insider trading), and mastered the art of junk-bond-financed takeovers. Though Boesky was the model for the villainous Gordon Gekko in the movie *Wall Street*, in real life Boesky was a bit player compared with Milken. Milken became more than a bond salesman, more than a financier. He became virtually omnipotent in the world of finance, almost as though he were . . . the Invisible Hand. At his peak, in 1987, people suspected he was making as much as $100 million a year. Foolish of them—$100 million is chump change for this guy. According to the government, Milken in 1987 was paid $550 million by Drexel, while the minimum wage in America held fast at $3.35 an hour.

How much is $550 million? Three times as much as the United States paid—even adjusting for inflation—for a tract of land back in the days of Thomas Jefferson. The property was called Louisiana.

It is also several times the budget of the Securities and Exchange Commission, which has been busy the last few years playing cops-and-robbers on Wall Street. The SEC in 1988 alleged that Milken and Drexel "devised and carried out a fraudulent scheme involving insider trading, stock manipulation, fraud on Drexel's own clients, failure to disclose beneficial ownership of securities as required, and numerous other violations of the securities laws." Criminal charges followed in March. Drexel agreed to pay $650 million in a civil settlement with the SEC, without admitting wrongdoing. Milken pled guilty to six felony securities violations and agreed to pay $600 million in fines and restitution.

Astonishingly, many Wall Street traders still revere Milken. He's a hero. Some think he went too far, but almost all think he earned—really earned—his $550 million. Such figures don't faze this world of wealth; at no point can an income become an injustice or an obscenity.

Robert K. Lifton, a corporate executive and friend of Milken's, said, "He made it in fees, the hard way."

A lot of Wall Street hands are saddened by the fall of Milken. He had vision. He wanted the world. The Invisible Hand, lording benignly and brilliantly over all mankind.

Now comes the leveraged buyout, or LBO, Milken's other favorite game. What happens is that someone who isn't very rich uses "leverage"—borrowed money, including lots from junk bonds—to buy a big, pricey, publicly traded company and take it private.

The assets of the newly acquired company become the

collateral for all those debts. Neat trick.

The genius of the LBO became apparent a few years ago when an investment group led by former Treasury Secretary William Simon bought Gibson Greetings for $80 million from RCA by putting up only $1 million of its own capital. A year and a half later the company went public again on the stock market; it sold for $290 million. According to a recent article in *The New Yorker*, Simon's investment of $330,000 turned into $66 million in cash and stock. Buy low, sell high.

But LBOs are dangerous. Critics say that heavily indebted companies are time bombs; they have performed well only because of the strong economy during the past seven years. As soon as there is a recession, they won't be able to pay the interest on their debts; they could fold.

LBO defenders say the technique is a fine way to steal a company from lazy, unimaginative, pudgy managers and make the company leaner and meaner. The idea here is that in order to service those huge debts, a company will have to be on its toes—debt, like greed, is good.

The truth is that some buyouts are good and some are bad, some breakups healthy and others cannibalistic.

Byron Dorgan, Democrat from North Dakota and a member of the House Ways and Means Committee, is an outspoken critic of LBOs, arguing that part of the problem these days is that the most attractive targets for takeovers are companies least in need of new management. They are alluring because they are likely to show only modest profits over the short run in exchange for long-term growth and capital improvements. As such, they are underpriced on the stock market. Their stock is cheap. A raider looks at that and his stomach growls.

And the securities industry encourages raiders. Last year $7 billion was paid in fees to Wall Street firms for handling leveraged buyouts.

It would be a mistake, however, to think that all anyone does anymore is try to swallow up companies. Another thing they do is try to rip them limb from limb. For example at one point we were in a major investment banking house talking to a twenty-three-year-old Smith College graduate whose job it is to try to figure out what companies will look like if they're torn asunder.

Enthusiasm poured from the woman like sweat from a boxer. She had big white voracious teeth.

She said, "My department is corporate restructurings. . . . We're looking at a company. I took the company's projections for, like, earnings and revenue, and, you know, like, operating income, and put them in a computer model. We're gonna, you know, look at different scenarios and look at how much debt capacity the company has, and how it would look if we spun off a division. . . . Would it be best if we levered it up? Would it be best if we sold it off?"

Does this company know that she's doing this? Probably someone does. But it doesn't matter. She's got the computer, she can do whatever she wants. Big gleaming teeth. No one's safe.

We also talked to one of her associates, who is older, wiser, more established—he's twenty-seven. He said he's in "merchant banking." This is the hot new trend. Instead of merely helping a client take over another company, the merchant banking department takes an "equity position" itself, meaning it cuts itself in on the action. The securities firm ends up owning a chunk of some distant company. There's a good reason why this is trendy on Wall Street: The firms have raked in so much money in the eighties that they want to get into some serious owning.

The associate said his job is wonderful: "It's one of the only Jobs where, straight out of school, you can be dealing with the heads of major corporations. There's a certain glamour factor."

Hi, my name's Biff, and I'm twenty-two years old. Let's bust up Texaco!

Despite a decade of rapid economic growth, the poor are getting poorer in this country. The income gap is spreading in part because certain types of American jobs are in greater demand in a newly integrated global marketplace. Some. But not others. Corporations can employ satellite technology to maintain headquarters in America while running their factories overseas, in places like Malaysia, where labor is cheap. This raises one of our outstanding questions: Will America cease to exist as an economic entity?

No, and yes. No in the sense that globalization doesn't affect every industry. Yes, because the great competition is not so much between the United States and Japan and the European Economic Community, as between Mobil and British Petroleum, Ford and Nissan, Spacely Sprockets and Cogswell Cogs.

In the global economy there is a demand for American-trained business students, for American know-how, for American musicians and filmmakers. Symbolic analysts, all. Their "value," and salaries, have gone up.

Not so for the average American blue-collar worker, who is a surplus item here. Value down. In the future he may have to find another line of work.

And finally the New York Stock Exchange. A horrifying place.

Michael LaBranche, an elegant man of thirty-four who is the "specialist" in AT&T stock on the floor of the Exchange, let us hang out with him one Friday morning. He's been the phone-company specialist since the day he got out of college. His job is to stand in a fixed spot, auctioning AT&T stock to the various brokers who come frothing along.

At 9:30 A.M. the market opened, and LaBranche told everyone that AT&T was selling at 35⅛, twelve cents higher than yesterday's close. Suddenly a gaggle of people appeared; simultaneously a clerk behind the counter yelled, "Fuck, the order's changed." LaBranche said, "I don't care, just give me the number," and finally turned to the drooling crowd and announced, "Five for 100,000! One hundred thousand at an eighth!"

A man said, "I'll take 10,000 at an eighth!"

Another man said, "An eighth at 10,000!"

And more voices:

"Fifty thousand sells at an eighth!"

"You guys just *bought* at an eighth!"

"Twenty-two five at a quarter!"

Only LaBranche can stand in this spot. Only he can be the specialist. Only he can say, with authority, what the going price of AT&T will be at a given moment. What is incredible is that he's a private businessman. LaBranche serves a public function, "creating a market," but in the meantime makes handsome profits through his own private account. He is supposed to try to prevent rapid movement of the price up or down. If he doesn't—as some specialists didn't during the 1987 crash— he could be stripped of his franchise.

The franchise is the legacy of his grandfather, who paid a nominal sum for the AT&T specialist position back in 1929. Since then the price of a seat on the exchange has risen above $500,000. Just to play the game, you have to fork over a massive entry fee.

Nearby, what appeared to be a rugby scrum had broken out in front of the Avon desk. Amway had dropped a takeover bid for Avon, and the stock was plummeting. The traders huddled, red-faced, forehead veins distended, in full scream, spittle flying.

"Twenty thousand at ⅝!"

"Whatever happens has happened!"

"I was the first on the sale!"

"Shut up!"

"I'm sick of you. . . ."

They were unhappy people. They had obviously bought high and now were forced to sell low.

So then, why did this market crash in 1987?

The answer presented itself right there at the Avon desk. The market crashes because investors crash the market. Investors crash the market because they realize the market is crashing. It's a circular dynamic. The initial descent came because the prices of stocks were obviously overvalued; the assets and income of all those companies listed on the Exchange could not justify the make-believe "value" of the stocks.

There is supposed to be a correlation between a stock's price and what a company is actually worth. But that stuff is irrelevant to the gamblers of the stock market. They don't buy stock in a company because they *like* it, they buy it because they think the stock is going to go up, up, up—easy money! So *what* if the company makes nerve gas? The stock is going up, up, up!

"Fifty thousand at a quarter!"

"Sold!"

Investors also watch the Leading Economic Indicators, which would be a great name for a rock band but is merely a list of such things as the latest wholesale price increases. If there's bad news, they rush to sell stock before everyone else sells stock and the price dips too far. Good news, the opposite. Before the Crash, there were predictions that the Dow Jones Industrial Average, an index of thirty major stocks, would continue to soar to record levels. So investors bought. The stock price increased. Investors bought more. And so on. Meanwhile the actual companies (somewhere out there in America, people are working, making something, helping people, many of them making upward of seven or even eight dollars an hour) were plodding along as always. The illusion was better than the reality.

Finally people began to cash in. They sold their stock. Prices went down. They sold more. The market began to dip precariously. Then it collapsed. The computers went to work and ordered everything sold. They had a simple function: If the market dropped 10 percent, sell, sell, sell. The night of Black Monday the traders had to stay on the Exchange floor until 3:00 A.M. trying to sort through the crush of sell orders, to figure out what happened during all that screaming.

Bob Hersey, a clerk who stands all day behind one of the Exchange counters, said, "All you're doing is working with numbers. It's just numbers. The companies don't matter, you don't care about the company you're investing in."

The stock exchange is perhaps a metaphor for capitalism on the whole. The drivers of the economy—everyone from the Wall Street gurus to the corporate chiefs who must answer to their stockholders—have neither the inclination nor the mandate to contemplate the out-of-earshot future. What matters is *right now*.

Nicholas F. Brady, the Wall Street executive who became secretary of the treasury, says the market has become too instantaneous: "It operates faster than the human mind can think."

Could the market crash again? Maybe. Wall Street is still wired to computer programs, Stock Exchange assurances to the contrary.

The final question: Is greed good?

We finally tracked down a man who could answer that: William Baumol, a professor of economics at New York University and Princeton.

He said, "It's perfectly clear that greed has always been central to how capitalism works and even to how many economies before it worked. The question is not whether there is greed, the question is whether it is harnessed to a mechanism that services the social interest. This was Adam Smith's point.

"Greed led the medieval robber baron to hold people up and murder them. And greed led Romans to conquer and destroy smaller nations and hold the captives for ransom. And greed also built up the steel industry and the automobile industry and made America competitive. Greed is a neutral thing—aside from its moral attributes—I'm just talking about whether it's good for the economy. It can be destructive and it can be useful.

"The rules of the game have to be refined so that the rewards for the destructive use of greed have been cut down."

It wouldn't be too hard. The government has a great tool for inspiring the marketplace to behave: taxes.

For example Robert Reich has suggested that the government consider putting a heavy tax on profits that are made on assets held for only a few weeks, making the quick, sleazy deal less alluring. The government could also ease taxes on profits made from assets held for many years. Another possibility is that Congress could decide to take away the tax benefits of LBOs, the ability to deduct interest payments on all that debt.

It does not appear that we are doomed, not so long as we remain vigilant and understand that capitalism is a wild boy, a juvenile delinquent who does not always heed the lash of the Invisible Hand. What makes the current situation scary to an outsider is that Wall Street, the motor in the economy, has become accustomed to massive profits. These firms have every reason to want to sustain the mergermania, the LBOs, the frenzied movement of money, the deals, deals, deals.

There is a mindlessness to it all, a heedlessness. Wall Street is not so much evil as it is unconscious. It doesn't want the income gap to increase between rich and poor, it doesn't want America to be purchased by overseas investors . . . but sometimes that's how things turn out. There's no time to ponder the consequences of a howlingly brilliant deal.

Wall Street has created a reality of its own . . . disengaged and aloof from the reality of the rest of us.

A moment sticks in the mind: It was late afternoon at Salomon Brothers, the bond floor still in a frenzy. Two traders, Bill and John, turned away from their screens, their phones, to talk for a moment about what they do. We asked Bill what a bond looks like. He thought for a moment. Then he turned to John.

"I've never even seen a bond. Have you?" he said.

John replied, "It looks like a certificate, with a pretty border."

LOOSE ENDS

(Odd stuff that comes to mind. And then, déjà vu-like, to mind again.)

Why Do People Experience Déjà Vu?

It suddenly hits you: You *know* you have been here before, in this same place, talking to this same person, who is wearing the same paisley shirt with the mustard stain on the lapel, making the same hackneyed observation—a past life! It must be from a past life!

Déjà vu is not caused by anything supernatural, extrasensory or extraterrestrial; it is more like a mental hiccup, a brief, harmless malfunction of a basic mechanism of memory.

Here's what happens: Normally when one is in familiar surroundings, two brain functions are triggered: a concrete memory of the place and a separate abstract feeling of familiarity. In a déjà vu situation the familiarity sensation is triggered without a specific attendant memory. Possibly you *were* in a similar situation, but you can't quite remember.

WHY ARE CAFETERIA TRAYS STILL WET AFTER ALL THESE YEARS?

A blower-dryer for precisely this purpose from Hobart Corporation costs about $5,000 and adds another four feet to what is likely an already expensive (say, $25,000) and long (sixteen feet) dishwashing setup. Some cafeterias won't spring for it. They expect the tray to air-dry, but that's nearly impossible in a steamy back room. Trays are made of plastic, which doesn't dry as fast as glass or ceramic. Since cafeterias have small marginal profits and don't overstock things like trays and plates, they must rush everything back to the serving line during the meal hour, wet or not.

To hasten drying, cafeterias add "drying agents" to the rinse cycle, such as a product called Rinse Dry. These drying agents cause the water to sheet rather than bead. Look at a wet cafeteria tray and you'll see it's true—the water is unbelievably flat. But even sheeted water has a hard time drying quickly, particularly when the water isn't hot enough. And this is the final problem: The Health Department requires that dishwashers be set at a minimum of 180 degrees, unless a chemical sterilizer is used, such as chlorine. Many cafeterias choose the latter technique because a "low-temp" dishwasher doesn't need an expensive water-heating booster from the Hobart Corporation.

Cafeteria owners presume that we, the customers, don't really care. No, we *like* to pick up something wet that's virtually been in someone else's mouth.

WHY DON'T PEOPLE TALK ON ELEVATORS?

S tare at shoes. Glance at ceiling. Study elevator button panel as though it's the Rosetta stone. One minute on an elevator with a stranger takes about as long as the Jurassic period.

Granted, not everyone is fazed and muted by elevators. Some are as voluble as they would be at a cocktail party. A few are positively boorish, and their annoying loquacity highlights the first and most important reason that most people refrain from talking on elevators:

1. It's rude. On elevators with more than two people it's not polite to talk to one person and ignore others with whom you are so intimately juxtaposed. Still, often you're silent when there's just one other person, which brings us to:

2. It's stupid. Elevator conversations are too abbreviated to be meaningful, so they're just wasted mental energy. We tend to hoard our mental energy. Consciously or unconsciously, we tend to limit the set of people in our lives to whom we owe the courtesy of conversation. If you do establish an elevator-talking relationship with someone, that might lead to uncomfortable conflicts during subsequent rides when you and your new elevator buddy are not alone and you neither want to be rudely silent nor rudely talkative.

None of this explains the tension of elevator rides that is so out of proportion to the brevity and triviality of the encounter. So we must look at:

3. The invasion of personal space. We all have a private space surrounding us, any intrusion into which causes tension or discomfort. How far out does it go? It can cover an entire elevator, but you begin to feel noticeably uncomfortable when someone comes within seventy centimeters, or about two and a half feet, according to a study by sociologist Leslie Hayduk from the University of Alberta. The discomfort is markedly increased at about fifty centimeters and virtually intolerable at thirty centimeters, though only when the intruder is in your face (your personal zone is smaller at your sides and back). That's why people who feel intruded upon will pivot and look away when they talk.

When your personal space is invaded, even from across an elevator, you become aroused. Not sexually. "Aroused" as in tense, alert, sensitive. This is why time passes so slowly on an elevator, and why you notice the silence.

WHY IS NORTH ALWAYS AT THE TOP OF MAPS?

We know what you're thinking. Because north is *up*. It just *is*. Like, that's how the earth goes around the sun, right?

You bonehead. In space there is no up or down. A map with south, east, or west at the top would be equally accurate, equally arbitrary. And despite scientific textbook drawings that indicate otherwise, the earth doesn't really orbit the sun counterclockwise any more than it does clockwise or end-over-end. Diagrams of the solar system show flat, level planes or planetary orbits only to help our feeble brains maintain equilibrium.

We have perused the cartography section of our local university library and learned the secret of north. First, some background: Eratosthenes (ca. 276–ca. 194 B.C.), the chief librarian at Alexandria in Egypt, made an early map of the known world with north at the top. Why he did that is unknown.

Then Christianity gave rise to maps with a religious inspiration, in which it made sense to put Paradise at the top. But where was Paradise in relation to the known lands of earth? In the mysterious Orient. So, east was on top, with Jerusalem dead center, Africa to the right, Europe to the left. The Mediterranean ran up the middle from the bottom. These maps gave rise to the expression "to orient yourself": It meant you faced east.

Around 1300, with the rise of sea navigation, there began to appear maps called portolano charts, which put north again at the top. The history books attribute this to the invention in Italy of the compass, which, we are told, points north. However, this explanation isn't quite adequate, because a compass really points north *and* south as the needle lines up with the earth's magnetic field. Why not put south at the top? Obviously the map makers were in the Northern Hemisphere during the Age of Discovery. They knew where they were on the globe. The northern prejudice was increased by Polaris, the North Star. It remains fixed at virtually the same point above the North Pole while other stars wheel across the sky, being a handy marker for sailors out in the middle of nowhere.

Incidentally, Polaris is a temporary North Star. There'll be another one in a couple of dozen millennia, as we hurtle a little farther through the Void.

WHY DOESN'T THE FEDERAL GOVERNMENT SELL ALL THE GOLD IN FORT KNOX TO PAY OFF THE NATIONAL DEBT?

A in't near enough. Fort Knox has about $6 billion in gold, which not only couldn't pay off the federal debt, and not only couldn't pay off the interest on the federal debt, but couldn't pay off the interest on the loan that we would need to pay off the interest on the federal debt. You dig?

The government could sell the gold if it wanted to. All Congress has to do is vote. We went off the gold standard in 1933. That means we no longer keep enough precious metal to back up the paper with George Washington and other folks on it. (From 1900 to 1914 a treasury note was convertible 100 percent to gold. The establishment of the federal reserve system in 1914 required that all currency have a 40 percent backing by gold.) Today currency is backed by government bonds—more pieces of paper promising that the government will pay up down the line. The old gold has become nothing more than money in the bank, a relatively small savings account. The reason no one panics is that the government's assets go far beyond the piddling pile in Fort Knox. In a pinch we could sell the Lincoln Memorial. We could sell the Smithsonian. We could sell Guam.

In fact that's been one of the government's secret tricks for attacking the deficit: selling pieces of America. Millions of acres of federal land are for sale at this moment. Army bases are being closed, and the land will go on the block. No one has suggested selling the gold in Fort Knox, but Congress recently authorized the sale of nine million ounces of silver. The proceeds will be poured into the absurd operating budget of the government. Assets go down, debt continues to rise.

This is faintly disturbing. You know a superpower is in decline when its budget is dependent on garage sales.

WHY DO WE PLAY TRICKS ON PEOPLE ON APRIL 1?

April Fools' Day is a lingering remnant of the Aztec civilization of pre-Columbian Mexico. The Aztecs considered New Year's Day to be March 21, the spring equinox, and would celebrate wildly for twelve days, concluding on April 1 with a human sacrifice to the Aztec gods. But when the Spanish arrived, they brought with them the bizarre custom of claiming January 1 as the New Year. In the resulting confusion among postconquest Aztecs, it became popular to "fool" someone into thinking he or she had been chosen for evisceration on April 1. At the last minute, with the knife poised over the victim's heart, the "priest" would say "April Fool!" thus eliciting raucous laughter.

Why Did Someone Get the Dumb Idea That the Length of Winter Could Be Forecast by the Actions of a Groundhog?

Groundhog Day was brought to America by English and German immigrants, none of whom had any apparent meteorological savvy. Granted, a sunny day in early February is likely to be an unusually cold one—the clear sky bespeaks an Arctic air mass. Thus one could make the most tenuous of claims for a logical basis to the fantasy of Groundhog Day: If the groundhog sees his shadow, winter lasts another six weeks. It's not exactly the kind of forecast you would want to plan your spring vacation around. You ask, Why a groundhog? The exact type of critter is optional, so long as it hibernates. In some parts of the world it's a badger, bear, or hedgehog. All these creatures have an interest in knowing how long winter will last. They're getting bored. Need a shower. Suffering from wicked "morning breath."

Why Do They Call It the "Ides" of March?

Every month has an ides. The word is from the Etruscans by way of the Romans, and roughly means "divide." It means the middle of the month. We think of the "ides of March" because of Shakespeare and Julius Caesar. Caesar was murdered on the 15th of March in the year 44 B.C., and Shakespeare invented a soothsayer who repeatedly warned "Beware the ides of March" in the play *Julius Caesar*. Caesar was a little rattled by the prophecy, but not enough to stop hanging around his fair-weather friends like Brutus and Cassius. The real question is, Why does Caesar say "Et tu, Brute!" in Shakespeare's play but talks the rest of the time in English?

WHY DID THE *MAYFLOWER* LAND IN MASSACHUSETTS INSTEAD OF SOMEPLACE WARMER AND MORE EXCITING, LIKE DAYTONA BEACH?

Before we answer this, we'd like to note that anyone who believed the rap about the Aztecs is truly an "April Fool."

The Pilgrims were aiming for a spot just south of the Hudson River, in what was then called Virginia, where there were other Englanders. They got off track a bit and hit Cape Cod Bay. Boat travel in those days wasn't exactly like a trip on the *Trump Princess*, so they didn't want to return to the water. Plus, they ran out of beer. Seriously the actual *Mayflower* log states, "Victuals most spent, especially our beer." As you know, no one ever goes to Daytona Beach without a lot of beer.

WHY DOES SANTA SEEM TO TURN UP IN EVERY DEPARTMENT STORE?

Because—children, leave the room—those guys are *imposters*. The fact is, Santa is a tiny man. The guys in the Santa suits at the department stores are preposterously big. According to the poem "A Visit From St. Nicholas," by Clement Clarke Moore, the whole enterprise of Santa and his minions is done in miniature: "What to my wondering eyes should appear/ But a miniature sleigh and eight tiny reindeer/With a little old driver, so lively and quick/I knew in a moment it must be St. Nick."

The small stature allows him to get in and out of chimneys. As for you guys at the department stores, we're on to your little game.

WHY DO PEOPLE BELIEVE THAT STARS CONTROL EARTHLY EVENTS?

Not since the seventeenth century has any scientist seriously believed that there could be a connection between the motion of heavenly bodies and the lives of human beings. Not only is the concept absurd on its face, but astrology succumbs to internal inconsistencies. For example why should the day of your birth be more significant than the day of your conception? Star-charters must also contend with the fact that the movements of the constellations are not precisely in sync with the progression of the calendar. Thus astrologers must make an arbitrary choice between following the stars and following the calendar. Your basic newspaper horoscope follows the calendar. It ignores the stars!

People probably find it easier to accept a predetermined world than one in which we are actually in control of our destiny. Determinism is liberating. The Roman astrologer Manilus put it well: "The fates rule the world, and all things are established by a settled law. . . . No one can renounce what he is given, or possess what he is not given, nor can he grasp by his prayers the fortunes denied him or escape that which presses on him: each must bear his own lot."

In other words, whatever happens, it's not our fault.

WHY DO EMPTY ROOMS GET DUSTY?

The dust situation was brought to our attention by six-year-old Joe Catrambone of Virginia Beach. For a good why question, you can always depend on the little people.

Every cubic inch of air in a house will have something like one million bits of particulate matter, most of them too small to see. Their biggest ingredient is soil, followed by salt, which somehow springs out of the ocean (true story). Dust particles float because the ratio of the surface area to weight is extremely high, as with an ultralight airplane. Even the biggest dust particle takes about three minutes to fall one foot, and the smaller ones—say, a quarter of a micron (a thousandth of a millimeter) in diameter—take about ten hours.

In this slow fashion dust is constantly precipitating out of the air, so unless an attic is absolutely airtight, there will be always be a steady invasion of airborne dust through the cracks under the doors, in the windows, and so forth. Plus you have all your degenerating cobwebs, bug hairs, and even molds and viruses that add to the dust mix.

Dust is a surprisingly detestable substance when viewed under a microscope. Perhaps for the sake of taste we should not describe too exhaustively the characteristics of dust mites. They sound cute, but under the microscope they look like beer kegs with roach legs. Hundreds of mites could fit on the end of a match, and about 42,000 in an ounce of mattress dust. The mites prowl for some of the 50,000 scales of skin that humans shed every day.

Oh yes: skin. Skin is a major dust ingredient. The mites eat the skin, which after passing through the mite intestines is excreted in the form of "mite pellets," which we then breathe. This gives us allergies. Vacuum the little suckers? Sorry, they cling to the carpet. Bug spray won't kill them. They tend to die of old age after a few months. In the meantime they've produced two hundred times their weight in excrement.

Not a pretty picture, eh, Joey?

WHY IS THERE SO MUCH RITUAL SUICIDE IN JAPAN?

Not many Japanese people kill themselves. Hungary and Czechoslovakia have higher suicide rates. In some years even the blissful Swiss are more suicidal than the Japanese. Japan's annual suicide rate is still high—often reaching 40 people per 100,000 citizens—when compared with Italy's, which is less than a tenth of that. But it's usually not too much higher than the average country, and the real question one might ask when looking at the numbers is, Why are the Italians so content? Is it the pasta?

Although the statistical frequency of suicide in Japan may not seem high, it remains striking given the low crime and divorce rates and general economic prosperity. Moreover the Japanese kill themselves in conspicuous ways and for reasons that most Westerners would deem unjustifiable. There is no question but that they have a more accepting view of suicide.

For example in 1978 a businessman named H. Heikichi, age fifty-five, went bankrupt and killed himself. So did his wife. And three children. And a daughter-in-law. And two grandkids. They all preferred death to the pain of losing face.

Yukio Mishima was probably the greatest Japanese writer of the twentieth century, if a bit of a flake. A weakling as a youth, the narcissistic Mishima eventually became a bodybuilder, adopted a samurai persona, and in 1970 gave a speech to the nation's Self-Defense Forces asking for an uprising to restore the Imperial Army. Immediately afterward, in ritual fashion, he disemboweled himself in a hara-kiri ceremony that ended when his best friend beheaded him with a sword. The man had flair.

"Mishima, Shintaro Ishihara (the writer) and Masahiro Shinoda (the movie director) maintained that beauty could be experienced only in violence and in its corollary of rapture, whether sadistic or masochistic. For them the utmost representation of masochistic ecstasy and, therefore, of beauty is suicide," writes Japanese-American scholar Mamoru Iga in *The Thorn in the Chrysanthemum: Suicide and Economic Success in Modern Japan.*

These are not Western concepts obviously. Iga cites a number of surveys showing the unique Japanese cultural philosophy. Asked "Do you agree with the opinion that man is by nature evil?", 33 percent of Japanese respondents ages eighteen to twenty-four said yes, twice as many as in the United States, Britain, and West Germany. In another survey one out of six stated that suicide is acceptable when facing "love without parental permission."

Japan's attitude toward suicide has been shaped by geography and demographics. It is a small, isolated, and heavily populated land. It is ethnically homogenous, and more so than in other countries, the family is the organizer and enforcer of social integration. According to Iga, "The Japanese cohesiveness is rooted in moral and social homogeneity, dominated by tradition. Its justice is directed toward the subordination of the individual to the collective conscience."

Suicides in Japan frequently result when an individual fails to achieve the goals he and his family have set for him, or falls into disgrace and scandal, or feels irretrievably alienated from the rest of society. In America he might simply feel like an outsider, a lonesome dove. In Japan he might choose to end his life.

WHY AREN'T AIRPLANES BLOWN OUT OF THE SKY BY LIGHTNING?

They are. Not often, though. In the ten years between 1970 and 1980, some 1,600 commercial and military planes recorded lightning strikes. The Boeing Co. reckons that in 1984 the average was one per plane per year. Normally the lightning strikes an extremity of the airplane, travels along the outer shell, and exits through another extremity.

Why does lightning travel through and out? Because the metal shell of the plane, usually made of aluminum and titanium alloys, forms something called a Faraday cage: Electric current flows around the metal but not into the interior space.

On occasion, however, fuel-vapor explosions have occurred. The last time it happened to a commercial airliner was when a Boeing 707 crashed in Maryland in 1963. The use of thicker metal over the fuel tanks has probably prevented any further accidents.

What bothers scientists most is that in the future planes will be made more and more from nonmetal materials, including graphite and epoxy. These materials will not carry an electric charge nearly so well, so they may not keep the lightning away from the inside of the craft.

Something else to worry about.

Why Do the Lights on New York Subway Trains Flicker Off Intermittently?

Stop the presses. Our investigation has revealed that the flickering subway-train phenomenon is careening toward extinction. Our pleasure at the prospect of no longer being shrouded in darkness fifty feet beneath the creepiest city on earth is muted by concern over what this will mean for American cinema. A film like *The Taking of Pelham 123* would have been sapped of much of its wonderful dreadfulness without the portentous winking of the lights.

The mechanics of the situation are simple. Subway trains are powered by the electrified third rail. But the third rail, unlike the tracks, is discontinuous, plunked down in thirty-nine-foot sections with large gaps in between. The train makes contact with the rail with an extension called a shoe. The momentary blackouts occur when the train is moving so slowly that the shoe lingers in one of the gaps between the rails, or when the train, speeding along, changes from one set of tracks to another and switches from a third rail on the right to a third rail on the left. Or vice versa.

Bob Slovak, spokesman for the New York City Transit Authority, told us that all new and refurbished subway cars are being equipped with a device to convert the DC current of the

330 ■ WHY THINGS ARE

third rail to AC current, which, for reasons that might bore us
if we were actually to research them, allows the motor alter-
nator to keep working and ensures that the lights will no longer
go out. The entire New York subway fleet will be thus equipped
by 1992.

New York will never be the same.

WHY DO AMERICANS TELL POLISH JOKES?

D idn't use to. The Irish were long the brunt of ethnic jokes
in which the antagonist was rendered as bumbling, dense,
unclean, and so forth. Irish jokes declined after World War
II and disappeared almost entirely by the early 1960s, when
an Irish-American was president of the United States. Then
Polish jokes became standard—but only in America. Other
countries have their own favorite whipping dogs.

The French tell jokes about Belgians.

In eastern Canada, especially Ontario, the joke is on New-
foundlanders, a.k.a. Newfies. In western Canada they mock
Ukrainians—who also get grief from Russians.

In India Sikhs are the target. In Brazil the Portuguese. Israelis
joke about Kurdish Jews, and Swedes yank the chains of Finns
and Norwegians.

Brits, Australians, and New Zealanders still make Irish jokes.

And the Irish tell jokes about Kerry men, residents of a part
of Ireland.

The list goes on and on and reveals a certain pattern: The
victims are usually immigrants or minority groups who are par-
tially but not totally assimilated into mainstream society. Different, but not too different.

The Irish came to America in large numbers in the 1800s,
the Poles in the early 1900s. Thus Irish-Americans had a head
start in losing their hyphenated status and becoming just
Americans.

"The Irish moved up, assimilated, intermarried with other ethnic groups and in time became Americanized to the point where only excessive Catholicism and alcohol consumption remained as distinctive traits that could be made the subject of ethnic jokes," writes Christie Davies in *Ethnic Humor Around the World: A Comparative Analysis*. "The groups who succeeded the Irish as the butts of ethnic jokes about stupidity were the descendants of the unskilled and illiterate immigrants from the poorest parts of Europe and Southern Europe who had migrated to America in the decades before World War I."

The decline of Irish jokes and the rise of Polish jokes in the early sixties is perhaps a compliment to both the Irish and the Poles, Davies writes. "The Irish are no longer ambiguous enough to be joked about, the Poles are no longer alien enough to be excluded from jokes. . . . Americans, like everyone else, tell jokes that export stupidity to the periphery of their society, and from the 1960s they used the Poles as a safe if somewhat anachronistic marker of the social boundary of American society."

WHY DON'T MOVIE THEATERS HAVE USHERS ANYMORE?

There's the obvious answer, and then the real, startling truth. The obvious answer is that it is a function of size. Until the 1970s every movie house was a barn with one screen, up to two thousand seats, balconies, and a corps of faithful ushers who guided patrons along with pen-sized flashlights. Now, in the age of the multiplex, there are only a couple of hundred seats per screen. Ushers still exist in name, but they don't do much ushering and instead spend their time patrolling hallways and cleaning bathrooms. The official explanation is that there are too many theaters to treat people the old-fashioned way.

Now for the truth. There used to be a concept called continuous performance. When a movie ended, there was a delay of only five or ten minutes, and then it started up again. This was because people used to routinely arrive at the theater long after the movie had started—maybe even during the second half of the film. They wouldn't even consult movie clocks. They'd wait out the brief interval between screenings and see what they missed. If you are over twenty-five years old, think back: You know it's true.

Because people came late, they needed ushers to seat them in the dark.

Audiences gradually grew more sophisticated, however, and it became social death to arrive late for a movie. The movie houses eventually abandoned the "continuous performance" policy, and there is now about thirty minutes between shows, during which the theaters are cleaned and, for popular movies, vacated. See, in the old days people would watch a movie twice, because life was slower then, and, besides, you were glued to the floor by someone else's Raisinets.

WHY ARE SOME QUARTERS RED?

One of the world's most baffling mysteries! Surely you have been in the possession of a red quarter, yes? If you haven't, then just trust us: They're out there.

Why would anyone want to color a quarter? And why do you find red quarters but not red nickels, or, except in the world of clichés, red cents?

The Why staff has been working slavishly on this puzzle for well over a year. We have repeatedly called the U.S. Mint. We have badgered the Federal Reserve. We have developed trustworthy sources at companies that make vending machines. We have contemplated the issue over long lunches at fashionable restaurants. The major break in the case came when we realized that the word for a person who has an unnatural obsession with coins—a coin hobbyist, in short—is *numismatist*. This allowed us to then track down the obligatory hobby publication, *Numismatic News*, published in Iola, Wisconsin. That publication's "Answer Man," Alan Herbert, put us out of our misery.

"I can tell you exactly what they are. These are so-called house or shill coins that a bar will use in a jukebox," he said. We had heard something like this before, but never from so reliable a source. The idea is that people won't feed the jukebox unless it's already throbbing. So the bar employees are given color-coded quarters to put in it, to start the music—and the fun. Later, when the machine is emptied by the jukebox vendor, it is obvious which ones were put into the machine by patrons and which ones by the bar employees. The bar keeps all of the red quarters and gets a share of the silver ones. Of course this system doesn't always keep everyone honest, which is why those red quarters sneak their way into general circulation.

What makes this seem like a credible explanation is that it explains why the only red coins you see are quarters: That's all a jukebox will take.

So why red? Why not green?

Because women don't paint their nails green. The coloring comes from nail polish, which sticks to a coin better than anything else.

WHY DO PEOPLE STILL GET ADVANCED DEGREES IN GEOGRAPHY EVEN THOUGH WE ALREADY KNOW WHERE EVERYTHING IS?

Geographers now study things like "why are so many barns painted red." Or—we're looking at an article here in the *Annals of the Association of American Geographers*—"Cattle and Sheep in Spain." Here's another one that looks equally riveting: "Spatial Associations of Midtropospheric Circulation and Upper Mississippi River Basin Hydrology."

Why those articles are not more representative of agronomy and climatology is, geographers would say, an irrelevant question. (Our guess: Because there's lots of maps.) Geographers have been a little defensive ever since the blank spots in places like Africa got filled in. They hate being quarantined and being regarded as little more than cartographers, so they boldly plunge into the turf of political science, economics, and history. Instead of maps they use flowcharts, graphs, branching trees, two-dimensional scales, standard deviations, and, for gosh sakes, *lists*.

Far from being a field in decline, geography is booming, thanks to the new "remote sensing" technologies, such as satellite-based radar and multispectral scanners. They can make better maps than ever before. As with all academic fields, there is intensive specialization: Biogeography, Industrial Geography, Geomorphology, Historical Geography, Biblical Geography, Native American Geography, and so on.

Isaiah Bowman, a Harvard geologist, said in 1936 that no one should ask, "Is this just pure geography or am I spilling over into sociology or history? Damn these boundary fellows who think the Lord created 'subjects' . . . Simon-pure geography is a blind man feeling the elephant's tail."

Unheeding, Harvard phased out geography in 1947–51. In more recent years Michigan, Northwestern, the University of Chicago, and Columbia have nuked their geography departments. Still, every year up to nine thousand students get a bachelor's degree in geography. Mary Lynne Bird, executive director of the American Geographical Society, told us, "Geography is a heightened and analytical consideration of places."

Still, you have to kind of long for the day when a guy in a pith helmet could stumble around with a compass and keep a journal with lines like, "Emerging from the dense forest, we finally saw, thirty miles away to the north-northeast, a jagged rise of metamorphic and igneous rock. We decided to call it Mount Bodacious."

WHY DO PEOPLE EXPERIENCE DÉJÀ VU?

I t suddenly hits you: You *know* you have been here before, in this same place, talking to this same person, who is wearing the same paisley shirt with the mustard stain on the lapel, making the same hackneyed observation—a past life! It must be from a past life!

Déjà vu is not caused by anything supernatural, extrasensory or extraterrestrial; it is more like a mental hiccup, a brief, harmless malfunction of a basic mechanism of memory.

Here's what happens: Normally when one is in familiar surroundings, two brain functions are triggered: a concrete memory of the place and a separate abstract feeling of familiarity. In a déjà vu situation the familiarity sensation is triggered without a specific attendant memory. Possibly you *were* in a similar situation, but you can't quite remember.

THE BIGGEST QUESTIONS

(Consciousness. Humor. God.)

WHY ARE WE SO SURE THE WORLD IS REAL, AND NOT SOMETHING THAT WE ARE HALLUCINATING WHILE OUR BRAIN FLOATS IN A VAT IN A MAD SCIENTIST'S LABORATORY?

Think about it. That whole Reagan thing might have just been a bad dream. You think you are living a relatively healthy fiber-rich life-style when in fact your brain is soaking in a vat of oxygenated blood in the laboratory of highly skilled if somewhat eccentric scientists who have hairdos like they just stuck their fingers in a light socket. (For more on this subject, see "Why Can't Scientists Keep Severed Heads or Disembodied Brains Alive by Percolating Fresh Blood Through Them?," page 169.)

You're certain you exist, but can't prove it. There is even a name for this: the Brains-in-Vats Paradox.

You say you feel stuff? Hear stuff? Smell? See? Those are just nerve impulses received in the brain. Experiments as early as the thirties showed that if a portion of a patient's brain is stimulated with an electrode, the patient may "experience" events with a vividness equal to ordinary life. The mad scientists could be prodding your brain right now. "Stick him in the optic nerve." "No, the medulla!"

The brains-in-vats epistemological dilemma is explored lucidly (unless we're dreaming) in William Poundstone's *Labyrinths of Reason*. Poundstone's recipe for making sure you are not dreaming is to keep a book of limericks handy at all times. If you ever have doubt, turn to a limerick you've never read. He reasons that in real life, and certainly in dreams, it is impossible to create instantly a perfect limerick.

Poundstone notes that the study of "what is real" (ontology) goes back to the seventeenth-century writings of mathematician René Descartes, who, we might note, was not a woman and is, somehow, the referent in the phrase "Cartesian philosophy." Descartes doesn't solve the mad-scientist problem and concludes he can't be certain that he's not dreaming. However he does argue that certain things in the universe must be real, independently of him, such as the color red. Red couldn't be invented. He also says that we can be sure of our subjective sensations and offers the famous saying, "I think, therefore I am," which unfortunately doesn't deal with the issue of whether or not we are, say, dogs dreaming of being human. (The Why staff came up with what it thought was a brilliant contribution to philosophy—"I drink their four yams"—but then learned that, wouldn't you know it, it's not original.)

Descartes extended "I am" to "God exists" and from that to "the real world exists" because God in his infinite wisdom would not have allowed evil geniuses or mad scientists to create an illusory universe.

The question we'd like to ask the long-deceased mathematician is, did numbers exist before the Creation? Is mathematics independent of matter and energy? If, after the Heat Death of the Universe, another universe were to somehow come into existence, would 2 plus 2 still equal 4? Could there be a universe without mathematics? And if so, how can we get there as soon as possible?

WHY DO WE ASSUME THAT OUR ACTIONS ARE THE RESULT OF FREE WILL AND AREN'T PREDETERMINED?

We realize that no one is really very interested in this subject. But we feel compelled to discuss it. It's almost as though we can't help it.

Let's say we're watching a Monster Truck race on ESPN and we suddenly "decide" to see if Mr. Ed is on Nick at Nite. Obviously we don't have a lot of brain synapses firing, but that's not the point. We say we have free will in this case because we have the luxury of choice: We can stick with the Monster Trucks, or switch to MTV, or turn off the tube and put an LP on the record player, or go out and shoot someone for no reason like that guy Meursault in The Stranger. We can do anything we want! We can invent dialogue that no one's ever spoken!

Butler: "Your noogie, sir."

The Master: "Very good. Now get that stupid piano out of my face."

See? But wait a minute. There's really no proof that anything we've done here is done "freely." Once we've switched channels to Mr. Ed, it is impossible to prove that we could have done anything else.

True, common sense says we had options. But common sense isn't proof. Some philosophers still contend that we behave as machines—that everything we do is the result of a sequence of causes-and-effects. Ideally free will is the power to go beyond the simple influences of brain cells, of predispositions, of outside forces, of *causes*. Free will is the power to go hungry when the body says to eat, to sing when the brain says to cry. But is this what actually happens?

A specific muscle contraction is caused by electrical activity in our brain cells. What causes that? Chemicals.

We quickly jump in here and say that our brain does this stuff because we want it to. We command our brain cells to fire. *Neep. Neep.* The thumb muscle contracts toward the button on the remote control. *Fzzht!* Mr. Ed is on TV. We want this to happen.

But as Thomas Nagel notes in *What Does It All Mean?* (we'd answer that question, too, except it's not in the proper "why" format), the existence of wants, desires, intents, and so forth does not meet the test of free will. They are just part of the computer program:

"The sum total of a person's experiences, desires and knowledge, his hereditary constitution, the social circumstances and the nature of the choice facing him, together with other factors that we may not know about, all combine to make a particular action in the circumstances inevitable."

Nagel doesn't actually believe this, nor do we. We're not daft. It's just an interesting idea, another unsolvable intellectual puzzle that will keep university philosophy departments in business for another thousand years.

Fortunately the scientific justification for determinism isn't what it used to be. Back in the eighteenth century mathematician Pierre-Simon Laplace and his ilk argued that if we could know the location, direction, velocity, and mass of every atom or electromagnetic wave in the universe at a given moment, we could then calculate precisely what the universe will be like into the distant future. We could know whether we were going to stick with the Monster Trucks or go to Mr. Ed.

Laplace was wrong. The world no longer obeys the strict, simple laws of Newtonian motion. In quantum physics, particles and waves behave mysteriously, randomly. When scientists study the movement of clouds, they speak of chaos. The physical world is getting harder to figure, not easier.

And finally there is a moral predicament raised by determinism. Lacking free will, we would no longer be accountable for our actions. We would have to shut down the churches, open the prison gates, and put a going-out-of-business sign on Heaven and Hell.

WHY DOES GOD ALLOW SO MUCH EVIL AND SUFFERING?

We will shy away from a definitive answer—we are nothing if not intellectually modest—and instead supply some of the standard wisdom on the topic (ignoring the easiest, least complicated supposition of all: because He doesn't exist.)

Theologians in the Old Testament era clung to what you might call the R-and-R version of suffering: It was the result of divine retribution and reciprocity. In this simple system you got what was coming to you. "He that soweth iniquity shall reap calamity" (Proverbs 22: 8, back when people knew how to speak dramatically).

The problem with the retribution concept was that it didn't explain the torment of the innocent, nor the occasional prosperity of the truly evil. Reality refused to follow the retributive model. So, along came a new, better idea: There had to be an afterlife in which the innocent will be rewarded, the evil damned. This would prove God to be just, even if a bit tardy.

A second explanation was that suffering, like H-bombs, made for a good deterrent, being God's way of keeping people in line. "And all the people shall hear, and fear, and not act presumptuously again" (Deuteronomy 19: 20).

Still, this hardly satisfied anyone. What about good people who didn't need the schoolmarmish discipline? The New Testament offered an explanation: Pain is good. Builds character, like cold showers. "Suffering produces endurance, and endurance produces character, and character produces hope" (Romans 5: 3–4).

This still leaves the question of whether God causes, approves of, or tolerates evil and suffering. One might argue that God is too big to worry about one species on a single planet around a typical yellow star in just one of the hundreds of billions of galaxies in the universe, but most religions reject the idea of such an impersonal God.

Jewish theologians, in particular, have puzzled over the suffering issue. *The Encyclopedia of Religion* says that Judaism "deals with this problem of mass suffering, of the undifferentiated fate of the innocent and the guilty, by claiming that this is an unfinished world in which justice and peace are not given, but have to be won." Why didn't God make the world fair? Says the *Encyclopedia*, "A tendency can be found in the rabbinic tradition to consider the problem of suffering as one of the areas beyond full human comprehension."

That's where it stands. Officially unknowable. It's just a mystery of unsurpassed inscrutability, rivaled only, we would say, by God's decision to make men and women fundamentally incompatible.

The seminal piece of writing on suffering is, supposedly, the Book of Job, which we have always found so bizarre and baffling that it seemed the wisest course to forget about the "message" and just remember that Job is not pronounced like the thing that makes you get up in the morning.

"When I looked for good, evil came," wails Job, a genuinely righteous and God-fearing man. Why does Job suffer so? Why does he lose all his children and his farm animals and his home and break out in a terrible pox? Because he was the unfortunate victim of a whimsical wager between God and Satan. They've got time to kill. Job is what they have instead of cards.

What happens is, Satan and God are sitting around talking—it really says this—and Satan says that people praise the Almighty only out of self-interest and would defame him if their fortunes soured. God says that wouldn't be true of Job. So, while God watches, Satan inflicts atrocities upon the humble farmer, who ends up leprous, childless, broke, and with nothing left of his life.

The dramatic conclusion: Job comes close to cursing God, but never does. Rather, in his misery, he challenges God to give a reason for his suffering, and God in effect tells him to hush his mouth. The moral of the story (as we read it): God can do whatever he wants, and we shouldn't arrogate to ourselves the wisdom to understand him.

Job, by the way, got his farm back, started a new family, and lived happily ever after with twice as much wealth, all in keeping with the you-get-what-comes-to-you reciprocity model of evil and suffering. And of course Satan lost the bet and got his comeuppance.

WHY IS HUMOR FUNNY?

Humor is the only type of human communication that results in a stereotypical physical response, specifically the contraction of fifteen facial muscles and altered breathing, in a pattern known as laughter. The comic effect is usually the result of a *conflict between overlapping but incompatible frames of reference*. Here is an example:

"My dog's got no nose."

"How does he smell?"

"Terrible."

We laugh hysterically, virtually weeping, at the moment our brain makes the delightful leap from one context to the next—from *smell* as a transitive verb to *smell* as an intransitive verb.

Another example:

"What's the difference between an oral thermometer and a rectal thermometer?"

"I don't know, what?"

"The taste."

Here the brain is jogged into perceiving the rectal thermometer in the incompatible context of an oral thermometer, but this time the joke is more visceral because of the scatalogical element. We know that society expects us to be offended and repulsed by the joke, but we take a crude pleasure in it, and the recognition of this disloyalty excites us. Our pleasure may very well be the result of repressed sadism.

When we laugh, we release the tension built up from living in an awful world. *Challenger* jokes were universal after the space shuttle blew up: "Why didn't the astronauts take a shower before the launch? Because they knew they'd be washing up on the beach later." Such "sick" jokes are in fact therapeutic to the teller, because they unburden the psyche of heavy emotions, the sorrow, the sadness. We might note that there is a rock band that calls itself My Dad Is Dead.

One requirement of humor usually is that it have an element of surprise. For instance: "My doctor says that if I start eating right, get plenty of exercise and avoid stress, I'll be dead in six months."

This one-liner is funny because as we hear the sentence, we expect it to end on an optimistic note, and yet it ends with utter bleakness. We recognize that this unexpected ending more properly describes the painful and desperate experience of life on earth, and our outrage is released in laughter.

A final example:

"Doctor, what's wrong with me?"

"Well, you've got hepatitis, mononucleosis, AIDS, tuberculosis, and the common cold."

"Can anything be done for me?"

"We can keep you in bed and put you on a diet of pancakes and flounder."

"Pancakes and flounder? Will that cure me?"

"No, but it's the only thing that will fit under the door."

This has elements of sadism, offensiveness, despair, and the surprise that erupts when the doctor suddenly leaps from his normal context—the reassuring professional—to the context of crude folk wisdom. Therefore we laugh.

WHY DO WE EXIST?

This one's easy.

We exist, first and foremost, to breed. The great Charles Darwin solved the world's greatest mystery: How did we get here? We now know that we are here through an evolutionary process, that we share the genes of other species, all of whom make up a single extended family of life. Billions of proteins inscribe the human genetic code, and though there is no overt intention in that language, we can easily imagine a subtle craving for survival. Thus we have a biological mission, to perpetuate ourselves, to live long and prosper.

Through survival we realize a collateral goal: the preservation of subjective values and ideas, things like love, goodness, beauty and faith. Kill ourselves and we might leave behind just atoms and molecules and electromagnetic waves and the unforgiving laws of physics. It would be too much like a machine. There'd be no laughter. There'd be no astonishment. There'd be no ice cream.

WHO IS THE AUTHOR?

J oel Achenbach, a native of Gainesville, Florida, is a reporter
  for the Style section of *The Washington Post*. His column, "Why
  Things Are," is nationally syndicated by The Washington
Post Writers Group. A graduate of Princeton University, he
worked for *The Miami Herald* from 1982 to 1990.